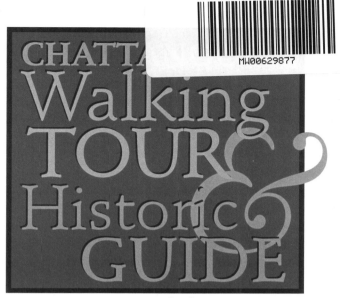

CHATTA... Walking TOUR & Historic GUIDE

Maury Nicely

STILLHOUSE **HOLLOW** PRESS

825 Mount Vernon Avenue
Chattanooga, Tennessee 37405

COPYRIGHT © 2002 Maury Nicely

Published in 2002 by
Stillhouse Hollow Press
825 Mount Vernon Avenue
Chattanooga, Tennessee 37405

Library of Congress Cataloging-in-Publication Data
2002093259

ISBN 0-9722523-0-4

PRINTED IN AMERICA

INTRODUCTION

HISTORY OF CHATTANOOGA, TENNESSEE

Chattanooga was not the first city to be located where the downtown area sits today. In reality, the flood plains along the banks of the Tennessee River were a prime location for the establishment of prehistoric Indian villages, and the area in the immediate vicinity of downtown Chattanooga has been the site of indigenous occupation for hundreds of years. The presence of prehistoric settlements throughout the Chattanooga area is evidenced by an important Mississippian mound and village site located 2 miles upstream from the present downtown area (the Citico site), as well as several Archaic, Woodland, and Mississippian Indian sites unearthed just downstream from Chattanooga, at Moccasin Bend. These "first cities" predated the arrival of white settlers as well as the Cherokee Indians, who came to inhabit the Chattanooga area at the end of the seventeenth century.

Between 1775 and 1793, a splinter faction of the Cherokee known as the Chickamauga Indians fought bitterly against white encroachment upon Cherokee lands. Led by the bellicose Dragging Canoe (1732-1792), the Chickamauga attacked settlers along the frontier in an attempt to discourage further white settlement. As a base of operations from which to strike settlers entering into East and Middle Tennessee, they established the "Five Lower Towns" in the vicinity of present-day Chattanooga; from this location, battles periodically broke out along the frontier until, following Dragging Canoe's death on March 1, 1792, the Chickamaugas finally rejoined the Cherokee Nation and agreed to peace with the United States.

In 1815, John Ross, the son of a Scottish trader and his Cherokee wife, joined with Timothy Meigs to establish a trading post, warehouse, and ferry on the Tennessee River at the site of present-day Chattanooga. The site soon became known as Ross's Landing (or "Ross's Warehouse") and grew to become an important market for several salt works established upriver in Virginia, as well as a trading point between the United States and the Cherokee Nation. Nevertheless, while river trade continued to increase at this spot, there was little substantial growth at Ross's Landing during this period, largely because the area remained the property of the Cherokee Nation.

On October 25, 1819, however, Hamilton County was created by an Act of the General Assembly of the State of Tennessee from lands ceded by the Cherokee Indians as part of the Hiwassee Purchase (1817). The county was named for Alexander Hamilton (1757-1804), who served as Secretary of the Treasury under President George Washington and was killed in 1804 in a famous duel with Aaron Burr. Following the Hiwassee Purchase and the creation of Hamilton County, the Tennessee River became the dividing line between the United States territory on the north bank and the Cherokee Nation across the river; at that time, the area on which downtown Chattanooga sits today was still part of the Cherokee Nation. This, however, would soon change.

Following the 1835 Treaty of New Echota, which ceded the remaining eastern lands of the Cherokee Nation to the U.S. government, Ross's Landing became the site of a military post established for the purpose of Indian removal. In 1838, the town witnessed the embarkation of thousands of Cherokees, both by river and on foot, for new lands in the west. While the removal of the Indians immediately opened Chattanooga for large-scale settlement and development, the forced removal remains one of the most tragic and regrettable episodes in U.S. history. Nevertheless, the period following the Cherokee Removal was a time of rapid growth and change at Ross's Landing.

In 1837, the name "Ross's Landing" was replaced by the new name of "Chattanooga," and during the remainder of the antebellum period a substantial foundation was lain for the future development of the town. As the physical layout of downtown Chattanooga indicates, the initial growth of the town was largely the product of 2 technological developments: the advent of steamboat travel and the arrival of the railroad. In 1828, the *Atlas* became the first steamboat to travel the entire course of the Tennessee River, and soon thereafter steamboat transportation made travel along the river a 2-way affair (unlike the flatboats and keelboats used previously, which could only travel downriver). In 1850, moreover, the town was selected as the northern terminus for the Western & Atlantic Railroad; this development, along with the arrival of several other rail lines during the 1850s, enabled Chattanooga to become an important rail junction in the Old South.

At the beginning of the 1860s, however, thoughts turned away from commercial growth as the nation braced for war between the North and South. As is the case with the South as a whole, one of the seminal events in the history of Chattanooga was the ensuing Civil War (1861-1865). Like much of Tennessee, Hamilton County was split with regard to its position concerning secession from the Union. The initial Hamilton County secession vote on February 8, 1861, resulted in 445 votes for secession and 1,445 in favor of the Union. In a second vote on June 8, 1861, Hamilton County voters again favored remaining in the Union, with 2,114 votes in favor of the Union and 854 for secession; as with the initial vote, most of the dissenting votes came from Chattanooga, which supplied soldiers for both armies throughout the conflict.

During the Civil War, Chattanooga was the site of 2 artillery bombardments by federal troops in 1862 and 1863, and after the nearby battle of Chickamauga (September 1863) the retreating federal army was surrounded and besieged by Confederate forces occupying positions along the mountains and ridges surrounding Chattanooga. Nearing starvation, U.S. troops opened a "cracker line" to bring supplies into the town, and on November 23-25, 1863, the Union army routed the Confederates in successive battles at Orchard Knob, Lookout Mountain, and Missionary Ridge. As the Confederates withdrew into north Georgia, Chattanooga became the "gateway to the Confederacy" and served as the Union army's base of operations for the Atlanta campaign of 1864.

This second phase of the war, the "occupation" of Chattanooga during 1864-1865, benefited the town in 2 significant ways. First, the buildup occasioned by the federal occupation led to the creation of new industries and city services, as well as a minor building "boom" throughout Chattanooga. 24 forts encircling the town were established during the federal occupation, and U.S. troops erected a total of 124 buildings, using 3,000,000 feet of board lumber, in the town during this period. Many of these structures were purchased by civilians at the close of the war and converted into private business enterprises, some of which were quite influential in helping Chattanooga to transform itself into a New South industrial center. In addition, the federal occupation introduced a number of federal troops to the town, many of whom elected to return after the war; along with Confederate veterans and other new residents to the town, these enterprising "carpetbaggers" helped Chattanooga to grow into a thriving industrial city on the heels of the military conflict.

The enthusiasm brought by these new citizens, Union and Confederate, resulted in large investments of capital and the creation of new business enterprises in Chattanooga in the years following the Civil War. Coupled with the general prosperity of the 1880s, this optimism boiled over into a substantial real estate boom in 1887-1888, which resulted in the construction of several large business "blocks" and the organization of a number of new commercial ventures. As evidence of this "boom," in 1886 alone

$1,076,347 was spent in building construction, and in 1887 real estate-related transactions totaled $13,264,555. The population of Chattanooga also increased greatly during this period, from 25,101 in 1885 to 36,903 by 1887.

One individual whose influence aided the "boom" in Chattanooga was Charles E. James, who developed a "belt line" (a railroad encircling the town) which offered opportunities for suburban growth on the outskirts of the town. As a result, several suburbs, including Orchard Knob, Hill City, Highland Park, East Lake, Ridgedale, and St. Elmo, underwent significant development during this period. In June 1889, moreover, the *Chattanooga Times* joined in the boom, announcing a give-away of 1,000 town lots to subscribers; an area located on Walden Ridge was opened up as "Timesville" as a result of this development. The biggest land speculator, however, was the Chattanooga Land, Coal, Iron & Railway Company (the "Over-the-Hill Company"), which worked to develop 25,000 acres in the surrounding area. Though the boom eventually stalled, officially ending during the financial panic of 1893, the event was instrumental in fostering dramatic growth in Chattanooga, and the important decade of the 1880s truly helped to transform Chattanooga from a town to a city.

During the latter decades of the nineteenth century, Chattanooga seemed to epitomize Henry Grady's vision of the New South – progressive, industrial, and forward-looking. The influx of new residents following the war – including nearby neighbors moving to town from outlying areas, transplanted Yankees, and foreign immigrants – resulted in significant industrial growth throughout the city, and Chattanooga became a southern industrial center in the latter half of the nineteenth century. Early on, Chattanooga's iron-and-steel-based economy earned it the nickname "the Pittsburgh of the South," at least until that title was usurped by Birmingham and the massive steel factories of north Alabama. Continued industrial development, in turn, led to the growth of commercial enterprises, including banking and insurance, and downtown Chattanooga was characterized by continued development (both outward and upward) as the nineteenth century gave way to the twentieth.

The spirit of conciliation and cooperation which pervaded Chattanooga during this period was epitomized by the creation of the Chickamauga & Chattanooga National Military Park (1893) by a group of Union and Confederate veterans; this park became the first and largest military park designated to commemorate the Civil War. Though visitors had long been drawn to "resorts" located on Lookout Mountain and other nearby spots, the creation of the military park was a significant step in transforming Chattanooga into a true travel destination for visitors. With the advent of automobile travel, this trend only increased, and in 1915 the Dixie

Highway Association was organized in Chattanooga for the purpose of creating a permanent highway from Chicago to Miami. The finished road drew thousands of visitors through Chattanooga, the halfway point in the trip, thus supplementing the city's industry with additional "tourism" opportunities in the early decades of the twentieth century.

Despite the growth of Chattanooga in the modern period, however, the implacable Tennessee River continued to hinder progress through frequent flooding as well as fluctuating water levels, which made river travel unreliable at best. Though Chattanooga residents had helped to fund the Hales Bar Dam (1913), which aided in removing some of the natural shoals and whirlpools frustrating river travel downstream from the city, flooding and navigation problems persisted along the Tennessee River well into the 1930s. In 1933, however, the federal government created the Tennessee Valley Authority (TVA), which endeavored to build a series of low dams along the length of the river to, among other things, control flooding and provide electricity throughout the Tennessee Valley. This project, the most tangible local result of which was the Chickamauga dam located upstream from downtown Chattanooga (1940), was likely the single most-important development within the Tennessee Valley in the twentieth century and has continued to promote commercial growth and economic development in Chattanooga to the present date.

The heyday for the "downtown" areas of most American cities occurred in the wake of World War II, when the city core became the true center of city life; Chattanooga was no exception to this rule. Replete with theaters, dining establishments, department stores, and a variety of retail shops, downtown was the place to go in Chattanooga during the 1950s and 1960s, a fact typically reflected by photographs from this era, which show crowds of automobiles and throngs of shoppers patronizing the numerous businesses lining Market Street and the other main thoroughfares of the central downtown area.

As with the remainder of the South, however, Chattanooga faced significant social hurdles in the 1950s and 1960s, as it struggled to address desegregation and racial equality. Although the city's record of racial progress is not without flaws, for the most part Chattanooga avoided the violent strife which characterized the response of some southern cities to the Civil Rights Movement. Recognizing the negative economic consequences of bitter resistance to desegregation, Chattanooga typically adopted a conciliatory, accommodating response to change, and in this sense the city avoided becoming saddled with a reputation for unrest and violence, as did many southern cities during that period of significant change.

In addition to social changes, the years between the 1950s and 1970s also witnessed dramatic physical changes within downtown Chattanooga. During this period, the city became the subject of serious efforts at "urban renewal," particularly on the west side of the downtown area. Sadly, the city's approach to historic preservation during this period was blisteringly short-sighted, as epitomized by the razing of the historic Union Depot (1972) which had stood downtown since 1882. During this period, Chattanoogans also witnessed the leveling of Cameron Hill and its fine Victorian homes, as well as the destruction of several structures with historic significance dating to before the Civil War. Many of the parking lots and "contemporary" structures which replaced these historic properties may leave residents and visitors shaking their heads, and a tour of downtown Chattanooga can at times lead to inquiries as to what "used to be there." While lost and demolished buildings can never be replaced, recent years have witnessed a reversal in Chattanooga's attitude toward the downtown area and its historic properties. Ironically, this change was occasioned, at least in part, by the growth of suburban shopping areas and the resulting departure of retail trade from the "core" of the city – between 1972 and 1982, the number of stores in the central city area declined from 175 to 95 -- which decreased the perceived need for larger, modern buildings to replace the older structures in the downtown area.

The latter half of the twentieth century has witnessed other changes in downtown Chattanooga as well. Although the New South development which had occurred in Chattanooga led to significant industrial growth and earned the city the title of the "Dynamo of Dixie," one of the consequences of heavy industry was pollution, a problem exacerbated by the city's location in an area ringed by mountains. As a result, in 1969 Chattanooga received ominous recognition as the city with the worst air pollution in the United States. By 1972, however, the city had taken significant steps to resolve its pollution problems, and Chattanooga became a model for the Federal Clean Air Act of 1970, a pattern which continues today with the designation of Chattanooga as one of the top ten environmental cities in the United States.

Subsequently, the 1980s and 1990s witnessed the additional redevelopment of downtown Chattanooga. Anchored by the Tennessee Aquarium (1992), which is located in the area where John Ross founded his trading post almost two centuries ago, downtown Chattanooga entered into a new period of growth based upon the premise of "sustainable development" – encouraging development which fosters preservation of the local environment and quality of life for residents. This riverfront resurgence and the redevelopment of the Southside area, which was originally occupied by the various railroads serving Chattanooga, has had a sort of "pincer" effect upon the downtown area as a whole, fostering additional growth and redevelopment within the "Market Center" lying between these two areas. This progress has been aided by Cornerstones, a local non-profit organization which has taken a guiding hand in protecting and renovating historic structures throughout the city, as well as by a strong public-private coalition which has provided the interest and optimism instrumental to create a vibrant city center in downtown Chattanooga.

The strides taken by Chattanooga in recent years have not gone unnoticed. Named "a place you might want to live" by Parade Magazine and labeled one of Outside Magazine's "Ten Dream Towns – perfect places to live big, play hard, and work (if you must)," Chattanooga has been recognized in a

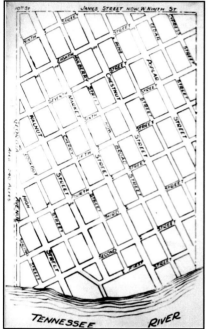

variety of magazines and journals as an exciting place to visit and a great place to live. The press accorded to Chattanooga culminated in the February endorsement of Chattanooga as one of National Public Radio's "Great Cities," and in 2002 more than 700 editors and writers at Fodor's selected Chattanooga as the number one "overlooked and underrated" family destination in or near the United States. As these reviews indicate, the changes which have taken place over the last decade in downtown Chattanooga have served to turn what had become a neglected downtown area into what is now – and once again – the vital core of the city.

THE 1838 CITY PLAT

The above image is the original city plat for Ross's Landing, which was lain out by Joseph Patty, of Kingston, Tennessee, in 1838. Like most cities, in its early years Ross's Landing had no urban design and, consequently, no established street system of which to speak. Houses and businesses were plopped down throughout the town, without a pattern of streets to guide settlers in placing buildings.

Early visitors to Ross's Landing noted the haphazard arrangement of the settlement. In 1837, Englishman G.W. Featherstonhaugh recorded his impressions of the town, describing "a small village hastily built without any regard to order or streets, every one selecting his own site, and relying upon the legislature of Tennessee to pass a law for the permanent arrangement of their occupations." This system (or lack thereof) was altered soon after the

Cherokee Removal in 1838. Joseph Patty was hired by the commissioners of the town to survey the 240 acres in the vicinity of the landing itself. Patty then established a grid of 9 streets running north-south, and 9 streets running east-west. The east-west streets were numbered First through Ninth, while the north-south streets were named, based upon the suggestion of Dr. Milo Smith and the obvious influence of the urban model of Philadelphia, for trees: Cypress, Cedar, Poplar, Pine, Chestnut, Mulberry, Cherry, and Walnut. The naming of streets did have one important exception: the central avenue leading from the landing (between Cherry and Mulberry) was labeled Market Street, though it was casually referred to as "The Road" in the early days of the settlement.

Soon after the establishment of this street system, new resident Ferdinand A. Parham described the town as follows: "The ground is elevated and somewhat rolling; the streets running at right angles with the river, will be comparatively level, but from the nature of the ground, commencing at the lower wharf, each succeeding street will be higher than the last, until it reaches the height of the bluff level.... The place has been settled in the last three years, and being public land, the inhabitants have only constructed the rudest log houses, thrown together promiscuously without any system whatever."

Though the natural surroundings throughout downtown Chattanooga have been altered through the grading of streets, the filling in of gullies and ditches, the raising of street levels, the damming of the Tennessee River, and the removal of the top of Cameron Hill for use as fill dirt during the urban renewal of the 1950s and 1960s, the original urban street system established by Patty has remained a generally constant stamp on the land in what is today downtown Chattanooga.

REUBEN HARRISON HUNT

Though the buildings located in downtown Chattanooga were designed by a number of architects and builders, some of whom – like Samuel McClung  Patton and Charles E. Bearden – exerted a significant influence upon the architecture of the city, the most noteworthy architect in downtown Chattanooga to the present day has been R.H. Hunt, the "master builder of Chattanooga."

Many of the buildings referred to throughout the tour of downtown Chattanooga bear the stamp of Hunt, pictured to the left. Hunt was Chattanooga's first significant architect, and his work was crucial in the architectural development of the city in the decades surrounding the turn of the century. After arriving in Chattanooga in 1882 at age 20, Hunt designed a number of buildings reflecting a variety of architectural styles — Gothic Revival, Romanesque Revival, Beaux Arts Classicism, Neo-Classicism, Georgian Revival, and Art Deco, among others.

Hunt's first major building was the First Baptist Church (1886) located on Georgia Avenue, which was erected just as the 1887-1888 real estate boom began to bloom. By 1890, Hunt began to advertise that "churches and public buildings are a specialty," and the buildings he designed in Chattanooga bear witness to his expertise in these areas. Among other structures, Hunt designed the Pound Building (where he maintained his offices for a period of time, as indicated by the advertisement to the right), Second Presbyterian Church, First National Bank, Georgia Avenue YMCA Building, James Building, MacLellan Building, Medical Arts Building, Chattanooga Bank Building, Carnegie Library, Municipal Building, Hamilton National Bank Building, Hamilton County Courthouse, Memorial Auditorium, Tivoli Theater, Miller Brothers Department Store, Frances Willard Home, and Joel W. Solomon Federal Building. Between 1895 and 1935, in fact, there was no major government building in Chattanooga which was not designed by Hunt.

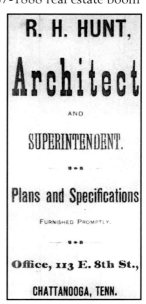

R. H. HUNT, Architect AND SUPERINTENDENT. Plans and Specifications FURNISHED PROMPTLY. Office, 113 E. 8th St., CHATTANOOGA, TENN.

In addition to the wealth of buildings erected in Chattanooga, Hunt also designed public buildings in virtually every southern state, and at the time of his death he was referred to as "the outstanding architect in the South." It has been said that "no man's life has been more thoroughly woven into the progress of Chattanooga during the past half century than that of R.H. Hunt," and it can surely be said that the architectural character of downtown Chattanooga is largely the product of Hunt's substantial talents and expertise.

WE WELCOME your suggestions and feedback! If you have any thoughts or suggestions concerning the materials in this guidebook, Please contact us at:

Stillhouse Hollow Press
825 Mount Vernon Avenue
Chattanooga, Tennessee 37405

Walnut Street Bridge

The historic Walnut Street Bridge (1891) is the oldest standing span across the Tennessee River at Chattanooga. The river itself has borne a number of names given to it by the nations and tribes which have passed through the Tennessee Valley – Caskinampo, Casquinambaux, Hogohegee, Callamaco, Cussatees, and Riviere des Cheroquis. The name Tennessee, derived from a word for a Cherokee town upriver called Tanasi, finally became the legal title of the river in 1789. After the Hiwassee Purchase (1817) ceded large portions of Cherokee territory in southeast Tennessee to the United States, the river became the boundary between the Cherokee Nation and the new white settlements. In 1819, Hamilton County was formed from part of these lands on the north side of the river.

Early on, river travel in East Tennessee was not without its difficulties – obstacles downstream, in the "Narrows" of the river gorge and at Muscle Shoals, made river travel difficult, and seasonal fluctuations in river levels hindered travel between July and October. In 1828, however, a momentous change occurred when the steamboat *Atlas* traveled upstream along the entire length of the Tennessee River, from Paducah, Kentucky, to Knoxville. This accomplishment inaugurated a period of intense river travel on the river, and after the Cherokee Removal (1838) Chattanooga developed as an important river port.

Though the development of rail, automobile, and air travel has over the years led to diminished reliance upon river trade, the changes wrought by the Tennessee Valley Authority (TVA) in the twentieth century have harnessed the river, preventing floods, producing electricity, and guaranteeing reliable river transportation on a year-round basis.

Battle of
Missionary Ridge

CONTEMPT
OF COURT

The Turn-of-the-Century
LYNCHING
THAT LAUNCHED A HUNDRED
YEARS of FEDERALISM

MARK CURRIDEN AND
LEROY PHILLIPS, JR.
WITH AN UPDATED EPILOGUE

Swing
Ferry

6 Battle of Lookout Mountain

Chair used by
General
Ulysses S. Grant
at Chattanooga

Note:
Take Riverwalk
to **Ross's Landing**
p. 135

Souvenir Programme
OF THE OPENING OF
The Walnut Street Bridge.

CHATTANOOGA, TENN.
WEDNESDAY, FEBRUARY 18TH,
1891.

THE BRACT PRINTING COMPANY,
CHATTANOOGA, TENN.

12

to **Fountain
Square**
p. 47

9 Captain S.J.A. Frazier

Charles H. Coolidge

11 Coolidge Park

12

Chickamauga Dam

3

4

3 MacLellan Island

Note: Take Riverwalk to **Bluff View** p. 25

13

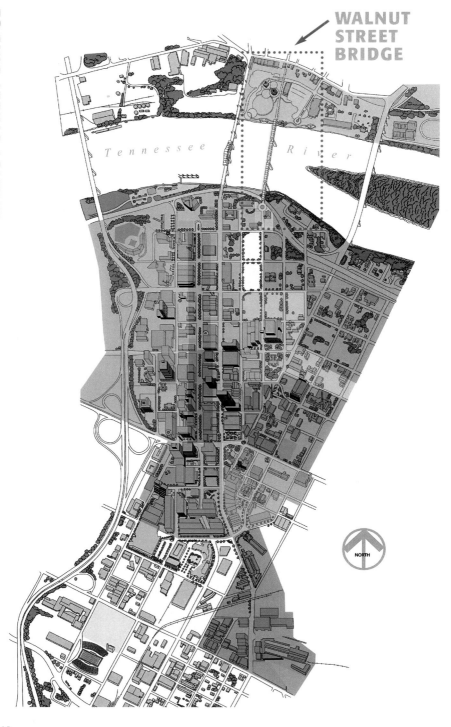

WALNUT
STREET
BRIDGE

Tennessee *River*

NORTH

The tour of the Walnut Street Bridge area begins on Walnut Street, at the south end of the bridge. To the left (west) of the bridge, on a lot currently occupied by a 1-story brick business building, ❶ formerly stood a 1-story frame house built by merchant T.J. Lattner prior to the Civil War. Also known as the **"Grant House,"** the home (pictured below) was reputed to have served as the headquarters of Union

General Ulysses S Grant after he arrived on October 23, 1863, to assume control of the federal armies in the western theater following the Union loss at Chickamauga. A chair reportedly used by General grant during the battles for Chattanooga is pictured below and on page 12. It is also reported that U.S. General William T. Sherman maintained his headquarters in the Lattner House at one point, a statement which is apparently verified by a circa 1889 Atlas of the City of Chattanooga, which lists the spot as "Hqrs of Gen. W.T. Sherman." At one time the oldest residence in Chattanooga, the house was eventually condemned and torn down in 1966, despite the efforts of local preservationists and placement of the house under the care of the Association of Tennessee Antiquities. After its destruction, some of the materials from the Lattner House were used by Johnny Cash for a home he constructed near Nashville.

The remainder of this tour takes place along the **Walnut Street Bridge** (above), ❷ the longest pedestrian bridge in the world (2,730 feet), which spans the Tennessee River at this point. Following the collapse of the Meigs Military Bridge in 1867, the only means of crossing the river was by ferry. As early at 1879, therefore, discussion began as to the construction of a new bridge over the river. After efforts were made to sound the river bottom, it was reported that an iron trestle bridge was to be built across the river at Market Street. However, the Decatur Bridge Company, which had been selected to build the structure, reneged on its promise, and the project was stalled. After Congress subsequently passed a bill granting permission for a bridge to be erected "at some point between the west line of Market Street and the east line of Georgia Avenue," architect Edwin Thatcher was employed to design a new span, and the Chattanooga Bridge Company presented a proposal in January 1889 to build a toll bridge across the river. With some changes (plans were finalized for a free public span, and the site was moved to the higher ground of Walnut Street to avoid the need for a drawbridge), the plan was approved. To raise money, the county issued $200,000 bonds, and the new Hill City development on the north bank contributed $25,000. The contractor for the structure was Confederate veteran John B. Neely, who also built the Cincinnati Southern railroad into Chattanooga.

The Walnut Street Bridge (also known as the "county bridge") opened on February 18, 1891, immediately driving the outdated river ferries out of business. The "Souvenir Programme" for the opening of the Walnut St. Bridge is shown above and on page 12. The city later inherited the bridge when Hill City was annexed by Chattanooga in 1929.

Serving as a streetcar line and automobile connector between downtown and North Chattanooga for several decades, in May 1978 the bridge was closed due to its deteriorating condition, and plans were made to construct a new bridge across the river. Discussions as to the future of this bridge included a variety of proposals – the creation of a trolley line across the structure, opening shops along the bridge, or transforming it into a pedestrian bridge. Eventually, the latter proposal was selected, and the "new" pedestrian bridge opened in 1991 following a $4 million restoration; the names of the individuals who donated funds to renovate the bridge are recorded on small plaques along the structure. Added to the National Register of Historic Places in 1990, the bridge, which is the oldest-surviving truss bridge in the South, offers a pleasant stroll from downtown to the north bank of the river; a number of annual events are held along the span, including Wine Over Water, an annual wine-tasting event which raises money for Cornerstones, a local historic preservation organization.

In addition to its role in conveying streetcar passengers, automobiles, and pedestrians across the Tennessee River, the Walnut Street Bridge has over the years been the site of numerous events, both humorous and regrettable. To illustrate the former, in 1902 a "Captain Stanley" of the Cincinnati Carnival Company proposed diving from the Walnut Street Bridge on a Sunday afternoon. Following protests by local residents that this would violate the Sabbath, the event was rescheduled for a weekday, and the daredevil dive took place before 500 onlookers. In 1915, daredevil Sir Charles Clift proposed to recreate this feat, but he was denied a permit by the county. Instead, he was placed in a steamer trunk and thrown into the river from the deck of the steamer *Chattanooga*, which had been tied at the foot of Broad Street for the event.

As for regrettable incidents, on the other hand, the bridge has witnessed 2 of the most tragic events to take place in Chattanooga during the Jim Crow period. On February 14, 1893, an "aged woman" was assaulted in her home by an African-American man described only as "slightly built." On McCallie Avenue, the police picked up a suspect, **Alfred Blount**, who was only tentatively identified by the victim. Though the sheriff sent out a flier asking for patience because the identification of Blount had not been satisfactory, a 1,000-person mob beat down the jail door, shoved aside the sheriff's deputies, and took Blount to the Walnut Street Bridge, where he was promptly hanged. With headlines reading, "The Ghastly Work of Last Night Accomplished by Cool and Deliberate Men Who, When their Work had been Accomplished, Quietly Dispersed," the *Chattanooga Times* decried the event as a violation of the law and the courts, and as one of the worst examples of lawlessness in the history of Chattanooga.

This, however, was not the last such incident to take place in Chattanooga. On January 23, 1906, a young girl was sexually assaulted in the St. Elmo suburb at the foot of Lookout Mountain by an African-American man. Two days later, a man named **Ed Johnson** was identified by a "witness" as the guilty party, after which he was taken to Nashville and "partially

identified" by the victim. Johnson was returned to Chattanooga for trial which, despite the ambiguous identification by the victim, ended in a guilty verdict. On March 19, 1906, the same night that the United States Supreme Court granted an appeal of the case, a mob broke into the county jail and took Johnson from his cell. Johnson was taken to the second span of the Walnut Street Bridge, where a trolley rope and bell cords were taken from a nearby streetcar and used to hang him from the bridge. His body was then riddled with 50 bullets. Prior to his death, Johnson proclaimed to the crowd, "God bless you all - I am innocent!" - a phrase which was subsequently etched on his tombstone. Again, the *Chattanooga Times* registered its outrage at this incident, with headlines reading, "Majesty of Law Outraged by Lynchers," "Mandate of the Supreme Court of the United States Disregarded and Red Riot Rampant," and "Terrible and Tragic Vengeance Bows Chattanooga's Head in Shame." For their role in allowing the lynching, Hamilton County Sheriff Joseph F. Shipp, jailor Jeremiah Gibson, and 4 other individuals who took part in the lynching were tried and found guilty of contempt of court, the only criminal trial in U.S. Supreme Court history. This event was the subject of a recent book by Leroy Phillips, Jr. and Mark Curriden, entitled *Contempt of Court: The Turn-of-the-Century Lynching That Launched a Hundred Years of Federalism* (pictured above), winner of the American Bar Association's Silver Gavel Award in 1999.

Continue across the bridge. To your right, immediately east of the bridge, is **MacLellan Island** (also known as "Chattanooga Island"). ❸ This island, which was occupied by prehistoric Indians for thousands of years, is described by archaeologists as a "multi-compo-

nent Archaic to Woodland open habitation site." Following the flood of April 1886, numerous skeletons were exposed, and Dr. Charles Wright and Professor H.D. Hyatt examined 6 prehistoric burials exposed by the high floodwaters at that time. A systematic archaeological exploration was subsequently conducted by the Jeffrey L. Brown Institute of Archaeology in 1983, and numerous artifacts have been removed from this site; the rattlesnake gorget (a medallion worn around the neck) pictured above and on page 13 was unearthed at nearby Williams Island downstream from Chattanooga, and is similar to the artifacts found on MacLellan Island.

Following the Cherokee Removal (1838), the 18.8-acre island was purchased by early Chattanooga resident Thomas Crutchfield. Originally, at the toe of the island was a swing

ferry, for some years the only means of crossing the Tennessee River at Chattanooga. A long rope from the ferry boat, supported at regular intervals by poles resting on small flatboats, was attached to the island; the boat was carried by the current into the river until a plank was dropped deep into the water on the upper side, which allowed the current to push the boat to the opposite shore. A *Harper's Weekly* illustration of the ferry is reproduced above and on page 12. Though the swing ferry remained in operation until the 1880s, it was eventually replaced by steam ferries, including the *Myra* and the *M.V. Read*. During this period, the island itself was operated as farmland, though at the turn of the century Charles E. James, president of the Chattanooga Estates Company, offered to give Maclellan Island to the city if it would create a high, level bridge over the river at that point. James offered to contribute $75,000 toward the construction of the structure, which was also to include stairs leading

down to a "summer garden" or "Coney Island on a small scale" on the island below. One additional condition, though, was that an additional bridge be built across the river at West Sixth Street; due to this requirement and the fact that the island overflowed at the low flood level of 35 feet, the offer was declined. The subsequent flood of 1917 completely submerged the island when it crested at 47.7 feet, validating that decision. In 1954, owner Robert Maclellan gave the island to the Chattanooga Audubon Society as a wildlife refuge, a function it continues to serve today.

Passing over MacLellan Island is the **Veterans' Bridge, ❹** the fifth bridge to be built across the river between downtown and North Chattanooga (and the fourth still standing). When the Walnut Street Bridge was closed in 1978, a new bridge was proposed in order to ease traffic problems involved in crossing the river. Following some controversy as to the location for this new span, a site connecting Georgia Avenue on the south side of the river to Barton Avenue on the north side was selected. Veterans' Bridge, which was completed in 1984, sits on one of the alternate sites proposed for the 1917 Market Street Bridge. Though the bridge crosses MacLellan Island, the piers do not actually touch the island, which remains a private bird sanctuary.

To the east, beyond the Veterans' Bridge, is a low, 300-400 foot-high ridge. Named for the Brainerd Mission to the east, **Missionary Ridge** (also called "Mission Ridge" in early days) was the site of the great Union victory on November 25, 1863, when federal troops abandoned their orders, rushed the ridge and routed Confederate troops entrenched at the crest of the hill. In this charge, the federal troops were aided by the efforts of a young Arthur MacArthur (the father of World War II General Douglas MacArthur), who seized his regiment's colors and, dashing to the top of the hill, planted the flag at the crest of the Confederate works, inspiring the federal advance. The Confederates had been misaligned, as they were placed at the extreme top - not the military crest - of the ridge; southern artillery was therefore useless, as cannon could not be depressed low enough to aim at the federal troops below, and the Confederate soldiers were forced to simply roll shells and rocks down the hill toward the advancing Yankees. The climax of the battle is depicted in a Currier & Ives engraving, reproduced on page 12. Though the rebel army suffered fewer casualties than the Union troops (the Union had 753 killed, 4,722 wounded, and 349 missing, while 361 Confederates were killed and 2,160 were wounded), the debacle at Missionary Ridge forced the southern army to retreat into North Georgia, setting the stage for the Union advance upon Atlanta. In 1929, Missionary Ridge was annexed by the city of Chattanooga. Originally, many ridge residents demanded beautification work as a condition of annexation, leading some to complain that Missionary Ridge residents "wanted gold-plated fire plugs." Though the initial vote went against annexation, ridge residents later reconsidered and re-voted after the nearby Brainerd area also approved annexation.

Further upriver (east) from the Walnut Street Bridge is the **Chickamauga Dam** (1940), part of a chain of dams erected along the Tennessee River by the Tennessee Valley Authority (TVA) in the 1930s and 1940s. On May 18, 1933, President Franklin D. Roosevelt signed federal legislation creating the Tennessee Valley Authority to harness the waters of the Tennessee River for the purposes of "relief, recovery, and reform"; news of this event reportedly caused whistles in Chattanooga to break out in a "bedlam of noise." At that time,

Chattanooga was considered the "great danger point on the river," and the prospect of flood relief was welcome news to many local residents. By the summer of 1935, final approval came for the construction of a dam several miles upriver from downtown Chattanooga. On Labor Day in 1940, Roosevelt dedicated this new dam, (pictured above and on page 13) concluding, "I, therefore, today on this very happy occasion dedicate this dam and these lakes to the benefit of all the people, the prosperity they have stimulated, the faith they have justified, the hope they have inspired, the hearts they encourage - the total defense of the United States of America" (the last phrase offered as a nod to the impending involvement of the United States in World War II). Built at a cost of approximately $39.8 million, the 5,800-

long and 129-foot tall structure created a 35,400-acre lake and required the purchase of 60,000 acres of land, as well as the relocation of 900 families and 425 grave sites. After completion, the dam was capable of producing 81,000 kilowatts of electricity and served to protect Chattanooga from floods such as those which inundated the city in 1867, 1875, 1886, and 1917. The former county seats of Dallas and Harrison, however, were submerged by this new, man-made lake. Although a number of names for the dam were initially proposed, the local word "Chickamauga" was eventually selected; this word is alternately translated as "river of death," "dwelling place of the war chief" (from the Creek Cukko-Mico), or "much muddy or red waters" or "much big waters, red" (from the Cherokee Tsi-gwa-amo-gi). In ensuing years, it became apparent that a mistake had been made in not building a bridge over the dam, a problem which was rectified on October 17, 1954, with the opening of the Thrasher Bridge, named for Judge Wilkes T. Thrasher, a prime supporter of the dam project.

The Tennessee River over which the Walnut Street Bridge passes has also been the site of a number of wild riverboat races, none wilder than the May 1900 race between the steamers *City of Charleston* and *Joe Wheeler*, which began to race after passing under the Cincinnati Southern railroad bridge near the present Chickamauga Dam. When the *Charleston* was called to the bank to make a landing, the crew on the *Joe Wheeler* passed by, jeering and yelling. Taking offense, the *Charleston* caught up to the other boat and began to crowd it into the shore, raking the wheelhouse with limbs which ripped the rails of the boat from the deck. Soon enough, shots were exchanged, although cooler heads eventually prevailed.

In addressing flooding problems in Chattanooga, the Chickamauga Dam served to compliment the earlier **Hale's Bar Lock and Dam** 35 miles downriver (to your left) from Chattanooga. ❺ Passing through the narrow

Tennessee River Gorge, the wild river originally created several natural obstacles referred to as the Tumbling Shoals, the Suck (also called the Kettle or Boiling Pot), the Pan, the Skillet, and the Pot. This whole 8 1/2 mile stretch of the river came to be known as the "Suck," a title first recorded in an 1768-1769 British army engineer's report of lands acquired in the French and Indian War, and it complicated navigation and hindered commercial transportation on the river, especially during periods of low river levels. In 1897, Col. Tomlinson Fort and G.W. Nixon proposed building a dam below the gorge, and in 1904 Congress passed legislation consenting to the project. Construction of the 1,200-foot dam was begun in 1905 by the Chattanooga and Tennessee River Power Company, which was organized by Chattanooga businessmen Charles E. James and Jo Conn Guild, along with New York financial backing. The final cost of the dam, which took years to complete, was around $10 million. The structure began impounding the waters of the river on November 1, 1913, raising the level of water at Chattanooga by 6 feet and extending the navigable season by 2 months. The new electricity created by this structure increased industrial opportunities at Chattanooga, as indicated by the new nickname "Dynamo of Dixie" adopted by the city, and also raised interest in recreational boating and usage. In the 1970s, this early structure was replaced by the current Nickajack Dam.

To the west (left) as you continue across the Walnut Street Bridge are a number of ridges and mountains which encircle Chattanooga. This is an excellent point from which to survey the city's surroundings. To the far left is the tallest peak in Chattanooga (2,126 feet in elevation), **Lookout Mountain.** ❻ Early on, this prominent peak was referred to by the Indian word *Chatanuge*, which means "rock that comes to a point" in the Creek tongue and "mountains looking at each other" in the Cherokee language. By the early 1800s, however, the term "Lookout Mountain" was generally used, though the origin is not known - some speculate that it refers to the excellent vantage point offered from the top of the mountain, while others believe that it refers to a warning given to boatmen concerning either the obstacles in the river ahead or robbers who preyed on boats in this stretch of the river. On September 20, 1782, the mountain played host to the "Last Battle of the Revolution" when militia under John Sevier encountered Chickamauga Indians under Chief Wyuka (or

Skyuka); although the battle took place almost a year after the British surrender at Yorktown, the fact that the governor of North Carolina had authorized "Continental credit" to be paid for this endeavor lent it official status, and it became known as the last battle of the American Revolution.

Following the Cherokee Removal (1838), local entrepreneur James A. Whiteside purchased a large amount of land on the mountain and established a toll road known as Whiteside's Pike along the old trail up the mountain. At the top of the mountain was Leonora Spring, named for Whiteside's wife, near which an early summer resort called Summertown developed.

On November 24, 1863, the second day of the Civil War battles for Chattanooga was set into motion when the federal army under General "Fighting Joe" Hooker swarmed Lookout Mountain in the midst of a thick fog which blanketed the mountain and caused the battle to be referred to as the "Battle Above the Clouds." After the Confederates withdrew from the Cravens' House, which is situated on a plateau midway up the mountain, the fighting petered out; the remainder of the rebel army withdrew across the mountain during the night, and the U.S. flag was raised at the top of the mountain to raucous cheers from the valley below. Pictured on page 12 of this section is a reproduction of a 30-by-13 foot painting entitled "The Battle of Lookout Mountain," which was completed by artist James Walker in 1874. The figure on the white horse in the center of the painting is General Hooker, who commissioned the work. The original artwork is today on display at the Point Park visitors' center at the top of the mountain.

Following the Civil War, Lookout Mountain became the site of a "Turnpike War" after a second road up the mountain (the "Johnson Turnpike") was created in 1879 by Col. A.M. Johnson, the founder of the St. Elmo suburb at the foot of the mountain. When this road began to charge a lower toll than its competitor, the Whiteside family instituted a fee for admission to the popular "Point" of the mountain, and armed guards with shotguns were placed at the entrance to that area. Soon thereafter, hotels began to be built at the top of the mountain, and the development of a cable car line to the crest spurred additional residential and commercial development. In 1898, it was announced that the Point would be purchased for inclusion in the Chickamauga &

Chattanooga National Military Park, and the last vestige of the Turnpike War ended. Interestingly, Lookout Mountain is also reported to be the first town in the South where women were allowed to vote (although not in state or national elections). Today, Lookout Mountain attracts visitors to a number of attractions, including the Incline Railway (which, with a gradient of 72.7%, is "America's Most Amazing Mile"), Rock City Gardens, Ruby Falls, and the Civil War battlefields at Point Park and Cravens' House.

North of Lookout Mountain, running along the western edge of Chattanooga, is **W a l d e n ' s Ridge, ❼** loosely named for a 1760s long hunter – his first name was Elisha, and his second has been reported as Wallin, Walling, Walding, Wallins, and Wallen - who entered into this area from Virginia. Walden's Ridge is a 2,000-foot escarpment, and its southern tip is known today as Signal Mountain, a residential area which was originally planned by Charles E. James as "Signal Point." The 1890s financial drought ended this plan, as well as a fine hunting club which had attracted a number of potential members, including Theodore Roosevelt. By 1913, however, James, who owned some 4,400 acres on the mountain, erected a hotel and established a streetcar line (pictured above) known as the Chattanooga Traction Company to the top of the mountain. The inn was expanded in 1916 (now it is the Alexian Brothers Retirement Home), and a casino, riding stables, and golf course (1918) were subsequently added. In 1919, a charter for the town of Signal Mountain (named for a signal station maintained on the mountain during the Civil War) was obtained, and today Signal Mountain remains a popular residential area.

Further north, the smaller ridge on the north bank of the river is known as **Stringer's Ridge**. ❽ This area is named for Captain William Stringer, a local resident who served in the Mexican War and died on the eve of the Civil War in 1860. This ridge was the site of 2 significant federal artillery bombardments during the Civil War. On June 7, 1862, federal troops under

Brigadier-General James Negley shelled Chattanooga for 2 days from the north side of the river, meeting fire from Confederate troops under General Danville Ledbetter (including the novice, 96-member Lookout Battery), who were entrenched on Cameron Hill before withdrawing on June 8, 1862. This event was repeated on August 21, 1863, when Colonel John T. Wilder's 18th Indiana Light Artillery set up a diversionary artillery attack from Stringer's Ridge to mask the movement of the federal army toward the town, reportedly sinking 2 steamers in the river and causing panic throughout Chattanooga. An ensuing artillery duel lasted for 2 weeks, during which the main federal army crossed the Tennessee River to the southwest, forcing the outflanked Confederate army to abandon the town in September 1863. In 1910, a tunnel was constructed through Stringer's Ridge; built by workhouse convicts without "a single expert tunnel builder," this tunnel opened additional land in north Hamilton County to residential and commercial development. In recognition of its Civil War heritage, Stringer's Ridge was added to the National Register of Historic Places in 1984.

Stringer's Ridge winds to the southwest along the north bank of the Tennessee River, terminating at a sharp bend downriver known as **Moccasin Bend**. Considered by many to be "the most important archaeological complex located inside a United States city," Moccasin Bend has been the site of continuous human occupation since the Paleo-Indian period (c. 14,000-8,000 B.C.). "The Bend" contains extensive evidence of Indian occupation and several town sites, including Mallard's Dozen, a Woodland town dating to 405 B.C., Vulcan (Archaic, 1335 B.C.), and Hampton Place (Mississippian, c. 1500). Abandoned by Mississippian populations after 1630, the area was sparsely occupied until 1817-1819, when John Brown, a mixed-blood Cherokee with "a reputation as the most skilled river pilot in the area," obtained a 640-acre reservation on the east side of the Bend to operate a ferry across the river at that point. After the Cherokee Removal, white settlers moved onto Moccasin Bend and operated several small farms on the land. In September 1863, Moccasin Bend was occupied by "the Crack Battery of Indiana," a 4-cannon battery which assisted in forcing Confederate forces to abandon Chattanooga prior to the battle of Chickamauga. After the federal retreat from Chickamauga, moreover, the site was utilized by the Union army as a "shield protecting the western approaches to

Chattanooga"; renamed "Fort Whitaker," the guns on the Bend traded cannon shots with Confederate troops on Lookout Mountain during the siege of Chattanooga. Today, Moccasin Bend contains evidence of this occupation, including a number of cannon emplacements, rifle pits, bivouac pads, a signal tower base, and, possibly, burials of federal casualties from the action which took place in the Chattanooga area.

In the early twentieth century, the town of Lookout Mountain petitioned the Chattanooga City Commission to buy Moccasin Bend for recreational purposes; due to protests from the Industrial Bureau of the Chamber of Commerce, however, this plan failed. In 1949, Congress, referring to the area as "one of the oldest and largest of the national historical areas," authorized the transfer of 1,400 acres to the Chickamauga & Chattanooga National Military Park; again, however, the plan failed when Tennessee Governor Clement vetoed a $100,000 appropriation to purchase the property due to the cost of the project, and by 1959 the U.S. government had lost interest in this plan. In ensuing years, the area became the site of a state mental hospital, golf course, radio towers, police firing range, and water treatment facility. Other subsequent proposals, including Ms. Sims Perry Long's 1958 proposal to landscape the area with artificial lakes, athletic fields, trails, and gardens, and a 1982 recommendation by the Urban Land Institute to build a zoo, marina, recreated Indian village, and public trails, never materialized. Named a National Historic Landmark in 1986, the site began to again generate discussion in the late 1990s, when the topic of preserving Moccasin Bend was again raised. At this time, a proposal to designate the area as a national park is pending before Congress.

At the end of the Walnut Street Bridge, the area on the north bank of the river is referred to as **North Chattanooga, ❾** a collection of early residential neighborhoods which sprang up across the river from downtown Chattanooga. During the Civil War, a young Confederate soldier, Captain S.J.A. Frazier, (pictured above) was cared for in Chattanooga after having been shot through the windpipe at Chickamauga. Following the war, Frazier purchased 70 acres on the north side of the river

from the pioneer John Cowart family, occupying the old Cowart homeplace ("The Cedars") on the slope of a hill overlooking the river at present-day Frazier Avenue; The Cedars were destroyed by an accidental fire on March 13, 1923, leaving only the 4 chimneys standing, and no remnant of the structure exists today. In 1884, the first organized attempt to build a community in this area took place when Frazier opened a steam ferry across the river and established the North Side Land Company, which then subdivided much of the land in this area as the "Hill City" development. The main road through the area was named Frazier Avenue; joining in this enterprise were Dr. R.W. Colville, James S. Bell, and R.M. Barton, Jr., for whom other main roads in the neighborhood were named. When 2 streetcar lines were opened across the new Walnut Street Bridge in the 1890s, residential development in the area blossomed, and today the area remains a convenient residential neighborhood across the river from downtown Chattanooga.

In 1925, the Dallas Heights Company was organized by W.S. Beck to develop a 125-acre tract northwest of Hill City, through which an old road had run to the early county seat of Dallas. This area, part of the "North Chattanooga" area, was annexed by Chattanooga in 1929.

Nearby, to the east of the Veterans' Bridge on the north bank of the Tennessee River, is the "Riverview" area. Pioneer David Beck (1765-1848) bought much of the land north of the river after coming from Rhea County, Tennessee, around 1822; the land subsequently passed to his son, Joshua Beck (1813-1886), a Union supporter during the Civil War. In the years after the war, stone from the Beck farm was used to build a number of significant downtown buildings, including the First Methodist Church at Georgia and McCallie Avenues. Part of this extensive farm eventually became the Chattanooga Golf & Country Club (1896), and the Riverview community thereafter grew up around the spectacular Lyndhurst mansion erected by John T. Lupton on another part of the old Beck farm. Few remnants of the former Beck estate exist today: though the former slave cemetery located on North Dartmouth Street was fenced and marked, the original Beck residence, erected in 1875 at the end of present-day Rivervista Drive, was destroyed by fire in 1974, and the antebellum family cemetery was accidentally bulldozed during construction of the golf course (it is now marked by a low iron fence & marker near the

As you near the north bank of the river, to your left, almost under the nearby Market Street Bridge, is the **Chattanooga Star Riverboat**. ❿ This 65-by-24 foot sidewheel paddleboat was built by John Hosemann and his sons, Pete and Mike, in 1982. Today the riverboat is complimented by a floating restaurant barge which serves patrons as they look out over the Tennessee River.

Near this spot lie the remains of the *Chattanooga* riverboat. This, however, was not the first *Chattanooga* to ply the waters in this area. The first *Chattanooga* was a 175-by-33 foot, 182-ton steamer built in Kingston, Tennessee, in 1857. This was the first boat owned by the prominent local steamboat line of James and William Williams. It was captured during the Civil War and put into service by the federal army, coming to be referred to as "Chicken Thief" by southerners due to its refusal to sink when in Union hands. Following the war, the boat was put into service as a civilian steamer.

In 1905, a second *Chattanooga* (the one lying at the bottom of the river here) was put into service by the Chattanooga Packet Company, which opened to compete with the Tennessee River Navigation Company to develop "through" navigation on the lower portion of the river. The *Megiddo* riverboat was renamed the *Chattanooga* at that time. Louis D. Pell captained the boat, which was 175 feet long, 33 feet at the beam, and had a 5-foot deep hold; this boat also included 25 cabins and had 2 steam boilers driving its aft paddlewheel. In 1918, the steamboat capsized at Ross's Landing due to careless unloading and a drop in river levels, and in 1920 the hapless ship sank in 12 feet of water on the north side of the river, marking the end of an era in Chattanooga. Today, the skeleton of the boat remains intact, and possible preservation efforts are being discussed at the present time.

This is not the only shipwreck in this part of the river. Also located underwater on the north side of the river is the hull of the steamer/ferryboat *Tellico*, which sank near here in 1886. The 75-by-16 foot steamer was built in 1880 as a tow boat and then converted into a ferry in 1883. Having sunk once near Soddy, Tennessee, when a pipe burst in 1884, the boat capsized and sank for good in 1886. In addition, near Chattanooga lie several wrecked federal pontoon boats which were used during the Civil War in crossing the river at Brown's Ferry, when the Union army opened the "Cracker Line" to break the rebel siege at Chattanooga.

On the north bank of the river, to the left (west) of the bridge is **Coolidge Park**, ⓫ a recreational park which opened in 1999. During the federal occupation of Chattanooga in 1864-65, a number of refugees, camp followers, and recently-freed slaves entered Chattanooga, throwing up tents and ramshackle huts in which to live. One such camp on the north side of the river, near where Coolidge Park is today, became known as "Camp Countraband," and a population estimate on November 7, 1865, put the number of people in the makeshift camp at 3,500 African-Americans, mostly former slaves following the advance of the federal army. Today, this spot is a 22-acre park dedicated in October 1999 and named for Technical Sergeant Charles H. Coolidge of Signal Mountain, Tennessee (pictured below), who earned the Congressional Medal of Honor dur-

ing World War II for his deeds on October 24-28, 1944: "With a handful of new reinforcements he directed a 4-day battle against a superior German force during which time he dueled two tanks with his carbine, advanced alone to stop a German attack with two cases of grenades and frustrated an attempt to turn the flank of his battalion."

This park was originally conceived following World War II (1946), and although dedication ceremonies took place at that time, completion of the project took until 1999. Coolidge Park features a restored carousel (pictured on page 13) as well as an interactive fountain encircled by sculpted lions, elephants, camels, and horses. The carousel was built in 1895 at the Dentzel factory in Philadelphia and shipped to Rochester, New York. A second level of horses was added in 1915; relocated to Massachusetts until 1940, the carousel was subsequently placed in Grant Park in Atlanta until the 1960s. It languished in storage until the 1980s, when it was rescued by Atlantan Charlie Walker, and 52 hand-carved animals were then added through the efforts of Bud Ellis' local "Horsin' Around" studio. Today, Coolidge Park is a popular recreational are which is filled with visitors throughout the year.

Backing up to Coolidge park is **Frazier Avenue**,

named for Hill City founder S.J.A. Frazier. Originally a self-sufficient community, today many former grocery stores, dry cleaners, hardware stores, and other business buildings dating to the 1880s have been renovated, and a variety of eclectic shops and restaurants have arisen along Frazier Avenue.

To the east (right), at the north end of the Walnut Street Bridge is the green-roofed **Chattanooga Theater Center**, ⑫ a community theater founded in 1923 as the "Little Theatre of Chattanooga." This facility underwent a recent $8.5 million renovation to complete a 45,000 square foot building housing 2 theaters of 380 (Mainstage Auditorium) and 200 (Circle Theater) seats. The Theater Center hosts approximately 18 shows per year, ranging from children's plays to full stage productions.

To the west, beyond the Chattanooga Theatre Center, is a large residential neighborhood on the bank of the Tennessee River known as **Heritage Landing**. This "Heritage Place" archaeological area, which sits opposite MacLellan Island, has been described as a "multi-component Late Archaic to Mississippian open habitation site." Surveyed by archaeologists in 1984, the site revealed the remains of numerous Amerindian burials, and Mississippian house floors and wattle-and-daub structures were found to have been scattered along the flood terrace. It is believed that this site was part of a prehistoric Indian town which predated the large Citico mound area across the river. This 96-acre site, which was formerly owned by the Hampton family, was purchased for $52 million by local developer Tommy Lupton. Opening in 1986, this project was subsequently labeled "Heritage Landing" (though it continued to be referred to early on as "Heritage Place"), and today the area contains a large condominium project with an estimated 345 units built along a series of interlocking lakes.

The beginning of the tour of the Walnut Street Bridge is located at the south end of the bridge.

Note: take Riverwalk to **Ross's Landing** (p.135) or **Walnut Street Bridge** (p.11)

Bluff Furnace

Citico Mound

14 *"Prodigal Son," by Leonard Baskin, River Gallery Sculpture Garden*

3 *D.M. Key*

2 *Thomas Richardson House*

THIRD STREET

WALNUT STREET

FOURTH STREET

286

At the title implies, the Bluff View tract sits on a prominent bluff overlooking the Tennessee River, to the east of the downtown core. Originally, a portion of this tract was owned by pioneer Jane Henderson, who operated an early inn nearby at the corner of Market and Second Streets. During the Civil War, both armies found the high river bluff to be a desirable spot on which to place artillery, and during the course of the conflict both Confederate and Union cannon looked out over the river from this excellent vantage point.

In 1885, a group of investors from New Orleans purchased from the Ker Boyce estate a tract of land on the bluff, where High, Lookout, and Walnut Streets converged at the edge of the river. The bluff was then surveyed for the construction of home sites, and a crew began work digging a well for a proposed distillery in the area. Concluding that Tennessee was moving toward the prohibition of liquor, however, the investors abandoned this enterprise. A second group of investors then bought the land (which is still listed on assessor's plats as the "Griffis & Evans Subdivision"), naming Sam R. Read as trustee to oversee its development as a residential area. As a result, around the turn of the century Bluff View began to become a fashionable residential district, a development highlighted by the 1904 construction of the impressive Ross-Faxon House (now the Hunter Museum of American Art) on the edge of the bluff.

The transition of this area from a residential neighborhood to an arts district began in 1952, with the opening of the art museum. In 1969, the Houston Museum of Decorative Arts also opened in the Bluff View area. Subseqently, between the late 1960s and the mid-1970s a number of original residences were torn down to make way for parking areas and park space in the vicinity of these museums. In 1989, Dr. and Mrs. Charles "Tony" Portera purchased a number of the remaining structures in the Bluff View area, transforming these old homes into a variety of art galleries and restaurants; this development was capped by the 1993 opening of the Bluff View Sculpture Garden. Today, the Bluff View Art District is a popular destination for local residents and visitors, and it offers a quiet, park-like haven adjacent to the downtown core.

10 Hunter Museum of American Art

13 Renaissance Commons

SECOND STREET

9　**8**　**13**　**12**　**14**

7

15

6

HIGH STREET

5

4

Snodgrass & Fields Sawmill

to **Fountain Square** p. 47

4

ancis Marion Walker

to **Brabson Hill** p. xx

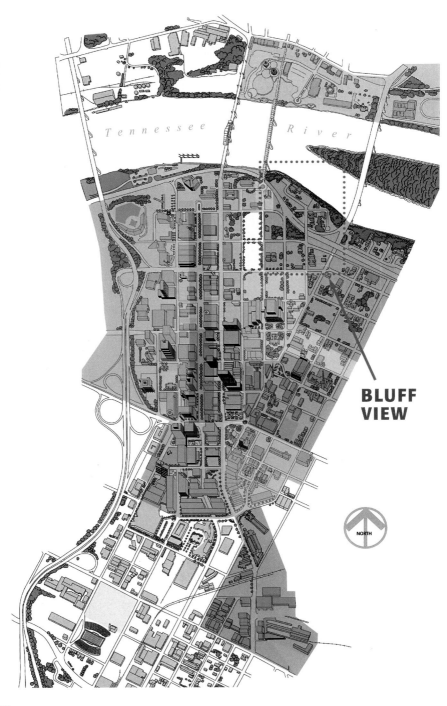

Tennessee River

BLUFF
VIEW

NORTH

The tour of Bluff View begins a few blocks from the bluff itself, at the southeast corner of Walnut and Third Streets. ❶ Previously located at this spot was the antebellum home of **Amos C. Van Epps** (302 Walnut Street), a 1-story frame home fronted by a wide veranda, fluted Ionic columns, and a white picket fence. Born in Schenectady, New York, Van Epps came to Chattanooga with his family from Alabama in 1848 to become a river merchant at the nearby Ross's Landing wharf. Following the Civil War, Van Epps relocated to Atlanta, Georgia, and the house was occupied for a time by David B. Ragsdale, owner of a local dry goods firm called the "New York Store". The house was then purchased by Captain J.P. Kindrick, a merchant who was involved in the newspaper and steamboat businesses in Chattanooga. The house was subsequently torn down and is now the site of a parking lot maintained by the UnumProvident insurance corporation.

From this corner, proceed south, away from the river. The 3-story brick building on your left (316 Walnut Street) is the site of the former **Thomas Richardson House**. ❷ Thomas Richardson was an Englishman who arrived in Chattanooga in 1854 to become involved in a

steam tannery on Chattanooga Creek and, later, the Chattanooga Leather Manufacturing Company. This 1-story frame house (above) was built for Richardson by John C. Glass. During the Civil War, the home was occupied by Confederate Generals John C. Breckenridge, Joseph E. Johnston, and John H. Morgan, and during the siege of Chattanooga in autumn 1863, the house served as Major General (US) William S. Rosecrans' headquarters; it was in this house that Rosecrans was informed that he would be replaced by Ulysses S Grant as commander of the federal army in Chattanooga following the Union loss at Chickamauga. Later, the federal assault on Missionary Ridge was reportedly planned here by Union Generals Ulysses S Grant, William T. Sherman, and George H. Thomas. Richardson returned to his home following the Civil War but eventually

sold the house to J.T. Williams, a Welshman involved in the coal business. The house was later taken down in the 1920s and replaced with the Tudor Revival Louise Terrace Apartment building, which is now listed on the National Register of Historic Places (1998). Currently owned by the UnumProvident insurance corporation, the building underwent a $4 million renovation in 1997 and now operates as a corporate "hotel" for use by visiting employees.

Proceed to the northeast corner of Walnut and Fourth Streets. ❸ This property, now vacant, was at one time the home of **David McKendree Key** (above), an attorney who came to Chattanooga from Kingston, Tennessee, in 1853 and moved to this location in 1859. During the siege of Chattanooga in 1863, the home became the headquarters of a future U.S. president, Major General (US) James A. Garfield. Returning to Chattanooga following the war (and only after his Unionist friend William Crutchfield promised that he would be "kindly treated" by local residents), Key, a Confederate veteran, was obliged to stay in temporary quarters; his health during this period was poor, and because all of his wealth was invested in worthless Confederate money, the family was obliged to sell their "finery" as well as his Confederate uniform to newly-freed slaves who had U.S. greenbacks to spend. Key, who later became a U.S. senator (1875-77), Postmaster General under President Rutherford B. Hayes (1877-80), and federal judge (1880-84), later relocated to a house at Fourth and Chestnut Streets, and the structure at this location was acquired by planing mill owner Robert Morrison and, later, by Alias Rosenhein, owner of a wholesale liquor and cigar business on Market Street. In the 1920s, much of this area came to be occupied by apartment houses, and the house was torn down at that time.

From this spot, turn left onto Fourth Street and go two blocks, to the corner of High and Fourth Street. ❹ Located at the southwest corner of High and Mott (East Fourth) Streets was another antebellum structure, the home of **Colonel Francis Marion Walker** (picutred on page 30), an early district attorney general from Kentucky who organized a company of Confederate soldiers at the outbreak of the Civil War. This group was originally known as the "Marsh Blues," named after the Marsh and Moore firm which gave uniforms and equipment to the men. Walker served under Brigadier General Otho F. Strahl's brigade at the battle of Chickamauga, and he commanded the 19th Tennessee regiment at Chattanooga and Missionary Ridge. However, he was killed on July 22, 1864, while leading his regiment at the battle of Atlanta,  one day after having been promoted to the position of Brigadier General; he was 37 years old. This early home, which was later occupied by the Cooke and Swaney families, was razed in 1967. Currently, the UnumProvident insurance corporation is in the process of erected a parking garage on this block.

Here, turn left and head north along High Street. Situated at the northeast corner of High and Fourth Streets **5** are the **Robert E. Lee Apartments** (320 High Street), which were built in 1920. Ironically, only next door (316 High Street) are the **Lincoln Apartments**, erected in 1939. Both buildings display the common brick-and-stone construction utilized for apartment buildings during this period.

Further down High Street are 3 brick homes **6** which survived the proliferation of new apartment housing and commercial development which accompanied the turn of the century in downtown Chattanooga. The first two houses (309 and 311 High Street) were erected around 1900, while the house at the southwest corner of High and Third Street (305 High Street) was built in 1895.

From this point, cross Third Street. As you cross the overpass, you are entering the Bluff View Art District. On your right is the Victorian **T.C. Thompson House** (212 High Street) erected in 1908. **7** Thompson was a South Carolinian whose father was governor of that state; during Sherman's march through Georgia and the Carolinas, Thompson, a child at the time, was carried to safety by an African-American blacksmith as the Union army arrived at the outskirts of town, a story which he often told when discussing the Civil War. Thompson came to Chattanooga with an Atlanta manufacturing business in 1893 and became involved in the National Life Insurance Company, where he later became state manager. He was subse-

quently elected mayor of Chattanooga, a post he held from 1909 to 1915. Today, a local children's hospital is named for Thompson; this hospital, which opened in 1928-1929 at a cost of $185,000, was an outgrowth of Thompson's charitable efforts for ill children. In the 1970s, this 2-story frame house was subdivided into apartments, and today it serves as a bed-and-breakfast hosting guests of the Bluff View Art District. To the left of this house is an alley through the art district. In this alleyway, behind the Thompson House, is Tony's Pasta Restaurant, which is located in the former carriage house of the home.

Next door to the T.C. Thompson House, at the southeast corner of High and Second Streets, **8** is a turn-of-the-century Spanish stucco home (400 East Second Street) which was the former residence of **W.L. Frierson,** who came to Chattanooga in 1890 and subsequently became city attorney (1912), mayor (1905), U.S. Assistant Attorney General (1917), and Solicitor General of the United States (1920). After functioning as a private residence for several decades, in 1977 the home was opened by Mr. and Mrs. Tom Moore, Jr., as "Gallery 210," a privately-owned art gallery. Greeting guests with a quaint, European atmosphere, the building now houses the River Gallery and Rembrandt's Coffee House.

Across High Street, at the southwest corner of High and Second Streets, **9** is the **Houston Museum of Decorative Arts** (201 High Street). This turn-of-the-century Victorian house was originally the home of Fenton A. Gentry, the great, great, great grandson of pioneer, Revolutionary War soldier, Indian fighter and first governor of the State of Tennessee (1786-1801) John Sevier. Today, the museum houses the antique glass collection of Anna Safley Houston, an eccentric character referred to as "Antique Annie," whose life's work was collecting antique glass. During the Depression, Ms. Houston, who is said to have had at least 9 husbands, was forced to choose between keeping her home and antique shop, or her antique collection itself; she chose the latter, moving into a little barn-like structure she built with her own hands on the outskirts of town, where she slept surrounded by her collection. Despite living in near-poverty, she saved her antiques, refusing to sell them even to buy food, medicine, or other essentials. At one time, she had 15,000 glass pitchers in her inventory, the largest collection of its kind in the world. At her death in 1951, Houston willed her collection to the city of Chattanooga, and in 1961 the collection was granted museum status. The museum opened nearby that year at the former home of local businessman E.Y. Chapin, Sr. (24 Bluff View); when this building was torn down in 1969, the collection, which is now valued at several million dollars, moved to its current location, which had been maintained as an apartment house for several years.

From this point, the tour splits into 2 directions. To the left, along the river bluff, is a spot with a commanding view of the Tennessee River; here, located at the edge of the bluff, is the **Hunter Museum of American Art.** ⑩ During the Civil War, the bluff was the site of Battery Smartt (CSA), a cannon emplacement which was part

of southern General Benjamin F. Cheatam's Division assigned to protect Chattanooga from the advance of the federal army. After the Union army took control of the town, this spot became "Redoubt Putnam," a defensive work named for Colonel Holden Putnam (Ninety-Third Regiment of Illinois Volunteers), who was killed on November 25, 1863, at the battle of Missionary Ridge.

Subsequently, as Bluff View became the site of significant residential development at the turn of the century, the current Classical Revival mansion (above & on page 27) was built in 1904 by local banker and insurance broker Ross Faxon. The home was designed by Chicago architect Abram Garfield, the son of U.S. President James A. Garfield, who had served in Chattanooga with the Union army in 1863. The 295-by-150 foot, 3-story home is built of cut stone and brick, with a large columned portico running the length of the house on the riverfront side. As with many buildings of the period, the mansion contains numerous classical ornamental details, including egg-and-dart, acanthus leaf, and fruit-and-flower motifs throughout the house. The mansion was subsequently purchased by Walter Henson, an officer of the Osage Cotton Oil Company, after the Faxon family moved to California; in 1920, Henson sold the home to Mrs. Annie Thomas, the

widow of Ben F. Thomas, one of the original founders of the Coca-Cola Bottling Company in Chattanooga. The home was later purchased by George T. Hunter, Thomas' nephew, who, following Thomas' death in 1914, became chairman of the board of the company, which was renamed "The Coca-Cola Bottling Company (Thomas), Inc.," in honor of Thomas and his innovative role in the soft-drink industry.

Following Hunter's death in 1951, the Faxon-Thomas mansion was given to the Chattanooga Arts Association (1924) for the creation of a local art museum. The Hunter Museum of Art then opened on July 12, 1952, with a loaned exhibition of famous artwork. The structure remained in its original architectural state until 1975, when a $2.3 million modern addition to the right of the original home, designed of poured concrete intended to "blend in" with the surrounding bluff, was added to the museum complex. At that time, the board of trustees of the museum also voted to shift the focus of the museum to a specialization in American art, thus allowing the museum to create an in-depth collection focusing upon one specific artistic area; today the museum maintains an impressive permanent collection of American artwork spanning the period from 1756 to the present. The museum was added to the National Register of Historic Places in 1980.

Passing in front of the Hunter Museum is a portion of the Tennessee Riverwalk (1992), a planned 20-mile trail system designed "to link the people of Chattanooga to their river and create a new mental image of Chattanooga in the minds of visitors." To the left of the museum (west), the Riverwalk descends from the bluff toward the river landing at the Ross's Landing Park (page 135); from the foot of the bluff, moreover, you can also access the Walnut

Street Bridge (page 11) across the Tennessee River. As you descend the bluff along the Riverwalk, to your right is the site of the antebellum **Bluff Furnace** (above), ⑪ an historic

industrial enterprise established in Chattanooga. The East Tennessee Iron Manufacturing Company was chartered in 1847 "for the purpose of manufacturing iron, machinery, and implements; and all articles composed in part of iron, steel, and wood." Robert Cravens, who had experimented with blast furnaces in Roane County, Tennessee, prior to coming to Chattanooga, constructed the Bluff Furnace, which was completed in 1854. In 1859, the stack was converted from a charcoal- to a coke-fired furnace, becoming the first iron coke furnace operated in the South. Though it produced in excess of 500 pounds of pig iron per day, the venture "chilled" after the subsequent owner, New Yorker James Henderson, left Chattanooga as civil war approached in early 1860. The subsequent owner, Giles Edwards, replaced the original limestone stack with the iron cupola pictured on page 26. In Summer 1862, shortly before the arrival of Union troops in Chattanooga, the stack and machinery were dismantled and removed to Anniston, Alabama. The federal army temporarily used the furnace as a lime kiln before tearing it down, using the stone of the furnace buildings in constructing the Meigs Military Bridge across the river. The site of the Bluff Furnace was later sold and subdivided, some of the lots becoming homesites in the late nineteenth century. In 1977, the original site was rediscovered by UTC archaeologist Jeffrey L. Brown and excavated (1981-1982), and it was placed on the National Register of Historic Places in 1980. Today, the site, as well as a model of the original Bluff Furnace complex, sits adjacent to the Tennessee Riverwalk.

Returning to the corner of High and Second Streets, turn left onto Second Street (east). On the bluff to your left ⓬ is the 2-story English Tudor **McLellan House** (28 Bluff View), erected circa 1910 on the edge of the bluff above the river. In 1958, the home was sold to J. Avery Bryan, after which it was operated as a funeral home for several years. Today, the home functions as part of the Bluff View Inn, a bed-and-breakfast serving guests of the Bluff View Art District. The lawn adjacent to the McLellan House includes a bocce court - an Italian game similar to lawn bowling - and next door, in the former basement garage of the house, is a glassblowing studio where guests can observe glass being blown and sculpted.

Across the street from the McLellan House is the 2-story brick **Renaissance Commons** banquet and conference center (402 East Second

Street), ⓭ a circa-1890 residence which features front doors obtained from a governor's mansion in Ohio, as well as mahogany paneling and heart pine-paneled columns on the interior. The home was utilized for several years in the 1970s as the Stanrich photographic studio before being renovated for use as an upscale meeting and reception facility.

Next door to this building is the **Bluff View Inn** (412 East Second Street), a 2-story brick Colonial Revival house erected in 1928 by local banker Cyrus Griffin Martin. The home features a "barn door" entrance and a rear addition which houses the Back Inn Cafe, a popular local restaurant. In 1984, the home became an early local reclamation project when it was renovated to become the "Bluff View Center," which housed several business offices. This home subsequently became one of the first portions of the Bluff View Art District to be developed by Dr. and Mrs. Charles "Tony" Portera, and today the building continues to serve as the centerpiece of this development.

Across the street from the Bluff View Inn, at the end of East Second Street, ⓮ is an **Overlook** above the Tennessee River. The entirety of Bluff View is an art district, with sculptures and artworks placed throughout the area, including a rotating exhibit situated at this overlook. The artistic highlight of the art district, however, is the **Bluff View Sculpture Garden**, which is located to the right, along Spring Street. In 1938, local businessman Scott L. Probasco offered the land at this

spot to the city of Chattanooga for use as a park, and in 1992 the land was deeded to the Portera family for inclusion in the Bluff View Art District. With the assistance of landscape designer Joe Baasch and sculptor Jim Collins, the 2-acre spot was transformed into a sculpture garden, which opened in 1993. The garden features three distinct areas, labeled formal, nature and meditative. The permanent works on location include sculptures by Leonard Baskin, Allan Houser, Isamu Noguchi, Richard Serra, Frank Stella, and Ernest Trova, as well as a sculpture entitled "Taigu Rocks," from Chattanooga's sister city, Wuxi, China. Printed guides of the sculpture garden are available in the covered pavilion at the entrance to the garden. In addition, a sculpture symposium is held each June as the sculpture exhibit changes.

From this point, the **Tennessee Riverwalk** climbs a set of stairs to an elevated walkway, from which it descends along the eastern side of the river bluff and continues along the bank of the Tennessee River. **⑮** In 1986, the *Chattanooga Times* announced the creation of this linear greenway, stating that "The Riverpark is a planned development of 20 miles of the Tennessee River shoreline from Chickamauga Dam south to the Marion County line near the Grand Canyon of Tennessee." The park was planned to include "jogging trails, biking trails, horse trails, visitor's center, aquarium, hotel, marina, 1700s trading post, 1800s farm, 1900s Chattanooga, townhouses, fishing piers, country inn and English garden, TVA museum, lake, restaurants, ferry boats, greenhouse, industrial exhibits, offices, archaeological digs, shops, ballfields, Martin Luther King Jr. Memorial Park, Cherokee village, historic bridges, new golf course, musicians, theater, amphitheater, Civil War museum, regional history museum, Amnicola marsh, local sports hall of fame, miniature railroad, aquatic garden, trolley [etc.]." Some of these plans have already been realized, while others are currently in the works. It is planned that the Riverwalk will eventually connect the Chickamauga dam with Moccasin Bend, with a variety of activities, historical markers, and exhibits along the way. The portion of the Bluff View tour along the Riverwalk in some ways feels like a trip back in time, taking visitors from present-day Chattanooga to the prehistoric settlements along the banks of the Tennessee River.

After crossing an elevated walkway over Veteran's Bridge, the Riverwalk begins to go downhill, along a row of houses sitting on the bluff above the river. Originally called Payne Street after Major Matthew M. Payne, a soldier stationed in Chattanooga during the Cherokee Removal, the street which parallels the bluff above the river was renamed **Battery Place** around 1910, in recognition of its use as a strategic artillery site during the Civil War. This street contains a broad range of homes, most of which were constructed between the 1890s and 1930. The oldest house on this street, 607 Battery Place, dates to 1869. During the Civil War, the northern segment of Fort Sherman, the main defensive line on the east side of Chattanooga, was located at this point; this portion of the works was later named Redoubt Bushnell in honor of Major Douglass Bushnell (Thirteenth Illinois Infantry), who was killed in the battle of Missionary Ridge on November 25, 1863.

At the bottom of this hill, diagonally across Battery Place and Mabel Street, the riverwalk continues past the **Manker Patten Tennis Center,** named for founder David Manker Patten. This tennis complex was constructed on the site of the Snodgrass & Fields Company, a steam-powered sawmill erected during the federal occupation of the city in the waning days of the Civil War and purchased at the close of hostilities by local entrepreneurs.

The land along the Riverwalk on the east side of the bluff was formerly an extensive farm owned by pioneer **William Gardenhire,** grandson of a German immigrant and an early settler of Chattanooga. Though white settlers were legally prohibited from moving onto the lands on the south bank of the river prior to the Cherokee Removal (1838), Gardenhire was allowed to live on this land earlier because his wife was a Cherokee Indian. The spot was located on the Indian trading route to Ooltewah, and for that reason Gardenhire also operated a ferry across the river.

An informal early proposal for a riverfront park was made by letter to the *Chattanooga Times* in May 1915, and concerned the area in this vicinity, along the bank of the river east of the river bluff. This proposal, which noted that "It is a remarkably strange thing to me that so few people have recognized the value of the banks of the Tennessee River a few blocks above the business section of the city for public park purposes," suggested a price tag of $200,000 for the development, and as a result it received no significant response. Today, however, this vision has to a large degree been realized by the creation of the Tennessee Riverwalk.

Continue along the Riverwalk to the **Tennessee-American Water Company,** which sits on a hill above the river. The original city waterworks were erected on Reservoir Hill, west of downtown Chattanooga. Pollution of the river by the city, however, forced the company to move its water intake lines upstream from the town. In 1888, therefore, the original waterworks were abandoned, and a new pumping station and filtering plant were erected at the mouth of Citico Creek by the Lookout Water Company, which adopted the new title "City Water Company." In 1892, Chattanooga became the second city in the South to have filtered water, and a new, 3-million gallon reservoir was built on the side of Missionary Ridge at that time as well. In 1913, the old Citico Furnace near this site was torn down, and the property was sold to the growing City Water Company, which then established intake pipes and a reservoir at this location as well. The company subsequently became the Tennessee-American Water Company in 1973, and today this private company continues to serve the Chattanooga area.

After passing the water company, cross **Citico Creek** on an iron-trestle walking bridge. Near this site, a company of cavalry under Captain Joel Hembry was stationed at the bank of Citico Creek during the Cherokee Removal. The soldiers erected a crude fort out of split trees, which were sharpened and set into the ground near this spot. Inside were log cabins and horse stables, and gun ports were placed around the perimeter of the building. The camp, which could house as many as 100 men, was occupied throughout the winter of 1836-1837 prior to the removal of the Cherokee from the area.

The cabin of Cherokee Indian **Water Lizard** was located to the south (right), in an area surrounded by a large peach orchard which was set on a hill back from the mouth of Citico Creek. Though the Cherokee were removed from the Tennessee Valley in 1838, this cabin remained for a number of years as a monument to the Indians who preceded white settlers in this area. Also on this side of Citico Creek is the Chattanooga Rowing Center, a large facility opened in 1994 and maintained by Chattanooga Rowing, Inc., a local non-profit organization; from this spot, numerous crew teams set out into the river to train and race throughout the year.

To the east of Citico Creek is the former site of the **Citico Mound,** a large Mississippian-era earthen mound which was 160-by-120 feet in size and stood approximately 20 feet high. It is

believed that this mound was the central feature of an Indian village occupied between 1350 and 1550 A.D., which may have served as the center of a chiefdom which included nearby villages at MacLellan Island, Williams Island, Moccasin Bend, and throughout the Chickamauga dam reservoir. The mound itself was likely crowned by a large log temple structure, and a fairly extensive village surrounded the site. During the Civil War, the Citico Mound was planted with gardens, and a gardener's shed was placed on top of the hill, as is seen in the photograph on page 26 and below. Haphazard excavations of the mound occurred in 1865 and 1915, and local curio seekers also looted the area for a number of years, locating a number of burials, rattles, shell beads, ceremonial blades, arrowheads, spear points, and

copper armbands, headdresses, and pendants. At the turn of the century, it was reported in speculation that the mound was the burial site of an ancient Cherokee Chief, referred to as "Citico"-this imaginative story, however, was little more than speculation, and today it is recognized as inaccurate. During the construction of Riverside Drive in 1915, the majority of the mound was razed for use as fill dirt, and in June 1915 the *Chattanooga Times* published an editorial letter lamenting as follows: "But, the mound is doomed. Modern commercialism and up-to-date road-builders care nothing for historic reminders of other races of people or of the beauty spots of the earth. One by one they are blotted out by what we call modern progress." Subsequent construction resulted in the eradication of this significant archaeological site. Today, construction continues to turn up additional artifacts, as evidenced by the discovery in 2001 of two burials during construction of a new restaurant on the edge of the river in this area. Findings such as these clearly illustrate that the Tennessee Riverwalk follows in the footsteps of history.

Currently, plans are in the works to complete

Currently, plans are in the works to complete the Riverwalk to the Chickamauga dam upriver; now, however, this portion of the park ends at the site of the Citico Mound. Beyond this point, approximately 2 miles further down Amnicola Highway, is the former site of the **Amnicola Farm** established by Tom Crutchfield, owner of the antebellum Crutchfield House. This 1,000-acre farm, where Crutchfield raised Jersey cattle, Cotswold sheep and Berkshire hogs, reached east from the river to Missionary Ridge and occupied approximately 2.5 miles of riverfront land. Originally, the boundaries were marked with a long plank fence with cedar posts; today, only 2 brick pillars remain to mark the entrance to the farm, part of which is today a wetlands area and park.

To return to the start of the tour, retrace your steps along the Riverwalk through the Bluff View Art District, turning left (south) on High Street. At Third Street, turn right (east) and proceed to Walnut Street, where the tour began.

Brabson Hill

The hills on the east side of downtown were an early site for residential development in Chattanooga. One of these hills was occupied by an early Chattanooga resident, attorney Reese Brabson, who moved from Sevier County, Tennessee, to Ross's Landing following the Cherokee Removal in 1838. A prominent local attorney, Brabson served in the Tennessee legislature (1851-52) and the United States Congress (1858-59); though he owned 8 slaves himself, Brabson was opposed to secession, and he served as the attorney for Union spy James Andrews following the "Great Locomotive Chase" which ended in Chattanooga. Brabson lived on a large piece of property overlooking the town, which became known as "Brabson Hill," upon which he erected a house which is today the oldest residence in the downtown area. Following the designation of Chattanooga as the county seat of Hamilton County (1870) and the construction of the Hamilton County courthouse nearby on Georgia Avenue, additional residential construction occurred in this area; this residential growth accelerated following the turn of the century, when D.B. Loveman purchased the Brabson property (1902) and subdivided a portion of the land to create 65 city lots in this neighborhood.

In the 1920s, several apartment buildings were constructed on Brabson Hill, which lay on the outskirts of the bustling downtown area. In ensuing years, suburban growth occasioned by the street-car and, later, the automobile led to a change in the character of the downtown area, and commercial development expanded and displaced former residential neighborhoods. As the Brabson Hill area demonstrates, many of the early homes which were constructed in this area are now utilized as business offices, and several former residential neighborhoods have been replaced by parking lots and newer commercial structures. However, partly due to the proximity of the University of Tennessee at Chattanooga, several of the buildings and houses in this area continue to be utilized as apartment buildings, and Brabson Hill today remains one of the main residential areas within downtown Chattanooga.

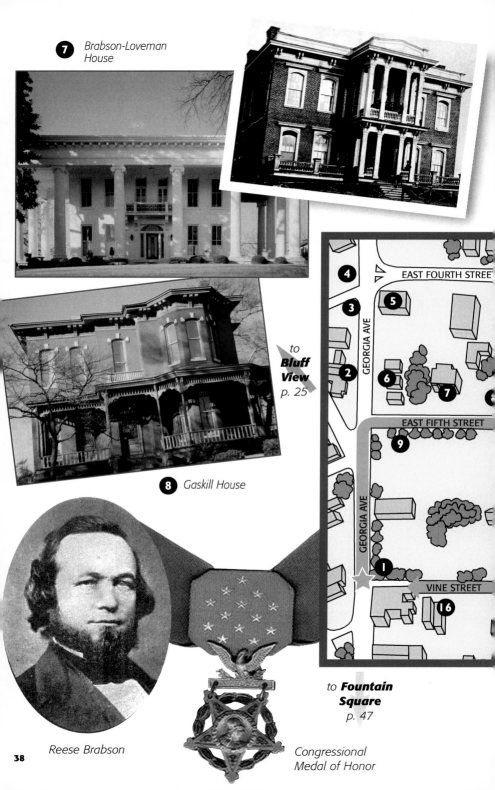

7 Brabson-Loveman House

to **Bluff View** p. 25

EAST FOURTH STREET

4

3

5

GEORGIA AVE

2

6

7

EAST FIFTH STREET

9

GEORGIA AVE

1

VINE STREET

16

8 Gaskill House

Reese Brabson

Congressional Medal of Honor

to **Fountain Square** p. 47

Civil War fortifications (U.S.) surrounding Chattanooga

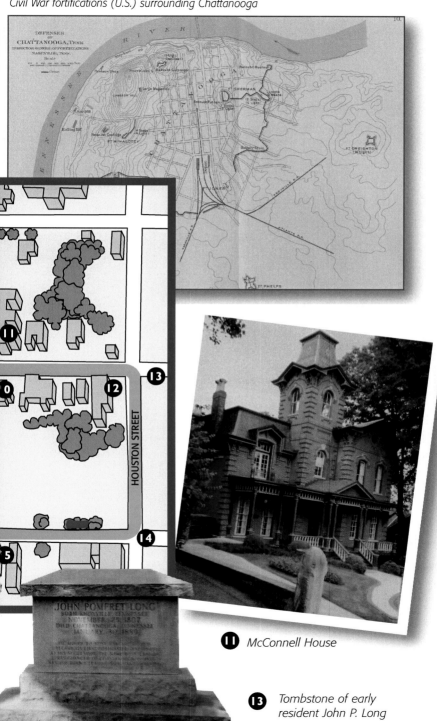

11 *McConnell House*

13 *Tombstone of early resident John P. Long*

Tennessee River

BRABSON
HILL

NORTH

The tour of Brabson Hill begins at the northeast corner of Georgia Avenue and Vine Street, ❶ at a **Parking Lot** maintained by the UnumProvident insurance corporation. Previously situated at this corner were several houses built in the 1880s, as well as the Fritts Apartments (409 Vine Street), a house which was converted into residential apartments in 1930. In 1959, this row of houses was torn down in order to create additional parking space for the Provident Life & Accident Insurance Company, which erected its head-quarters nearby. Several years ago, the insurance company announced plans to build a research center in partnership with the University of Tennessee at Chattanooga on this corner; this plan is said to be progressing at the present time. In 2000, moreover, it was announced that UnumProvident had joined with a local downtown developer to begin the first phase of a $10 million development intended to place 5 single-family homes, a 14-unit condominium building, and 3 carriage houses on this 2-acre site; this is an extension of the Lindsay Court developments located nearby, at East Fifth and Houston Streets. At the present time, these plans are still proceeding, though delays have precluded construction at the site to date.

From this corner, proceed north to East Fifth Street. A number of interesting homes clustered on Georgia Avenue between Fifth and Fourth Streets around the turn of the century. ❷ On your left, the brick house at **417 Georgia Avenue** was built around 1890 by architect William H. Floyd for Judge Charles Dickens Clark, a Confederate veteran and federal judge. At the turn of the century, the home was occupied by businessman John Faxon, whose brother later built a fine bluff mansion which is now the Hunter Museum of American Art, and in later years this house was subdivided for use by a number of businesses. Next door, at **415 Georgia Avenue**, is a 2-story brick home erected in the 1880s and occupied around that time by Wilford Caulkins, professor of Greek and Latin at Grant University (the University of Chattanooga). After Caulkins left the school due to a controversy in which African-American students were denied admission to the university, he opened a school for boys in the house. Later subdivided into apartments, today the house is occupied by legal offices.

Beyond these homes, at the southwest corner of Georgia Avenue and East Fourth Street, ❸

is a parking lot once occupied by the **Confederate Memorial Hall** (above), a 2-story brick building erected around the turn of the century and since torn down. Incidentally, East Fourth Street, which intersects Georgia Avenue at this point, was originally known as Mott Street; the name was changed, along with several other original street names, in 1912.

Across Fourth Street, at the northwest corner of Fourth Street and Georgia Avenue, is an **herb garden** maintained by the Bluff View Inn. ❹ Following the turn of the century, this lot was occupied by the Virginia Apartments, one of several apartment buildings erected in this area as residential development spread east of downtown. In the center of the herb garden is "The Watcher," a sculpture crafted by artist Jim Collins and placed at the top of a 22,000 pound piston from an offshore drilling rig which was forged in a local Chattanooga foundry.

Nearby, the parking lot at the southeast corner of Georgia Avenue and East Fourth Street ❺ is the former site of the **National Medal of Honor Museum**, which originated in 1991 as an exhibit at the Soldiers and Sailors Memorial Auditorium on McCallie Avenue. With a World War II-era tank and machine gun nest greeting visitors at the entrance to the museum, the building housed memorials to the 3,400 men and 1 woman - Civil War nurse  Mary Walker - who have received the Congressional Medal of Honor. This medal has special significance in Chattanooga, as the first individuals awarded the medal were the members of Andrews' Raiders, who were involved in the "Great Locomotive Chase" between

Marietta, Georgia, and Chattanooga during the Civil War in 1862, and whose bodies today rest in the National Cemetery in Chattanooga. In 2002, the museum building was torn down as part of a street-widening project intended to reintroduce 2-way traffic to Fourth Street, and the museum is currently in the process of relocating to larger quarters nearby.

Adjacent to this spot are several older houses which front on Georgia Avenue. ❻ Records in the Hamilton County assessor's office indicate that the house at **418 Georgia Avenue** was erected circa 1865, although the style of the building appears to be later in design, and city directories first list a residence at this address in 1886. Next door, the house at **422 Georgia Avenue** was built circa 1890, and the house at the northeast corner of Georgia Avenue and East Fifth Street (**424 Georgia Avenue**) was erected around 1900. Today these buildings (along with an 1953 addition to the latter structure) serve as private offices.

From this point, turn onto **East Fifth Street**. This street, which was originally known as Caroline Street (and, later, "Carolina Street"), served as a popular early residential area, in part due to the elevated hill upon which houses in this area were built. The area north of East Fifth Street was known as "Lindsay's Extension," so named for Colonel William Lindsay, a U.S. soldier who came to Chattanooga during the Cherokee Removal to command the forces (2nd U.S. Artillery) stationed at Ross's Landing. Following the Removal, Lindsay purchased a 104-acre tract of land east of the original town boundaries in his wife's name, and part of the area continues to bear his name today. The area south of Fifth Street is known as Long's Addition, named for early citizen and first postmaster of Chattanooga John P. Long.

This elevation made Brabson Hill an advantageous spot for the establishment of military fortifications. During the period immediately preceding the Cherokee Removal, the U.S. army established a camp on the crest of the hill at this location. One of the soldiers who participated in the Cherokee Removal was U.S. Lieutenant Braxton Bragg, who would return to this very spot 25 years later as commander of the Confederate Army of Tennessee during the Civil War. During that war, Brabson Hill was used as a camp by both Confederate and Union troops, including the Forth-Third Tennessee Regiment (CSA) led by Colonels David McKendree Key and J.W. Gillespie, which arrived by rail in Chattanooga in May 1896 and estab-

lished a bivouac on the hill. The hill was picked clean as trees, gardens, and outbuildings were torn down for use by the soldiers stationed in the town. In fact, the deteriorated condition of the land in Chattanooga following November 1863 led to a popular soldiers' anecdote concerning a dead soldier who asked the Devil to take him straight to Hell rather than tarry in Chattanooga, as "he did not want cruel and unusual punishment."

Subsequently, as indicated by the map of Union defenses on page 39, in 1864-65 the main interior defensive line established along the east side of the town crossed over Brabson Hill. Known as Fort Sherman (named for U.S. Major-General William T. Sherman), this line, which included tall walls of earth and stone and a deep, wide ditch, began to the west, in the vicinity of East Fifth and Walnut Streets, and proceeded across Brabson Hill toward the river bluff. At Brabson Hill was placed a battery of 6 light cannon and 2 siege guns, and the spot was labeled Lunette O'Meara in honor of Colonel Timothy O'Meara (Nineteenth Illinois Infantry), who was killed at the battle of Missionary Ridge on November 25, 1863. From this spot, the defenses of the city proceeded north to the river bluff and south to Battery Ervin.

To your left, the centerpiece of Brabson Hill is the columned **Brabson-Loveman House**, located at 407 East Fifth Street. ❼ In 1858, attorney Reese Bowen Brabson (left) built this home, which was brick with a small collonaded portico above the front door (as seen in the Civil War-era photograph on pages 38 & 43); the interior included fine woodwork of carved oak and white mahogany. During the Civil War, the house served as a hospital for Confederate troops following the battle of Stone's River (Murfreesboro), and General Braxton Bragg (CSA) used the home as his local headquarters during the Confederate occupation of the city in 1862. During the federal siege of the city in 1863, Brabson's widow (Brabson had died of typhoid fever earlier that year) was forced to leave the home after shells landed in the front yard, and it became a hospital for Union troops following the battle of Chattanooga. During this period, books, carpets, furniture, and curtains were taken away, the trees on the property were cut down, and slaves' quarters were dismantled in order to build a blockhouse nearby

for Lunette O'Meara. When returning to the house following the battle, Ms. Brabson was injured in a fall from her carriage; she was taken to the house, where she was cared for by a Union physician, Col. Peter Cleary. When she inquired as to how she could afford to pay him for his medical services, Col. Cleary replied, "Madam, I will take you and the children in payment for the bill," and the pair were married soon thereafter.

The house itself, which was later remembered as "a place of cordial hospitality and delightful entertainment," again served as a hospital during the 1878 Yellow Fever epidemic. Ms. Brabson later added Victorian stylings to the structure in 1879. However, the home was partially destroyed by fire on January 9, 1881. After having been rebuilt using the original bricks, the home was purchased in 1902 by David B. Loveman, the owner of the Loveman's department store on Market Street, who sold off part of the property to form approximately 65 city lots in the surrounding neighborhood. Loveman then added a broad front porch with fluted Ionic columns to the house in the 1930s, as seen in the photograph on page 38. In 1937, the house was sold to A. A. Dragoo and became the Mt. Vernon apartments. The house was later sold in 1942 to Drs. Cecil and Ed T. Newell, who utilized the building as a medical clinic; it was subsequently used as a restaurant and an art gallery. The house thereafter fell into disrepair until the 1970s, when it was purchased by Dr. and Ms. Yukata Kayo, who restored the building. Today, the Brabson-Loveman House is utilized as office space for several small businesses.

Next door to the Brabson House, at the northwest corner of East Fifth and Lindsay Streets, is the **Gaskill House**. ❽ Placed on the National Register of Historic Places in 1979, this Italianate house was constructed in 1883 by Clinton and Sally Lee Gaskill. Mr. Gaskill was involved in the organization of the Third National Bank in Chattanooga, as well as the

Chattanooga Street Railroad Company. As was recognized in the application for historic status for this site, the style of this house is interesting, in that it falls between the more functional buildings of early Chattanooga and the "full Victorian flowering" which came at the turn of the century. From 1908-1930, the house was occupied by John J. Mahoney, manager of the local Cahill Iron Works, after which it passed to his daughter. Currently, the building (below), which was renovated by the Betts-Lutin consulting firm in the 1970s, houses several private offices.

Though they are no longer standing, across East Fifth Street from the above historic buildings, where currently is located a parking lot, were several apartment buildings established in the first part of the twentieth century when residential apartment construction blossomed in this area. At the southeast corner of Georgia Avenue and East Fifth Street was a home built by contractor **S.B. Moe**, ❾ next door to which he erected an apartment building known as the Moe Apartments (404-406 East Fifth Street). Next door to those apartments, at 408 East Fifth Street, were the Morningside Apartments.

Across Lindsay Street, at the southeast corner of East Fifth and Lindsay Streets, ❿ is the former site of a home built by Tennessee Supreme Court Judge **David Snodgrass**. This 2-story frame house, which had a prominent wraparound porch, was erected in 1884-1885; the building was subsequently torn down and replaced with the current brick office building in the 1970s.

Next door to this building are several apartment buildings erected early in the twentieth century. At 510 East Fifth Street are the **Brabson Hill Apartments** erected in 1920. On either side of these apartments are homes built in 1885 (508 East Fifth Street) and 1895 (518 East Fifth Street), which today house residential apartments and private offices.

Across East Fifth Street, at the northeast corner

of East Fifth and Lindsay Streets, ⑪ are the **Jefferson Apartments** (501 East Fifth Street), which were erected in 1928 and include 36 apartments. Next door to this building are the **Wanda Apartments** (507 East Fifth Street), which were erected circa 1915.

Adjacent to the Wanda Apartments is the intriguing **McConnell House** (517 East Fifth Street), which was built in 1882 by Chancellor T.M. McConnell, who also owned the McConnell Block in the downtown core. This

mid-Victorian brick building, which was named to the National Register of Historic Places in 1992, features a tower which was originally ringed with seats for viewing the city, as well as a man-made pond in the back which guests could cross via a small footbridge. Interestingly, McConnell hired a group of Cincinnati artisans to come to Chattanooga to construct the elaborate frescoes located on the ceilings of the entryway to the house. Today, the building is home to the Lyndhurst Foundation, a local non-profit organization founded by T.C. Lupton in 1938.

From this spot, continue to the foot of the hill. Here, at the southwest corner of East Fifth and Houston Streets (522 East Fifth Street), ⑫ is a 2-story frame house erected in 1885 by **William Snodgrass**, who owned the Snodgrass & Fields sawmill on the riverbank at the foot of the bluff nearby. Although Mrs. R.F. Snodgrass remained at this location for several years after her husband's death, in the 1930s the house was subdivided into residential apartments, a use it continues to serve today.

At this corner, turn right onto Houston Street (this is a one-way street; if you are traveling by car, turn left, then go right on Fourth Street until

you reach Palmetto Street, and then turn right again). To the east, beyond the end of East Fifth Street, is the campus of the University of Tennessee at Chattanooga (UTC). The large structure across Houston Street is the **McKenzie Arena**, also known as the UTC "Roundhouse." ⑬ This $15.5 million, 210,000-square foot structure was built in 1982 and plays host to a variety of sporting events and concerts throughout the year.

The majority of the area east of Houston Street was originally the farm of William Gardenhire, an early settler who operated a ferry at the mouth of Citico Creek, along an Indian trading path. The historic **Citizens Cemetery** (bounded by Third, Fifth, Collins, and Douglas Streets) was established on land purchased from the Gardenhire and Lindsay properties for $75 per acre. First used in 1837, many of Chattanooga's founding pioneers and early residents are buried here, including Reese B. Brabson, for whom Brabson Hill is named. The grave of early resident

John P. Long is also located here, as see in the photograph (above). During the Civil War, a number of Union spies were also hanged at this location. It is believed that hundreds of stone markers were taken from the cemetery for use by the federal army in building fortifications in the city; in fact, one house torn down on Water Street in the 1930s had a large foundation stone with two inscriptions: "Erected by the First Regiment of Michigan Engineers 1864"; and, below that one, "Alphonse Henri, died 1851."

Adjacent to the Citizens' Cemetery is the **Confederate Cemetery**. During the Civil War, several Confederate soldiers who had died during the winter months of 1863 following the battle of Stone's River in Middle Tennessee were buried in a low, swampy plot near the river. Subsequently, in September 1867 a group of Confederate veterans acquired a 2-acre deed of land near the old city cemetery for $750, and the graves of these and other Confederate soldiers were searched out so that they could be reinterred in the cemetery. The subsequent dedication of a monument to the Confederate dead in 1877 was attended by veterans of both armies. Today, approximately 1,200 soldiers and their wives are buried here.

Next to this cemetery (east) is the **Jewish**

Cemetery, which was established in 1867 after a cemetery association purchased land next to the Citizens and Confederate cemeteries.

Beyond the cemetery tract is the historic **Fort Wood** district (bounded by McCallie and Central Avenues and Palmetto and Fort Wood Streets), which was annexed by the city of Chattanooga in 1851 as the first residential suburb of the town. During the Civil War, this site was occupied by a large fort with high walls and deep ditches (also referred to at the time as a "moat"), which was labeled Fort Wood in honor of General Thomas J. Wood. Along with Major Frank Bond, Wood was considered responsible for opening the hole in the Union line which led to the Union defeat at Chickamauga; though Wood knew that the orders he had received (to move his men to a new location) would leave a hole in the federal line, a recent tongue lashing by General William S. Rosecrans for failing to follow orders prompted him to adhere to these orders at all costs, and the Union was defeated as a result.

The initial Union attack at Chattanooga on November 23, 1863, came from soldiers stationed at Fort Wood; a 32-pound Parrot gun was periodically fired from the fort toward the battlefield at Orchard Knob during the battle, and Generals Grant and Thomas (U.S.) watched the battle from the fort. On April 27, 1864, General Thomas issued an order assigning official names to the defensive works established throughout Chattanooga, and the official name of the fort was changed to Fort Creighton, in honor of Colonel William R. Creighton (Seventh Ohio Infantry), who was killed in action at Ringgold, Georgia, on November 26, 1863. This large fort later came to possess 14 light cannon during the federal occupation of Chattanooga in 1864-1865, and it stood for several years after the war before eventually being torn down in 1888.

Cut off from town by a railroad embankment, the Fort Wood area became an early African-American settlement after the Civil War. Following the dismantling of the fort in 1888, however, the area became a fashionable residential address, and a number of Victorian-era homes were erected throughout the area. This late-nineteenth century neighborhood still includes a collection of fine homes designed in a variety of styles, including Queen Anne, Dutch Colonial, Tudor, Foursquare, Greek Revival, Neo-Classical, Italian Renaissance, East Lake, and Eclectic. Though the neighborhood declined to some degree after the 1950s, it has witnessed a rejuvenation in recent years. Following a restoration effort by the Fort Wood Community Association, the 120-home neighborhood, which is listed on the National Register of Historic Places, became Chattanooga's first historic district in 1990.

Returning to Houston Street, proceed south to **Vine Street,** ⓴ where local attorney John Livingston Hopkins built a tall frame house prior to the Civil War on a tract of land he purchased in the area of Vine and Houston Streets. Hopkins maintained his law offices in a 2-story brick building located behind his house, which has since been torn down as well.

From this spot, head east to Lindsay Street. Here, at the southeast corner of Vine and Lindsay Streets, ⓵ is the **Central Church of Christ** (400 Vine Street), erected at this location in 1924. Turning left onto Lindsay Street, at 615 Lindsay Street, is the former **Frances Willard Home**. Named for the founder and national president of the Women's Christian Temperance Union, the Frances Willard Home was established in Chattanooga circa 1885 to provide a home-like environment for working girls coming to Chattanooga from outlying rural areas. In 1928, it was determined that the organization had outgrown its earlier headquarters (1895) on Oak Street, which were then sold to the First Baptist Church. R.H. Hunt then endeavored to design a new building at this spot. This 3-story brick building included a reception hall, 4 large parlors, a kitchen and dining room, and 20 bedrooms on each of the upper floors. Due to rising maintenance and heating costs, the home, which is listed to the National Register of Historic Places (1980), closed in 1976. The building was thereafter deeded to the Central Church of Christ, which planned to convert the building into a home for the elderly. This plan was not completed, however, and the building was sold to Green Acres of America in 1979, which renovated the interior for conversion into "luxury office suites," a use it continues to serve today.

From the corner of Vine and Lindsay Streets, proceed west, to Georgia Avenue. On your left as you proceed along Vine Street are 2 homes erected near the turn of the century (**312 and 314 Vine Street**), ⓶ each of which is maintained today as a private office in the vicinity of the county courthouse and Fountain Square.

To return to the start of the tour, continue

west along Vine Street to Georgia Avenue.

Fountain Square

Though Chattanooga never had a central "town square" in the truest sense of the term, the Fountain Square area could be said to represent the heart of downtown Chattanooga in many ways. Early on, this area was the site of an important log structure which served as schoolhouse, church, and meeting house for the entire community; it was at this site that the name "Chattanooga" was selected for the town.

Following the selection of Chattanooga as the county seat of Hamilton County (1870), the knoll on which the county court-house now sits became the symbolic "center" of the county as well. The centerpiece of the area – a 3-tiered fountain dedicated to the memory of 2 firefighters who died while fighting a fire nearby on Market Street – was installed in 1888, giving the area the name by which it is know today. Situated between the downtown core and the University of Tennessee at Chattanooga (UTC) campus, the Fountain Square area, like other neighborhoods on the eastern flank of downtown, was clustered with homes and apartment buildings following the turn of the century, and today it remains an important residential center within the downtown area. For a number of years, moreover, local historian and newspaper columnist Emma Bell Miles ran a local column in the *Chattanooga News* entitled "Fountain Square Conversations," highlighting local events and happenings.

In 1976, a proposal was made to close Georgia Avenue in order to create an "expanded Fountain Square," replete with a new base pool and "simple basque of trees," to compliment a new "Historic Park" filled with cannon, statues, and informational plaques at this spot. According to this plan, "sidewalk cafes and band concerts are among the new activities appropriate to the new Fountain Square." This portion of the new urban design for the city, however, was never implemented, and the square, which was added to the National Register of Historic Places in 1979, has remained largely unchanged since the early portion of the twentieth century.

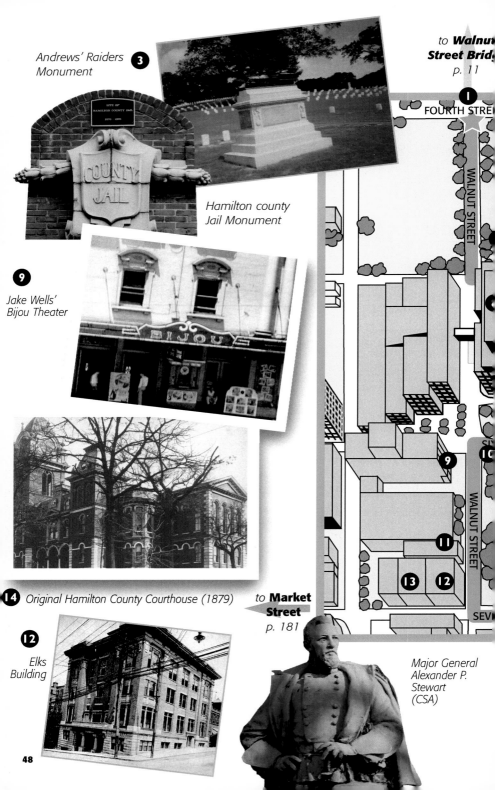

Andrews' Raiders
Monument **3**

SITE OF
HAMILTON COUNTY JAIL
1870-1890
COUNTY
JAIL

Hamilton county
Jail Monument

9
Jake Wells'
Bijou Theater

BIJOU

14 Original Hamilton County Courthouse (1879)

to **Market
Street**
p. 181

12
Elks
Building

to **Walnut
Street Bridge**
p. 11

I
FOURTH STRE

WALNUT STREET

9

II

13 **12**

WALNUT STREET

SEV

Major General
Alexander P.
Stewart
(CSA)

48

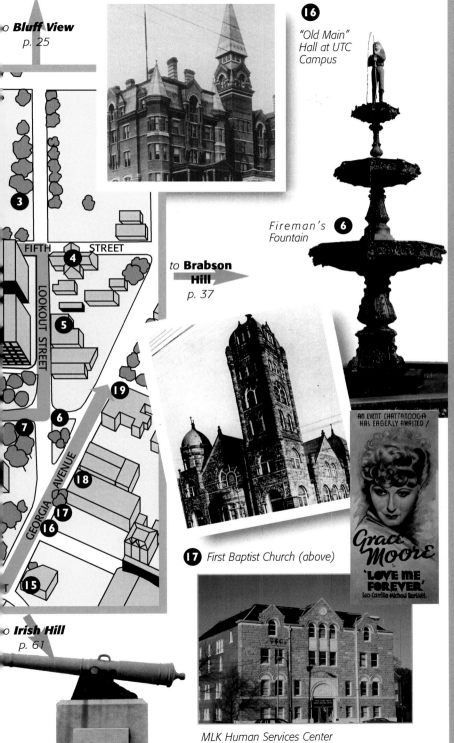

to **Bluff View**
p. 25

16
"Old Main"
Hall at UTC
Campus

3

FIFTH STREET

4

to **Brabson Hill**
p. 37

*Fireman's
Fountain* **6**

LOOKOUT STREET

5

19

6

7

GEORGIA AVENUE

18

17

16

T **15**

17 First Baptist Church (above)

AN EVENT CHATTANOOGA
HAS EAGERLY AWAITED /

*Grace
Moore*
in
'LOVE ME
FOREVER'
Leo Carrillo·Michael Bartlett

to **Irish Hill**
p. 61

MLK Human Services Center

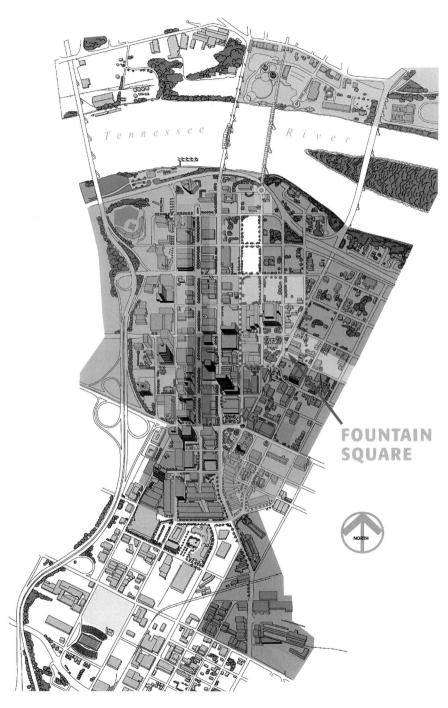

Tennessee River

FOUNTAIN
SQUARE

NORTH

The Fountain Square tour begins at the southeast corner of Walnut and Fourth Streets. ❶ Though the spot is today located in the middle of a busy downtown area, when pioneer **William Walker Anderson, Sr.**, arrived in Chattanooga in 1840 from Athens, Tennessee, he remarked that the area was still "an almost unbroken forest." Anderson and his family settled in a small log cabin at this spot, erecting a general mercantile business near Market Street between First and Second Streets.

From this spot, head south along Walnut Street. Near Fifth Street, ❷ the 300-seat **Mizpah Congregation Temple** (421 Walnut Street) opened in 1882, using bricks from the antebellum First Presbyterian Church building located at Market and Seventh Streets. After the congregation built a new temple nearby at the northwest corner of Oak and Lindsay Streets, the building was renovated in 1904 for use by Professor Joseph Ottokar Cadek as the Cadek Conservatory of Music, dedicated to "training individuals in the fine arts, cherishing high standards, and encouraging active group participation in community projects of a cultural nature." This project merged with the University of Chattanooga in 1948, and the building was renamed Cadek Hall. Many Chattanoogans fondly recall after-school music lessons at this building, though in the 1950s a new conservatory was built on the UTC campus, after which the original building was razed in conjunction with the construction of the nearby Provident Building.

Turn left on Fifth Street and proceed to the northwest corner of Lookout and Fifth Streets. ❸ Nearby is a historic plaque marking the site of **Swaim's Jail** (also referred to as "Swim's Jail"), established at this spot in 1862. In 1851, an amendment to the Chattanooga city charter

called for the city to "erect a lock-up house or calaboose for the safekeeping of prisoners." In 1852, therefore, a committee was established to build a jail house at a cost of no more than $200, and in 1858 plans were completed for a 12-by-12 foot pen of hewn logs, with iron-barred windows, an iron door, and a 22-foot high pen around the building. These plans were altered in the final construction, however, and the jail, which initially served as a local "lockup" for runaway slaves, was a small 2-story brick building surrounded by a high board fence; the ground sloped upward so much at this spot that the building was built into the side of the hill itself, as seen in the drawing below. The family of jailer John Swaim lived upstairs at the north end of the jail, while the rooms on the south end were reserved for prisoners. A trap door and ladder led down to the basement level, a 13 square-foot room with no windows - only 2 openings in the walls - and no furnishings, aside from some candles and buckets for water and slop.

After their capture by Confederate soldiers in 1862, the Andrews' Raiders - Union spies who began the "Great Locomotive Chase" in Kennesaw, Georgia - were jailed at this location. Though some of the men paid Swaim money to get them better food than the cornbread and rancid meat they had been given, the next day the same food came down on a rope; when the prisoners inquired about the food, Swain jeered, "Boys, I lost that money." Over time, the Raiders were moved to the upper story and given some additional freedom; after receiving death sentences following their trials, however, an escape plan was hatched, though only James Andrews and John Woolam escaped. Both were later recaptured, and leg irons were fitted to the prisoners to prevent another jailbreak. Andrews was eventually executed by hanging on June 7, 1862, in Atlanta, Georgia; in 1887, his body was reinterred in the National Cemetery in Chattanooga, along with 7 of the Raiders. A memorial to the Great Locomotive Chase (pictured on page 48) was placed adjacent to the graves of the Andrews' Raiders, who are notable also for being the first recipients of the Congressional Medal of Honor established during the Civil War. As for the jailhouse itself, it was destroyed by vengeful federal troops upon their arrival in Chattanooga in 1863, and no trace of the building exists today.

The southeast corner of Lookout and Fifth Streets ❹ is one of the most historic spots in Chattanooga. An historic plaque at this spot marks the site of an important **Log Community Building** erected here in the early years of the Ross's Landing settlement. Among the lots sets aside for community purposes when the town of Ross's Landing was established was this corner lot, on which was erected a structure described as follows: "about 16 x 20 feet in size, made out of logs and chinked and daubed with mud. The seats were puncheon benches without backs, the floor was the bottom of an old and abandoned flatboat, taken from the river, and the roof was made of split boards. Instead of a spire, there was at the north end of the building a stick and mud chimney." A pestle striking a suspended spice mortar called members to worship at this impromptu church, which also served as a schoolhouse and community meeting house in the early years of the Ross's Landing settlement.

It was at this spot that the name "Chattanooga" was selected for the community. Following 1815, the area had simply become known as "Ross's Landing," because John Ross had established a landing and store here. By 1838, however, it was agreed that the growing town needed a new name, and residents met at this spot to discuss a permanent name for the town. Several initial proposals were discussed and rejected. As early resident John P. Long later recounted, when the title of "Lookout City" was offered, objections arose that "it was too pretentious; that a city in the woods never came to anything; that it was time to add the city when the town became worthy of it."

The name "Montevideo" was also suggested, as a reflection upon the view of the surrounding mountains from the town. This proposal, however, was also overruled: one resident remarked that it was too farfetched, someone else pointed out that it was not an American name, and others objected that it was not local. This then led to the proposal of the name "Chattanooga," of which it was initially said that "it was home-like, it was local and the name of a valley and creek in the neighborhood, and . . . was the original name of Lookout Mountain." Early maps, in fact, label Lookout Mountain as "Chatanuge," a word of mysterious Creek or Cherokee origin.

One resident, however, objected, claiming that the word "was too uncommon, too uncouth; that strangers would miscall it, and [he] remarked that a visitor from a distance a few days before, on ascending Missionary Ridge, when the magnificent view of the valley and the white cliffs of Walden's Ridge burst upon the

view, [suggested] that Albion would be an appropriate name for the town." At once, an enthusiastic member of the audience exclaimed, "Oh yes, let us call it that, Albun, that would be splendid." This mispronunciation spelled the end for the proposal that the town be called Albion, and discussion renewed concerning the name of "Chattanooga." One settler then proposed what would be the clinching argument: "The name might sound outlandish and strange to some ears, but if our city was a success, it would become familiar and pleasant, and there would not be another name like it in the world." A vote then confirmed the change of the town name to Chattanooga, a change which was officially recognized when the U.S. Post Office named its local outpost "Chattanooga" on November 14, 1838.

A second historic plaque at this corner marks the site of the point of **Fort Sherman**, a defensive fortification erected along the east side of town during the Civil War occupation of Chattanooga by the federal army. Fort Sherman was essentially a long line constructed of stone and earth, adjacent to which was dug a wide ditch. Named for Major General William Tecumseh Sherman (US), the fort began at this point and ran northeast, over Brabson Hill toward the high bluff above the Tennessee River.

Today, this corner is the site of the **Wiley Memorial Methodist Episcopal Church** (504 Lookout Street). In 1847, early resident John P. Long conveyed a lot in this vicinity to the Methodist congregation, and $3,500 was raised to build a 32-by-52 foot frame building with a shingle roof and an odd-shaped cupola which led the building to be referred to as the "Pepper Box Church." The structure was framed upriver, at Soddy, Tennessee, and floated downriver for placement at this spot. This biracial church had 100 white and 12 African-American members during the antebellum period. The building was used as a Civil War hospital for ill and injured Confederate soldiers and as a military prison by the Union army, and following the war it was left in such poor condition -- the bell was gone, weatherboarding stripped, furnishings removed, and floor broken in -- that the congregation abandoned the building. The building was then sold to an African-American congregation for $1,000. Subsequently, the Wiley Memorial Methodist Episcopal church building was erected at this spot in 1886-1888, at a cost of $18,000. At the turn of the century, a new pipe organ was purchased for the church, making it the first African-American congregation in

Chattanooga to have one. The brick church building, which sits on a limestone foundation, has witnessed a number of structural alterations over the years: the original northwest spire, once believed to be the tallest in Chattanooga, was removed due to its weakened condition; the southwest bell tower was taken down; and several second-story arched openings have since been bricked in. In January 1978, the church was padlocked by city officials, who concluded that the structure was too dangerous for continued use; however, member John Dodds led a campaign to restore the church building, which is now listed on the National Register of Historic Places (1979).

Head north along Lookout Street. On the left, at 520 Lookout Street, ❺ is the **Patten & Patten Building**. Formerly the site of the O'Donohue Funeral Home and the Betts-Lutin consulting firm, this renovated 2-story brick building has been occupied by its current tenant since 1980.

Continue north along Lookout Street. Located in a small triangular plot bounded by Georgia Avenue and Lookout and Sixth Streets ❻ is **Fountain Square**, a small memorial park dedicated in 1888. On June 9, 1887, the most tragic fire in Chattanooga history broke out at the Bee Hive Store at Fourth and Market Streets, in which an explosion inside the building claimed the lives of 2 firefighters, Matthew Peak and Henry Iler. Led by the *Chattanooga Times*, townspeople raised funds to establish a memorial to the firemen, and a "Fireman's Fountain" designed by the J.L. Mott Company of New York was placed on this site. The 27-foot tall fountain has a 25-foot wide catch basin, with decorative features including scrollwork, acanthus leaves, flowers, and animal heads on each level. The area surrounding the fountain soon became known as "Fountain Square," a name which it retains today. Early on, small alligators were exhibited within a short iron fence surrounding the fountain; after the reptiles repeatedly escaped from the enclosure, however, this practice was discontinued.

At the north end of this triangular block is a **Cannon** which was used by the Spanish army during the Spanish-American War, firing upon attacking American soldiers in the bay at Santiago de Cuba. The cannon (pictured below & on page 49) was captured by the U.S. army on July 16, 1898, and it was subsequently loaned

to the city by the U.S. government and placed within Fountain Square.

Across Lookout Street, at the southwest corner of Lookout and Sixth Streets (on the courthouse lawn) ❼ is a small memorial to the original **First Baptist Church** erected at this spot during the antebellum period. One of the original 53 citizens of Chattanooga was Matthew Hillsman, a Baptist minister from Knoxville who, despite having come to Chattanooga for commercial reasons, soon began to organize Baptist services in the town. Because the local Baptist congregation was scattered throughout the town, construction of a formal church building was delayed until 1852, when a small frame church with a cupola was erected on a lot set aside at this spot during the original allocation of lots in Ross's Landing. During the Civil War, the church was used as a federal hospital and, subsequently, as the post chapel. It was left in ruins following the departure of the Union army, and meetings were then held for a time at the house of deacon Foley Vaughn. In 1887, the property was sold to the city for $30,000, and the First Baptist Church moved to a new site nearby.

From this spot, proceed west down Sixth Street. On your right, on the block bounded by Lookout, Walnut, Fifth and Sixth Streets, ❽ is the massive **UnumProvident Building** (above). By the turn of the century, this area had become a fashionable address on the east side of town, and banker T.G. Montague erected a large frame home, along with barns and stables, on much of this block. In the 1950s, the Provident Life & Accident Insurance Company, the first private insurance company to offer hospital surgical insurance to the public, began to outgrow its headquarters on Broad Street. The company then constructed a 7-story, 270,000 square-foot headquarters, the largest office structure in town, at this spot. This move required the demolition of the Montague and Gillespie residences (the latter of which had been last used as the Chattanooga Bible Institute), as well as numerous other older homes. Designed by Otto Eggers and Daniel Higgins of New York City, the Provident building is faced with Georgia marble, and at the time of the building's construction the company directed a large-scale landscaping program to be conducted on the grounds. In 1959, the company also tore down several 1880s-era houses on Vine Street to make room for additional parking; a similar fate faced a row of old homes which stood on Walnut Street to the west of the new building, where in 1980 a 6-story, 300,000 square-foot building was erected across Walnut Street from the original building (which as a result occupies 2 full city blocks today).

Proceed along Sixth Street to the southwest corner of Sixth and Walnut Streets, ❾ the present site of the Hamilton County Justice Building. This is the former site of **Jake Wells' Bijou Theater**, pictured above and on page 48. Built at a cost of $100,000 by Jake Wells, a Virginia theater-chain owner, the Bijou (Greek for "little jewel") Theater opened in 1906 with the Vaudeville comedy "Bankers and Brokers." The 1,600 seat theater was constructed of brick trimmed in stone, and the interior included a lobby wainscotted in marble and finished with tile floors. In the theater, 12 boxes and 8 loges were fronted by plaster figures representing the "delights of the drama," and artistic designs comprised of hundreds of glass tiles accompanied a huge glass chandelier in the center of the

domed ceiling. The initial cost for orchestra seats was 50 cents, and gallery seats for "colored patrons" cost 25 cents, with the owner's cryptic promise that "especial attention will be given to preserving order in this gallery." It was at this location that D.W. Griffith's controversial epic film "Birth of a Nation" was first shown in Chattanooga. By 1916, financial problems led to the closing of the theater, which was then leased for a period of time to the Pilgrim Congregational Church. Although the theater was subsequently reopened, hosting such visitors as Tallulah Bankhead, the Marx Brothers, Ethel and John Barrymore, and William Jennings Bryan, the theater never regained its original stature, eventually advertising second-run movies, road shows, and wrestling matches. In its latter days, the balcony of the building was condemned, leaving a total of 975 seats in the theater. On December 19, 1940, a backstage fire complicated by freezing conditions which made firefighting difficult resulted in substantial damage to the structure. Although the owners originally planned to rebuild, this never occurred, and the remnants of the building were demolished in 1949 to make way for a county employee parking lot. In the late 1970s, the multi-million dollar Hamilton County Justice Building, designed by architect Jack Tyler, was erected on this spot to house the county jail, civil and criminal courts, and county offices.

Across Walnut Street, at the southeast corner of Walnut and Sixth Streets (on the lawn of the Hamilton County Courthouse), ❿ is a monument to **John Ross** (1790-1866), founder of Ross's Landing and Principal Chief of the Cherokee Nation at the time of the Cherokee Removal of 1838. The monument reads, "Faithful to his trust, he spent his life in service to his nation, a loyal Cherokee, a great American."

Next door to the Justice Center, where today is located a county parking garage, is a concrete scroll marking the former site of the **Hamilton County Jail**. The building was erected in 1879, after Chattanooga was named the county seat of Hamilton County, at a cost of $33,530; it was designed by T.J. Dolan and Son of Fort Wayne, Indiana. The scroll sat above the main entrance doors to the jail and was preserved as a monument to the building when it was torn down in 1976.

The county jail was the site of several noteworthy incidents, one of which occurred during the Jim Crow period of racial segregation. In 1892, a local African-American resident, Frank Weims, was arrested for attempting to assault a white woman in a wooded area in Hill City on the north bank of the river. Thinking quickly, Sheriff John Skillern immediately sent the prisoner out of town, and a mob which stormed the jail that evening found no one there. Though the deputy and jailer escorted Weims from jail to jail throughout Tennessee, telegraph lines stayed one step ahead of them, so that they were almost always met by a mob demanding that Weims be turned over. Many jails refused them access - Middle Tennessee jails placed "standing room only" cards outside, and a Memphis jail shook a red rag at the suggestion that Weims could be taken there. Finally, hearing that a mob was awaiting them at Wauhatchie, on the outskirts of Chattanooga, the lawmen and the prisoner leapt from the train and hiked to Chattanooga over Raccoon and Lookout Mountains. They then proceeded to Knoxville (which had no room), and Morristown, Tennessee. When Weims was eventually returned to Chattanooga for trial, he was accompanied by 75 guards. He pled guilty to assault with intent to rape, receiving a 21-year sentence.

North of the old jail site is the 3-story **Title Guaranty & Trust Company** (617 Walnut Street), ⓫ a Beaux Arts building erected in 1925 next door to the 2-story, towered brick building at 619 Walnut Street (1892) which was the original location of the title company. Today, the latter building is part of the County Courts complex at the corner of Walnut and Seventh Streets.

Attached to the 1892 title company building, at the northwest corner of Walnut and Seventh Streets, ⓬ is the 4-story **Elks Building** constructed in 1907 for the Benevolent and Protective Order of Elks (BPOE), as indicated by the initials etched on the front facade of the building. The Elks Building (above & on page 48) was designed by local architect Charles E. Bearden, who also designed the early Mountain City Club, Chattanooga Golf & County Club, Hardwick-Hogshead Apartment Building, First National Bank building, and the American Trust & Banking Company structure. This stone-and-brick building was renovated in the 1970s and now houses a number of county offices.

Next door to the Elks Building is the **Park Hotel** (117-119 East Seventh Street), ⓭ a 9-story hotel building designed by R.H. Hunt and erected by the Royalty Trust Company in 1915, at a cost of $200,000. This 105-room Renaissance-style hotel boasts a facade of the "richest gray brick and terra cotta," concrete, and brick; the lobby features silver-gray Tennessee marble wainscotting and tessellated marble floors. Originally, the ninth floor included a large solarium looking out over the city. In 1963, the building was leased out by its Chicago owner for use as a retirement hotel, which was then determined to be financially unfeasible. In 1970, the building was purchased by a local company for use as office and apartment space, and in 1978 Hamilton County bought the structure for $260,000 in order to add it to the growing complex of county government buildings in the vicinity of the courthouse. The structure was then added to the National Register of Historic Places in 1980. Renamed the "Newell Towers" after county officer Frank Newell, the building underwent a $850,000 renovation in 1981, at which time silver porcelain-enameled panels were added to the upper stories of the building. Today, this structure continues to house county governmental offices.

To the east, at the northeast corner of Walnut and Seventh Streets, is the **Hamilton County Courthouse.** ⓮ Hamilton County has had 6 courthouses since the founding of the county in 1819. According to tradition, the first courthouse was located at a tavern and stock stand owned by Hasten Poe at Poe's Cross Roads

(now Soddy-Daisy). In 1823, the court was moved approximately 1 mile to the home of John Mitchell "until a permanent seat of justice could be selected." A log courthouse was subsequently erected at the farm of Asa Rawlings in the town of Dallas (now under the waters of Chickamauga Lake), and the community at that spot was named "Hamilton County

Courthouse." The county seat was then moved to Harrison (now under Chickamauga Lake as well) in 1840, and relocated to the growing town of Chattanooga in 1870. After utilizing temporary quarters for several years, a new courthouse was completed in 1879 at this location, which had been formerly occupied by residential homes and the First Baptist Church. Interestingly, a 1967 article claimed that this site was originally occupied by a rock fort built by ancient Welsh settlers who predated the Indian populations of Tennessee and also built complex rock fortifications on Lookout Mountain, Fort Mountain (near Dalton, Georgia), and at Old Stone Fort (Manchester, Tennessee); this report is intriguing, if unlikely. Designed by A.C Bruce, the Second Empire-styled courthouse pictured on pages 48 and 55 was constructed of brick and stone, with arches of dressed fossiliferous limestone and polished marble pillars; the entrance (on Walnut Street) led to a large vestibule with a mosaic tile floor. The highlight of the $64,625 structure, however, was its 120-foot tall bell tower, which was fitted with a 6,000-pound clock and a 3,000-pound bell which rang out across the town on the hour.

The site of numerous trials and public ceremonies, the courthouse was also the site of a macabre public display in 1881. On September 14, 1882, Hamilton County sheriff William T. Cate, along with a deputy, John J. Conway, set out to escort several prisoners to a hearing in Knoxville; one of these prisoners was the notorious riverman John Taylor, who had killed Captain John W. Fletcher aboard the *Tellico* steamboat on February 23, 1881. Though Cate was warned to take extra men with him, he naively responded that he had "not an enemy on earth" and proceeded to board the train to Knoxville. At Sweetwater, Tennessee, however, 3 men - including brothers Bob and Andy Taylor - boarded the train. Deputy Conway was shot in the back and died instantly. A man in the front shot Cate, then shot him again as he tried to draw his gun; he was shot several more times as he staggered to his feet and was shoved to the platform outside, where he died. Retired Hamilton County Sheriff Jack Springfield then returned to office solely to hunt down the murderers. After John Taylor reportedly died in Missouri, Springfield had his body exhumed to be certain it was him, and when Bob Taylor was killed in Missouri, his body was taken to Chattanooga and placed in the portico of the Hamilton County Courthouse.

In 1910, a bolt of lightning started a fire at the courthouse, which quickly spread to the bell tower and destroyed the building; the fire was referred to at the time as "by probably the most conspicuous and dramatic fire" in the town's history. Temporary quarters were then secured while a new courthouse designed by prolific Chattanooga architect R.H. Hunt was erected on the same spot. Opening in 1913 at a cost of $350,000, the current Beaux Arts courthouse, which was advertised as "fireproof" at the time of its construction, is composed of gray Tennessee marble with terra cotta trim; the entrance to this new structure was moved from Walnut to Seventh Street at the time of construction. The courthouse was added to the National Register of Historic Places in 1978. Today, the building (which was enlarged in 1937) continues to house county courts and offices, though the need for additional space has led to expansion and construction of other county buildings nearby.

Surrounding the courthouse is a Rock Wall which was built by stonemasons Mike Minnigan and J.J. Sullivan during construction of the original county courthouse in 1879. Constructed of stone quarried from the nearby Stone Fort, the wall was retained in the design for the current structure.

The courthouse lawn is the site of several historic monuments, including a bust of Major General **Alexander P. Stewart** (CSA) which greets visitors at the front of the courthouse. Known to his men as "Old Straight," Stewart (pictured above and on page 48) roomed with future Confederate general James Longstreet at West Point, and as a teacher at the same school he lectured students George McClellan (future general of the Union Army of the Potomac) and Thomas J. "Stonewall" Jackson. A Tennesseean, at the outbreak of the Civil War Stewart was torn between his opposition to slavery and his loyalty to his home state, eventually choosing to accept an appointment as a major in the Confederate army. He served in the battles of Shiloh, Perryville, Stone's River, Chickamauga, Missionary Ridge, Atlanta, Nashville and Franklin, earning a reputation as a hard fighter and good administrator. It is reported that, at Missionary Ridge, Stewart grasped a Confederate flag and rallied his men, crying

"Men of Tennessee! Rally to your flag and protect your army!" The line then held until the defeated southern army could retreat into North Georgia. He assumed control of General Leonidas Polk's corps after Polk was killed during the Atlanta campaign, and he continued to serve with the Confederate army until the end of the war, commanding the last remnants of the rebel army at the battle of Bentonville in 1865. Following the war, Stewart served as chancellor of the University of Mississippi (1874-1886), and he was the Confederate representative to the commission established to create the Chickamauga & Chattanooga National Military Park. At the time of his death in 1908, Stewart was the highest-ranking Confederate survivor of the war, and he is remembered by this monument for his actions in and around Chattanooga, both during and after the war.

From the courthouse, cross Georgia Avenue. At the northeast corner of McCallie and Georgia Avenues **15** is the former site of the imposing 5-story **Elizabeth Apartments**, named for Elizabeth Patten Lupton, the wife of owner John T. Lupton. Built at the location of a home owned for years by early resident Foley Vaughn, the 40-suite apartment building (each suite had 4-5 rooms) was designed by W.T. Downing and cost $150,000. In the early 1950s, the building was sold to realtor E. Cecil Phillips, who converted it into commercial space and renamed it the "Professional Building." Struck by fire in 1976, the building was later purchased by the city and torn down; McCallie Avenue was then diverted to curve into Seventh Street, in order to ease traffic flow in this area.

Near the Elizabeth Apartments, on Georgia Avenue between McCallie Avenue and Oak Street, was the former **Calumet Club** (660 Georgia Avenue), which was erected circa 1905 and took its name from an Indian term for "peace pipe." Located in a 3-story house formerly occupied by local resident W.E. Baskette, the club added Greek-Revival columns and a large portico, and the building was the only structure in town to boast a rooftop garden and separate cafes for ladies and gentlemen. Occupied for many years after 1912 as a funeral home and as the headquarters for the Olan Mills Company (a locally-based portrait studio business founded in 1932), the structure was torn down in 1954, and today the property is occupied by a parking lot.

From this spot, head north to **Oak Street**. **16**

Originally occupied by farms and pasture land on the edge of town, Oak Street began to be developed during the real estate boom of 1887-1888, and it is one of the earliest residential expansions in the city of Chattanooga.

On Oak Street was the first site of the local **Girls' Preparatory School** (GPS), which was founded in a frame house at 106 Oak Street in 1906 by Grace Eliza McCallie, sister of one of the founders of the local McCallie School. The school began with 4 teachers and 50 students and included daily exercise, in order "to prevent that nervous breakdown so common among girls." In 1915, the school moved nearby, to Palmetto Street, and in 1947 the school relocated to its present location in North Chattanooga.

At the northeast corner of Georgia Avenue and Oak Street **17** is the former site of the **First Baptist Church**, erected in 1887. This Romanesque church (pictured above and on page 49), which was designed by R.H. Hunt and completed at a cost of $50,000, featured a pink sandstone exterior and 140-foot bell tower. The congregation's original, 1-ton bronze bell, which had been painted black during the Civil War to disguise its value and thus discourage its removal by the federal army, was placed in the new building. Although a destructive fire in 1894 caused substantial damage to the church, the structure was reopened in 1895 with new sandstone trim, cherry pews, and fine interior woodwork. During its tenure at this site, the church played host to several notable events, including 4 Southern Baptist conventions and a presidential visit by Theodore Roosevelt. Although some church members thought as early as 1929 that the church "should recede before Chattanooga's expanding commercial life and seek a location farther away from the heart of the city," the congregation elected to

stay in this location, undergoing periodic renovation and expansion. To that end, several additional buildings were added to the original structure in the 1920s, and in 1957 the church acquired several additional properties along Oak Street for $160,000. By 1962, however, the tide had turned, and the church, citing congested facilities, crowding, and trash-strewn alleyways, announced that it had purchased 8.43 acres in the Golden Gateway development on the west side of downtown for construction of a new $1.5 million building. Groundbreaking for the new church took place in 1965, and in 1967 Fred Robinson purchased the old building, which was then razed to provide parking for his apartment building next door.

The only remaining portion of the First Baptist Church is a 4-story brick U-shaped building with a Tennessee pink sandstone facade, which is located on Oak Street. This structure (pictured on page 49) was originally constructed in 1928 as a Sunday School building for the First Baptist Church. The Romanesque building was designed by R.H. Hunt, the same individual who had designed the original church building in 1888. This building was saved from destruction and purchased by the City of Chattanooga, and in 1981 the building, which was added to the National Register of Historic Places in 1980, was renamed the Martin Luther King, Jr., Human Services Center.

AN EVENT CHATTANOOGA HAS EAGERLY AWAITED /

Grace Moore

'LOVE ME FOREVER'

Leo Carrillo · Michael Bartlett

One significant local event which occurred at the First Baptist Church was the 1947 funeral of opera/film star and prima donna Grace Moore. Called "the daughter of the hills of Tennessee" and the "Tennessee Nightingale," Moore (pictured below and on page 49) was born in Slabtown, Tennessee, and moved from Jellico, Tennessee, to Chattanooga with her parents in 1932, after her father became owner of the Loveman's department store. She debuted with the Metropolitan Opera in 1928, as Mimi in *La Boheme*. She became the first motion-picture star to receive the Medal of the American Academy of Arts and Sciences in 1934 for her role in *One Night of Love*, and in 1939 she received the chevalier of the Legion of Honor of France. She was also actively involved in several USO tours which entertained U.S. troops during World War II. Moore died in a plane crash in Denmark on January 25, 1947, during a European tour.

From this corner, you may choose to proceed down Oak Street to the **Caleb Isbester House** (551 Oak Street), located at the northwest corner of Oak and Douglas Streets. Erected in 1896, this brick structure is typical of the residential buildings erected in this area at the turn of the century. This Queen Anne structure includes a brick turret, as well as a number of architectural features reminiscent of the Chateauesque style which was also prevalent during this period. The home was originally built for Caleb Isbester, a Scottish emigrant who arrived in Chattanooga in 1868 and formed the Chattanooga Foundry & Pipe Works in 1877. After Isbester died in 1898, the home was occupied by William Riley Crabtree, the husband of Isbester's daughter, Ginny. Crabtree subsequently became mayor of Chattanooga in 1907-1909, during which a number of significant developments took place, including the creation of a city commission form of government, the construction of a new city-owned water works, and several important public works projects. In the 1930s, ownership of the house passed to the University of Chattanooga, during which period it was operated as a men's dormitory known as "Varsity Hall," which possibly housed members of the university's athletic teams. Today, the home is utilized as private commercial space.

Beyond this home, where Oak Street dead-ends into Douglas Street, is the campus of the **University of Tennessee at Chattanooga**. Founded in 1886 by the Methodist Episcopal Church as "Chattanooga University," in 1889 the school merged with East Tennessee Wesleyan College (Athens, Tennessee) to create "Grant College," named for U.S. President Ulysses S Grant. The sole campus building at that time was Old Main, pictured on page 49 and 58, which contained the classrooms, dormitory rooms, faculty apartments, kitchen, mess hall, chapel, and library for the school. Old Main was eventually torn down in 1917 to make room for campus growth and the construction of several new buildings. In 1907, the college was renamed the University of Chattanooga, and in 1969 it (and a junior college, Chattanooga City College) merged into the University of Tennessee system.

Back at the corner of Oak Street and Georgia Avenue, next door to the former site of the First Baptist Church, are the **Robinson Apartments** (622 Georgia Avenue). ⓯ One of the first "luxury" apartment buildings established in Chattanooga (1907), this Classical Revival structure (above) features a 3-story pedimented portico with fluted Corinthian columns. Recently renovated, the building continues to house downtown apartment residents today.

Next door to the Robinson Apartments is a low, 1-story building which displays an eclectic mix of classical and Spanish elements (**614-618 Georgia Avenue**). Renovated in the early 1970s, this building was divided into 2 separate restaurants, each of which employed in its design historically-significant architectural elements from earlier Chattanooga buildings. To the right, the Brass Register restaurant utilized the original stand-up bar and cash register from the popular Rathskellar restaurant located nearby, while the brass revolving doors at the former Gazebo restaurant to the left were salvaged from the original American Trust & Banking Company building at Market and Eighth Streets. Due to continued redevelopment of the Ross's Landing area in the early 1990s and a resulting shift in traffic patterns, these long-tenured eating spots were eventually closed; today, the Gazebo building is currently used as a private

business, and the Brass Register building is again a restaurant, the Vineyard.

Next door to this building is the 2-story brick **Claridge Building** (608-610 Georgia Avenue). Constructed in 1924, this building features Spanish details, as well as limestone accents on the quoins and windows of the building. For a numbers of years after its construction, the building housed the Coffee Shoppe, a "popular social center" run by Gertrude and Bessie Oehmig. Remodeled in the late 1970s, this structure continues to house a number of private offices today.

From this spot, continue north to Vine Street. Here, at the southeast corner of Georgia Avenue and Vine Street, are the **Hardwick-Hogshead Apartments** (604 Georgia Avenue), ⓰ which were completed in 1912-1913 and named for owners F.T. Hardwick and Dr. J. McChesney Hogshead. The "H and H" motif on the iron grillwork at the entrances and balconies of the building represents the Hardwick and Hogshead names. This Classical Revival apartment building was designed by local architect Charles E. Bearden. This 6-story brick building, which was designed to house residential apartments as well as Dr. Hogshead's Chattanooga Eye, Ear, Nose & Throat Clinic, has dual facades on the east and north sides, with limestone lintels, keystones, and block courses. The building also features a rooftop garden for residents. Like other buildings in this area, this apartment building underwent renovation in the 1970s and continues to be utilized for both residential and business purposes today.

To return to the start of the Fountain Square tour, head north to Fourth Street, then turn left (west) and proceed to Walnut Street.

As the name indicates, the area known colloquially as "Irish Hill" is a noticeable elevation located on the southeast fringe of the original town boundaries of Ross's Landing. Cresting at the spot where McCallie Avenue meets Georgia Avenue, the hill falls away toward Martin Luther King Jr. Boulevard, where originally sat a low, swampy area.

This tract of land was originally referred to as "Branham Hill," named for an early resident who lived in the area, and the southern portion of the area was listed in early Chattanooga maps as "Griffin's Addition," in reference to an early developer of this portion of the downtown area. It is best known, however, as "Irish Hill," a title given to the area in reference to the large number of Irish railroad workers who stayed in Chattanooga following the arrival of the railroad in 1850.

When Father Henry V. Brown purchased a piece of property in this area on which to build a Catholic Church, he offered to sell lots in the surrounding area at cost to church parishioners, many of whom were Irish. A number of these new residents clustered nearby, and the area soon became known as "Irish Hill." Today, several significant buildings and historic spots in this area trace the development of downtown Chattanooga from its beginnings to the present day.

17 The Original Krystal Restaurant

18 Masonic Temple

to **Fountain Square** p. 47

13 Market Square

MARKET HOUSE

to **Market Center** p. 167

Turner Hall

to **Big Nine** p. 75

9 St. Peter and Paul's Catholic Church

15 Keystone Hotel

62

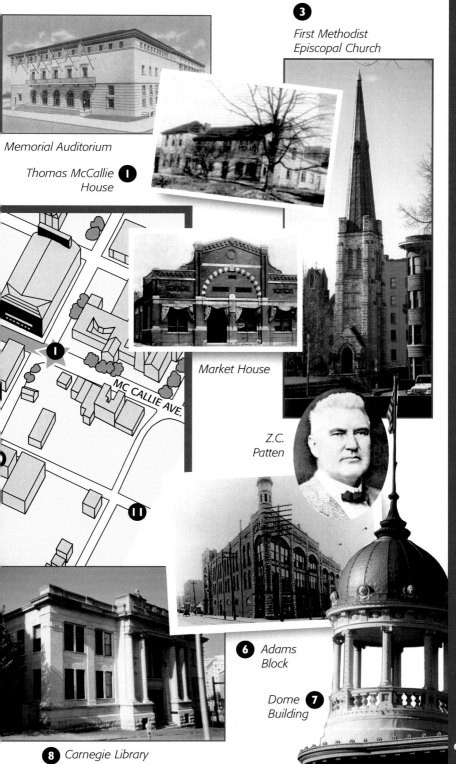

Memorial Auditorium

Thomas McCallie **1** House

3 First Methodist Episcopal Church

Market House

Z.C. Patten

6 Adams Block

Dome **7** Building

8 Carnegie Library

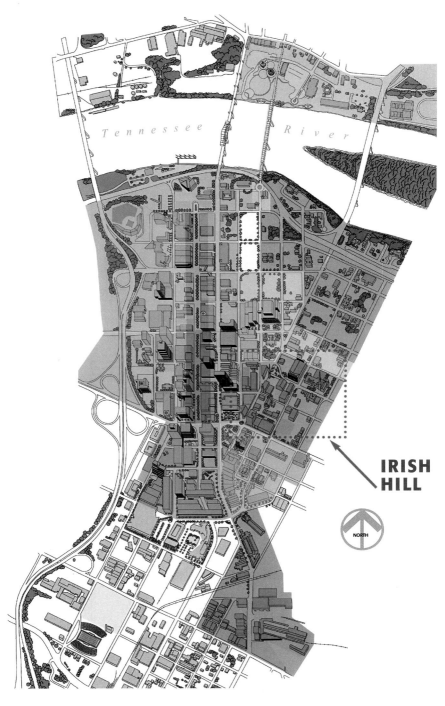

IRISH HILL

NORTH

The walking tour of Irish Hill begins at the corner of McCallie Avenue and Lindsay Street. ❶ Initially the site of farmlands lying on the outskirts of town, this area began to attract a variety of homes in the latter half of the nineteenth century, when it became a convenient residential neighborhood with easy access to the downtown area. While continued expansion of the downtown "core" led to the replacement of several of these early homes with newer buildings throughout the twentieth century, a few older homes and apartment buildings still attract residents to this part of the downtown area.

The block at the southeast corner of McCallie Avenue and Lindsay Street, currently the site of the First Centenary Church annex, was previously the site of the **Thomas McCallie House**. Thomas McCallie was the son of a Scottish immigrant who came to Philadelphia in 1775; McCallie himself (1795-1859) was born in Blount County, Tennessee, and came to Chattanooga in 1841 in a flat-bottom boat. One

of the early residents of Ross's Landing, he established a mercantile store at the corner of Market and Fourth Streets and arranged for a large, 2-story frame house (above) to be built at this site. The road which linked Ross's Landing to the old Brainerd Mission passed this house, and it thereafter became known as "McCallie Avenue." The 25-acre property, which covered much of the land in this area, included orchards, a stable, hog pens, a smokehouse, and large corn cribs; also situated around the house were several small buildings which housed the 5 slaves McCallie owned. During the Civil War, the house served as a "hotel and hospital" as well as the headquarters for Union General L.H. Rousseau; the outlying sheds and pens were torn down for use by the federal army, leaving the house standing alone on the property. Although Union General J.B. Steedman initially ordered that house to be torn down to make room for placement of a fort, Mrs. McCallie's pleadings caused him to lift

the order, and the home survived the war intact. Later, the house became the first site of the local Baylor School for boys (1893). Purchased by the Centenary Methodist Church in 1908 for use as an annex, the house was torn down in 1920 to make way for a new church building (1921) fronted by 6 massive columns and a large flight of stone steps. This structure, in turn, was torn down after the Centenary Methodist Church merged with the First Methodist Church and erected the present building on the southern portion of the block (1973); an annex was then built at the site of the old McCallie home in 1978.

Directly across Lindsay Street from the McCallie farm site is the **Soldiers and Sailors Memorial Auditorium** (399 McCallie Avenue). Following World War I, the local Kiwanis Club suggested that a memorial be erected to the men who fought in that conflict; due to the pressing need for an adequate city auditorium (the prior auditorium had burned down in 1916), it was felt that such a building would be a fitting choice for a war memorial. The home of local attorney, clerk-and-master, and businessman James Caldwell, who came to Chattanooga in 1867 after serving in the Confederate army, was chosen as the site for this 5,000 seat auditorium, which was designed by prolific local architect Reuben Harrison Hunt. The cornerstone was lain in a city-wide ceremony on November 11, 1922. Today, this distinguished building (above) continues to serve as an important local performance and ceremonial hall.

From this point, cross McCallie Avenue to the northwest corner of McCallie Avenue and Lindsay Street. Replacing yet another house that had previously stood at this spot, the **Albemarle Apartment Building** (324 McCallie Avenue) was completed in 1914. It recently underwent a program of renovation and continues to operate as an apartment building at the present time.

Directly across Lindsay Street, at the southwest corner of McCallie Avenue and Lindsay Street, is a parking lot which was previously the site of a large home erected by Chattanooga entrepreneur and early millionaire **Charles E. James**. The home (above), which at one point featured a large wrap-around porch, was subsequently occupied by the Interstate Life and Accident Insurance Company and the local Red Cross chapter, after which it was torn down in 1969. The only portion of the property which remains today is the attractive 2-story building at the back of the lot, which was erected as a carriage house for the James home; this building, which has seen a variety of uses, is currently a private residence.

East of this parking lot is an interesting 3-story brick building located at **414 McCallie Avenue**. Originally constructed as a residence circa 1900, this Victorian building most recently housed Southeast Tennessee Legal Services, a non-profit legal aid organization. Next door to that building are the **Ayrshire Apartments** (416-418 McCallie Avenue), occupying 2 brick buildings erected in the early years of the twentieth century.

From the corner of McCallie Avenue and Lindsay Street, proceed west (toward downtown) along McCallie Avenue. After approximately one block, the road splits; in the center of the street at this point is **Phillips Park,** ❷ named for local realtor E. Cecil Phillips. Originally, McCallie Avenue dead-ended here at Georgia Avenue; in order to ease congestion and divert traffic to Seventh Street, it was decided in the 1970s that a portion of the northeast corner at McCallie and Georgia Avenues would be removed (as can be seen in the map of this spot), and Phillips' Professional Building at that spot was sold to the city and torn down. Following this decision, in 1975 the creation of a "Market Center" in the downtown core was proposed as part of an Urban Design Plan and

Improvements Program for the City of Chattanooga; as part of this program, the triangular park at the confluence of McCallie and Georgia Avenues, named for Phillips, was created as an "exciting and dramatic flag plaza" to signify the eastern entrance to the downtown core.

Across the street from the park, the tall stone tower at the southwest corner of McCallie and Georgia Avenues ❸ marks the former site of the **First Methodist Episcopal Church**, organized in 1865 under the leadership of a former Union army chaplain, the Rev. T.S. Stivers. After meeting in several temporary locations, in 1867 the 16-member congregation moved to a new, $1,400 frame structure built on brick pillars at the corner of Pine and Sixth Streets; this worship hall featured steep steeps leading to a double-door entrance and "windows glazed as if it were a saloon." In 1882, however, work began on a new stone church, which opened in 1885 at this spot. Located on a lot where presidential candidate Stephen A. Douglas spoke to Chattanooga citizens during his 1860 campaign, this new church was constructed of limestone from the Joshua Beck farm on the north side of the river. It also included a 176-foot steeple, 3 spiral staircases, exposed ceiling beams of virgin pine, and the first pipe organ in Chattanooga. In 1926, a $150,000 auxiliary building, the "John A. Patten Memorial Parish House," was erected next door to the church building. In 1966, however, the church membership voted to consolidate with the Centenary Methodist Church, which had recently purchased the block bounded by McCallie Avenue and Oak, Lindsay, and Houston Streets; following the construction of a new church build-

ing at that location, the original bell from the stone church was relocated, and the church was vacated in 1972. Unable to find a purchaser for the building, its new owner, Gordon P. Street, tore down the church structure, although the "landmark" stone tower (pictured on page 63) was retained as part of North

American Royalties' rejuvenation plans for this area.

From this point, turn left (south) onto Georgia Avenue and proceed downhill. On the right, at the northeast corner of Georgia Avenue and Walnut Street, is a triangular block occupied by the **Flatiron Building** (1911). ➍ Originally occupied by of the First Presbyterian Church and the homes of early Chattanooga residents Daniel Kaylor and Dr. Philander D. Sims, in 1911 architect Charles E. Bearden designed a "diminutive replica of the famous New York structure," i.e., the Flatiron Building, at this location. This red brick, stone-trimmed building has 5 stories on its Walnut Street side and 4 on the Georgia Avenue facade; the upper stories were originally devoted to residential apartments, and the lower floors were redesigned to house businesses. As you can see, the glass-walled apex of the building is only a single story tall; this portion of the structure initially housed a cigar stand. The building underwent a multi-million dollar renovation in the late 1980s and continues to house several businesses today.

Across Walnut Street from the Flatiron Building is the site of the **Kindred Hospital.** ➎ In the 1880s, this lot at the northwest corner of East Eighth Street and Georgia Avenue was occupied by the Arlington Hotel. Subsequently, however, it became the site of a long-lived downtown hospital. The Newell Infirmary, operated by Drs. Edward T. and E. Dunbar Newell, opened in 1908 with 15 patient beds. In 1920, it moved to the former Knights of Pythias Hall at 711 Walnut Street, after which it came to be referred to as the Newell Sanitarium. In 1951, the name again changed, this time to the Newell Clinic Hospital; at that time, the original building at 707 Walnut Street was renovated, and a new 3-story wing was added to the building. In 1975, a new 54-bed building was completed here at the northwest corner of Walnut Street, Georgia Avenue, and Eighth Street, to house a new non-profit hospital, the "Downtown General Hospital," and the original building was then torn down to create a parking lot. Today, the building continues to house a medical facility.

From this point, head down Georgia Avenue. The parking lot at the southwest corner of Georgia Avenue and Eighth Street is the former site of the **Adams Block** (1881), ➏ constructed by John Wesley Adams, an architect, contractor, and builder who was instrumental in investing large amounts of capital into Chattanooga during the 1880s real estate boom. The

Richardsonian Romanesque-styled building (above4) included 4 business rooms on the first floor and residences on the second story. While Adams initially planned to build a number of similar buildings nearby under the name "Union Block," the waning of the real estate boom curtailed interest in this plan, which was never realized. In 1930, the original stone facade was replaced by a modern-styled exterior after the widening of Georgia Avenue and Cherry Street forced the owners to tear back the building 10 feet from the street. In 1980, moreover, the building, along with the adjacent Ferger and Salvation Army buildings, was torn down to make way for additional downtown parking, a use the property continues to serve today.

Across Georgia Avenue, at the northeast corner of that street and Eighth Street, is the distinctive **Dome Building** (1892), ➐ one of the architectural icons of Chattanooga. This 6-story building, which was erected on a lot where previously sat a 4-room frame house and low wall (1872), displays a mix of Romanesque and Italian Renaissance styles and features a main entrance with Tuscan pilasters and a keystone arch. The build-

ing (right) was originally the headquarters of the *Chattanooga Times* newspaper (founded in 1869 and consolidated with the *Daily Dispatch* in 1878) owned by Adolph S. Ochs (1858-1935), an enthusiastic and influential supporter of Chattanooga who also owned the *New York Times*, which received the first Pulitzer Gold

Medal in Journalism in 1918. For its part, the *Chattanooga Times* was instrumental in promoting Chattanooga in the years surrounding the 1887-88 real estate boom, which in turn influenced the growth and development of the Irish Hill area. In 1917, an unadorned 3-story addition was added to the rear of this building to house the printing offices of the newspaper, which occupied the building until 1941. As part of a "modernization" program for the building, in the 1960s advertising signs were fixed to the facade and black material was placed over the stonework of the first floor. In the 1970s the building, which is listed on the National Register of Historic Places, was acquired by North American Royalties, which renovated the structure and ensured its status as a key feature of the Chattanooga skyline.

Across Eighth Street (originally known as Gilmar Street), at the southeast corner of that street and Georgia Avenue, is the **Carnegie Library,** ❽ which housed the Chattanooga Public Library for a number of years. Chattanooga did not have a formal library building until this structure was completed in 1905, although early library associations arose in 1867 and 1887 (the latter of which was stymied by the 1893 financial panic). In 1900, following the destruction of several private law book collections in a destructive fire at the nearby Richardson Block, a Bar and Law Library Association was founded, and by 1909 the city voted additional funds to supplement the library. In 1905, northern philanthropist Andrew Carnegie donated $50,000 for construction of a library in Chattanooga (several Carnegie libraries were built during the period following 1881, with Carnegie donating $2 per local resident for construction of the buildings). A lot was purchased from the Catholic church, and a 2-story Italian Renaissance structure (above and on page 63) was built at this spot. Some debate continues as to whether local architect

R.H. Hunt or famed New York architect Stanford White designed the structure, which has a rough stone base onto which was placed a 2-story Neo-classical marble structure. The building has Ionic columns and an interior rotunda reaching upward to a skylight in the roof, and the plain frieze of the entrance to the building is accented with a cornice carved in a modified egg-and-dart design. Incidentally, at the time it was completed the building was the only structure in Chattanooga with wall radiators. In 1940, the library moved to newer quarters in a building now on the campus of the University of Tennessee at Chattanooga (UTC), and this building, which is now listed on the National Register of Historic Places, subsequently housed the non-profit Community Chest (a forerunner of the United Way) and a YMCA youth center. It was purchased by North American Royalties and renovated by the Los Angeles firm Cannell & Chaffin in the 1970s for use as corporate offices.

Next door to the Carnegie Library is the **St. Peter and Paul's Catholic Church.** ❾ In 1854, Father Henry V. Brown began construction of a stone church, which neared completion as the Civil War began. In order to protect the unfinished structure, Union General William S. Rosecrans, himself a Catholic, ordered the federal soldiers occupying the city to safeguard the building materials earmarked for the church, adding that "the penalty for the violation of this order is death." Upon Rosecrans' replacement by General Ulysses S. Grant (US), however, the soldiers immediately tore down the walls for use in fortifications. The

parish then used temporary facilities until the building boom of the late 1880s, when the construction of a new building was undertaken. Seating 1,000 parishioners, the St. Peter and Paul's Catholic Church was said to be one of the finest Catholic church buildings in the South. This gothic structure (above) is constructed of limestone, pressed brick, and berea stone, and a stained glass shamrock was placed above the central entryway to greet parishioners, many of whom were Irish. The church building originally featured two towers 174 feet tall, with crocketed pinnacles and turrets. In 1917, a new Tudor rectory was added next door to the church building. An interior renovation of the church in 1936 was followed by an exterior remodeling in 1939, at which time the 2 original sandstone towers were replaced with the single, shorter limestone steeple which is seen today on the left side of the church.

From this spot, continue along Eighth Street, crossing Lindsay Street. When the roads in this portion of Chattanooga were originally laid out, the cross streets south of McCallie Avenue were given alphabetical labels, and this portion of Lindsay Street was known as "A" Street. In 1912, however, these street names were replaced, and A Street became Lindsay Street; to the east, B Street became Houston Street, C became Mabel Street, and E became University Street.

Here, at the southeast corner of Lindsay and Eighth Streets, is the **Chattanooga Y.W.C.A.** building (1912), located at 300 East Eighth Street. ❿ The third Y.W.C.A. chapter in the South (after Atlanta and Nashville), the Chattanooga Y.W.C.A. was organized in 1902. After having operated in various temporary facilities, in 1912 the organization moved into this building, which was designed by Clarence T. Jones. The 4-story brick building included several amenities, including a basement swimming pool, cafeteria, and birch-paneled dining hall. The building currently houses the Family & Children's Services of Chattanooga, a local non-profit corporation.

Next door to the Y.W.C.A. Building is the **Notre Dame de Lourdes Academy** building (1926). Founded in 1876 under the guidance of 4 Dominican sisters brought to Chattanooga from the St. Cecilia Academy in Nashville by Father Patrick Ryan, the school first occupied a gabled building (1854) that had served as the rectory for the Catholic church. In 1886, the 250-student school erected a new building at the southwest corner of East Eighth and Lindsay Streets; that $25,000 building was a 2-story brick structure with a stone basement. In 1926, the current Gothic building was completed at this spot across Lindsay Street from the older structure, which was then torn down. While the school later moved to a new, suburban location in 1956, the building subsequently served as the All Saints Academy for elementary students; it is currently home to the Dismas House, a local non-profit corporation.

From the corner of Lindsay and East Eighth Streets, turn right and proceed down Lindsay Street (south) toward Martin Luther King Jr. Blvd. First, however, you may wish to continue down Eighth Street to the **Shiloh Baptist Church** (506 East Eighth Street), ⓫ a church founded in 1866 by a number of former African-American soldiers in the Union army. After meeting in a blacksmith shop and a temporary frame structure which later burned, the cornerstone was lain for this church, intended to be the largest of its kind in the South, on October 8, 1885. Although the stone basement for the church was completed, financial troubles and internal dissension subsequently struck the congregation, and several groups split off from the church. The name was changed from Shiloh Baptist to First Baptist, and the original title was scratched from the cornerstone. This building, which was constructed largely by former slaves, took approximately a decade to complete. Listed on the National Register of Historic Places, the structure continues to operate as a church today.

Next door to the church building is the **Walden Hospital** (528 East Eighth Street). Founded by Dr. E. R. Wheeler in 1918, this structure operated as an African-American hospital for 38 years until its closing in 1952. Although in 1938 Chattanooga began to allow African-American doctors to treat African-American patients at Erlanger Hospital (the first instance in the South of such a practice in a municipal hospital), this hospital nevertheless provided a critical early facility for African-American doctors in the city, including 19 African-American members of the Mountain City Medical Society who treated patients at this location. The historic building, which subsequently served as residential apartments for a number of years, is currently undergoing restoration.

From the Y.W.C.A Building, proceed down Lindsay Street; before you reach Martin Luther King Jr. Blvd., turn right onto **Patten Parkway,** an open area between Lindsay Street and Georgia Avenue. ⓬ Initially, the center of this

parkway was occupied by the city **Market House** (pictured on pages 63, 69, and 71). ⓭ An early market house at Market and Sixth Streets (1853) was removed to make way for the First National Bank Building in 1871, and during the real estate boom of 1887-88 it was decided that the town needed a new public market. Led by newspaperman Adolph Ochs, a group of businessmen pledged $20,000 to the city in exchange for the right to select the site for this new market house; they then selected this spot, located on land deeded for educational purposes and known as the "Georgia Avenue School Lot." The city then enacted an ordinance prohibiting the sale of meat anywhere other than the market house (and limiting the sale of vegetables, eggs, and poultry at other stores prior to noon). The one-story brick building then was erected in the center of "Market Square," which had 20-foot streets (North Market Place and South Market Place) on either side of the building. The structure was adorned with various motifs depicting fruits, vegetables, and flowers, and elaborate decorations of sheep, cattle, and hogs were placed above the doors and windows of the building. Around 1898, when it was determined that the market had become economically infeasible, the building was remodeled for use as a city hall, police headquarters, jail, and engine house. A lawsuit was filed by several Cincinnati businessmen who owned surrounding buildings, but the attempt to prevent this development failed. However, in 1908 a new city hall was completed at Eleventh and Lindsay Streets, and in 1914 the building reverted to its original use as a market house, at which time a new 254-foot long shed was added to the building to house additional vendors. Over time, however, it became apparent that the city had outgrown the market house, and the narrow lanes surrounding the building fostered traffic problems. In 1942, therefore, the Market House was razed to make way for a new park at this spot.

To that end, in 1942 a new "comfort station" was planned on this site, and in 1944 it was proposed to name the park after prominent Chattanoogan Z.C. Patten (left), the founder of the Volunteer Life Insurance Company and other significant local ventures. In 1948, a World War II memorial was

added to the park, and a stone base with four shallow pools of Quartzite, granite, and brick was placed in the center of the parkway (these pools were later filled in and converted to the current planting areas in 1959). Though the monument was unveiled in 1950, a planned bronze statue was omitted due to cost concerns, with plans to complete it when additional funds were raised; to date, it has not been added to the park. Subsequently, a 76mm anti-tank gun was brought from Anniston, Alabama, as a monument to those who fought in the war, but the Executive Committee of the American Legion vetoed its placement at the park. In 1969, a 24-inch gas-burning "Flame of Freedom" was added to the center of the monument; though it can still be seen (along with a symbolic brass eagle), the flame itself fell victim to the Energy Crisis of 1973 and no longer burns. One interesting proposal made in the 1970s offered that "The northern portion of Patten Parkway is proposed to be closed to vehicles to permit full pedestrian circulation and a variety of activities including outdoor cafes, crafts and art shows and strolling troubadours"; it was also proposed at that time that a new fountain be placed on the northern portion of the parkway. These plans, however, were never implemented. However, memorials to the veterans of the Korean and Vietnam wars have been added to the park in recent years, and the parkway itself was placed on the National Register of Historic Places in 1978.

Situated along the north side of Patten Parkway is a row of 2- and 3-story brick buildings erected by Cincinnati investors whose interest in Chattanooga was sparked by the completion of the Cincinnati Southern Railway in 1880. These buildings, which were erected for $90,000 as an "adjunct" development overlooking the market square, were originally intended to house small shops and apartment spaces, uses which continue today.

At the left (west) of this row of buildings are a plaque and historic marker commemorating the site of the **Original Coca-Cola Bottling Facility** (the plaque is located at 17 Patten Parkway, although some early advertisements list the location as 23 Patten Parkway). This facility was located in 1900 in a small building at this site, which has since been torn down. In 1899, two local men, Ben F. Thomas and J.B. Whitehead, acquired from Atlanta resident Asa Candler the exclusive right to bottle Coca-Cola, paying one dollar for the right to do so. As early as November 12, 1899, the *Chattanooga Times*

announced the arrival of this novel product with the refrain, "Drink a bottle of Coca-Cola, five cents at all stands, grocers, and saloons." By 1902, the firm produced 100 cases of Coca-Cola per day; while several competitors were also located in Chattanooga, including Cherco-Cola, Tenn-Cola, Coca-Ginger, Grape Fizz, Tripure Cola, and Whistle Cola, the Coca-Cola franchise soon outdistanced its competitors, creating an internationally-recognized product as well as financial fortunes for several Chattanooga residents in the first half of the twentieth century.

From this spot, head to the northeast corner of Patten Parkway and Georgia Avenue, where is located a 4-story building emblazoned with a bright sign reading "Yesterday's." This structure, which was constructed in 1888 and initially operated as a boarding house or hotel known as the Delmonico Hotel, was converted in 1925 to the 70-room **Hotel Ross**, which advertised itself as "Chattanooga's newest and most elegantly appointed Hotelry." This hotel featured a 40-by-100 foot ballroom (the "Grotto") on the ground floor, a second-floor parlor with grand piano and rich tapestries, private baths, and an ice-water fountain on each floor. Notably, in the wake of the Scopes "Monkey Trial" in Dayton, Tennessee (1925), 3-time presidential candidate and attorney William Jennings Bryan spent his last night in this hotel before dying the following day in Dayton. By 1966, when the property was sold for $75,000, the building housed mostly permanent residents; despite a voluntary rent hike by residents in 1978, however, financial losses caused the new owner to close the residential portion of the building in 1979. As for the corner restaurant located on the first floor of this building, this spot housed D.C. Kenner's meat market (pre-World War I), a Piggly Wiggly food store (1920s), and an A&P food market (1930s), before becoming Edmund's Restaurant, named for owner Edmund B. Raines, in 1945. In 1973, the restaurant changed its name to "Yesterday's," which

continued in operation until closing its doors in 1998. Currently, the building is empty and awaiting plans for restoration.

Up Georgia Avenue from the Hotel Ross is an enclosed parking area next door to the hotel building; this spot is the former site of the Chattanooga **Y.M.C.A. Building**. The oldest volunteer organization in the city, the Chattanooga chapter of the Y.M.C.A. was founded in 1871 and was originally housed in the Adams Block across the street. After temporary moves in 1882 and 1902, the Y.M.C.A. moved to this location at 812 Georgia Avenue in 1909. The 5-story brick building, which was designed by R.H. Hunt and built at a cost of $150,000, housed a gymnasium, assembly rooms, great hall, and dormitory rooms. The building was torn down in 1972 after the organization elected to move to a new location in the Golden Gateway urban redevelopment project; the space was subsequently converted into the current parking garage by North American Royalties, which owned and renovated a number of historic buildings in this area.

From Patten Parkway, turn left and proceed to the northeast corner of Georgia Avenue and Martin Luther King Jr. Blvd. (832 Georgia Avenue). ⓮ Located at the southern edge of the original town limits (and at the bottom of Irish Hill), this area was situated near a low-lying pond and a "deadly swamp" where early residents are said to have gone to do their washing. In 1883, two Confederate veterans, James Gillespie and L.J. Sharp, built a livery stable and undertaking business on this spot, although it was initially necessary for Gillespie to convince Sharp that placing a business in this location "so far out of town" was a good idea; it was also necessary to fill in the marshy lot before the frame structure for this business could be built. After operating at this location for a number of years, in 1913 the undertaking business was relocated, and the property was sold to Z.C. Patten for construction of offices for the Volunteer State Life Insurance Company (founded in 1903). The 12-story **Volunteer Building** was completed in 1917, at which time it was the tallest building in the city. Prior to its opening, the building was barricaded by police guard, for reasons which are now unclear — either to safeguard against theft of construction materials, or to prevent possible violence or sabotage associated with lingering payment issues between the insurance company and the building's contractors. This Neo-Classical building is detailed with pilasters, oval medallions, and an ornate arched entrance, over which is placed a circular bronze tablet depicting President Andrew Jackson, symbolizing the company's motto of "Strength, Stability, and Integrity." The lobby, moreover, features elaborate marble decorations and a molded ceiling. This building was intended to provide "an appearance of monumentality and elegance," and, viewed in comparison to the earlier buildings erected in the vicinity of the Market House in the 1880s, it is an interesting testament to the increasing commercial development of downtown Chattanooga in the early decades of the twentieth century. The building, which was subsequently acquired by the Chubb Life Insurance Company (1984) and the local Corker Group (1998), is now listed on the National Register of Historic Places and continues to house a number of professional offices at the present time.

From this point, cross Georgia Avenue and, at MLK Jr. Blvd., turn right onto **Cherry Street**. Unlike the other north-south streets in the original city plat, which were designed to be 100 feet wide, Cherry Street was initially somewhat narrow — 68 feet wide. To complicate matters, in 1849 the mayor and board of aldermen narrowed the width of all city streets in order to alleviate the cost of street maintenance and upkeep, and Cherry Street was cut to 48 feet in width. Following the arrival of the automobile and the resulting need for additional street space, however, the city enacted the Metropolitan Improvement Act, and in 1930 the portion of Cherry Street between Ninth and Fourth Streets (excluding the section between Seventh and Eighth Streets, which had previously been expanded) was widened at a total cost of $647,902. As a part of this plan, numerous trees were chopped down, and various businesses and residences were demolished or scaled back from the road. As a result, few buildings along this portion of Cherry Street predate 1930.

At the northeast corner of Cherry Street and MLK Jr. Blvd. is the **Keystone Block**. ⑮ Initially, a 4-

story brick building erected at this spot in 1887 housed a number of businesses, including the Provident Life & Accident Insurance Co. and the local library association. In February 1930, however, when Cherry Street was widened to take into account its transformation from a residential area to a growing commercial thoroughfare, the original Keystone Block was razed. In its place, Sarah Key Patten built the 32,000 square foot Hotel Key, a 7-story structure with 95 rooms which was built at a cost of over $100,000. Though the building was constructed as a hotel, the bottom floor of the structure was reserved for the M.B. Eaves & Brothers food store. Subsequently, the squared apex of the building, as seen in the picture below which depicts the hotel following its completion (in 1930), was replaced by the rounded glass elevator shaft which can be seen today. In 1963, the hotel was purchased by Towne House Properties, which initially planned to renovate the building for use as a Hilton hotel; when the Terminal Station was instead selected as the site for this "Chattanooga Choo-Choo" project, the possibility of undertaking a $1 million transformation to condominiums was discussed. Originally proposed in 1973, the concept of subdividing this property persisted until 1983, when the building was bought by the local Quadel Corporation. Today, the "Union Planters Bank Building" operates as a commercial bank and office building.

From this point, proceed down Cherry Street toward Eighth Street. Although portions of Cherry Street were developed commercially in the early years of the town (particularly on the west side of the street, which connected to the businesses fronting on Market Street), Cherry Street as a whole was never fully developed as a commercial area. In fact, in 1885 the only buildings along Cherry Street between Eighth and Ninth Streets were listed on maps as "shanties," and few significant buildings were erected along this street. Due to the widening of Cherry Street in 1930 and the demolition of several buildings in 1980 to create additional parking for the Loveman's Building (the rear portion of which sits at the southwest corner of Cherry and Eighth Streets), much of this block remains sparsely developed today, although the Loveman's Building is currently under renovation, presenting a new opportunity for residential and commercial growth in this area.

At the corner of Cherry and Eighth Streets once sat a structure where, it is believed, the **Yellow Fever Epidemic** of 1878 began in Chattanooga.

In June 1878, word reached Chattanooga of a Yellow Fever epidemic which had begun in New Orleans after the disease arrived on a steamer from Havana, Cuba. Though it was reported that the disease was spreading northward, Chattanoogans were assured that the high altitude and healthful climate of Chattanooga would prevent the spread of the disease here; even when a few cases of an unspecified illness turned up, physicians dismissed the possibility that the disease had reached the town, labeling the illnesses as "pernicious bilious fever." During this period, Chattanooga continued to accept numerous refugees and participated in fundraising and relief efforts for cities afflicted with the epidemic. On September 6, 1878, however, a few deaths were reported in the area; these initial deaths were eventually traced to an individual who had come to Chattanooga from Memphis and stayed in a house near this spot, in the vicinity of Cherry and Eighth Streets. Nevertheless, residents were still urged that "the air in the night is too cool here to allow the fever to spread," and reports in the *Chattanooga Times* urged people not to flee; medicine companies also assured consumers that "Simmons Liver Regulator" and the "Iron and Alum Mass" could prevent yellow fever. Despite these pleas, the number of deaths rose, and Chattanooga was eventually quarantined, its river and rail travel lines cut. An exodus from the town then began in earnest, leaving only 1,800 residents in the town, and relief efforts poured in from cities as far away as New York and Paris. Before dissipating in late October 1878, the epidemic claimed a total of 366 lives, including those of Mayor Thomas Carlile and Father Patrick Ryan, who died after "going from house to house in the worst-infected section of the city to find what he could do for the sick and needy,". Many of these victims now lie buried in the historic Citizens' Cemetery nearby.

From this point, cross Eighth Street and continue along Cherry Street. The block between Seventh and Eighth Streets is occupied by a number of 2-to-4-story brick buildings erected in the 1930s after the street was expanded to its present width. At the northeast corner of Cherry and Eighth Streets is the 3-story Gothic **Heritage Building** (736 Cherry Street). ⓰ Occupied at one point by the Union Realty Company and later sold to William A. and Ernest Martin in 1955 for $100,000, the terra cotta building (below left) was purchased by Heritage Investment Properties (1982) and upgraded at a cost of $1.5 million to 20,000-square feet of offices. Next door, at 732 Cherry Street, is a beige brick structure which, after housing various companies (including the Employees Finance Company, Service Finance Company, Baptist bookstore, House of Music, and the Little Shopper), was renovated in 1983, as was the beige brick building located at 722-730 Cherry Street. These buildings currently house various private offices and retail stores.

The left (west) side of Cherry Street was occupied by several early businesses; in 1917, for example, this stretch of the road included a pool hall and hotel (721-723 Cherry Street), cigar factory (715), cabinet and carpentry shop (713), and warehouses (709-711). In the 1920s and 1930s, these early structures were razed and replaced by the current row of 3-story brick buildings, which continue to house businesses and professional offices at the present time.

Continue to the corner of Cherry and Seventh Streets. At the southwest corner of this intersection (701 Cherry Street) is the site of the **Original "Krystal" Restaurant** founded in 1932 by Chattanoogans Rodolphus B. "Rody" Davenport Jr. and J. Glenn Sherrill. ⓱ The restaurant (above), which was named after a small crystal lawn ornament Davenport's wife noticed in a neighbor's lawn, served hamburgers for a nickel, exhorting customers to "take home a sack full." The 25-by-15 foot building originally located at this site was designed by

local architect Gordon Laidlaw Smith, who utilized porcelain enamel on the exterior walls in order that the building would be washed clean each time it rained. A chrome-plated crystal ball was situated on top of the prefabricated structure, which was manufactured in Chicago and shipped to Chattanooga for assembly. By 1952, growth of the restaurant chain, which had spread to 16 cities in 6 southern states, led Krystal to replace the original restaurant with the current 2-story building, which housed corporate offices located above a first-floor restaurant. By the 1970s, however, additional growth (a total of 200 restaurants in an 8-state area) required the construction of a new corporate headquarters, although the restaurant at this location remained open until recently. Currently, the building houses a variety of offices, and the former Krystal restaurant location is occupied by a diner serving breakfast and lunch.

Across Cherry Street, the parking lot at the southeast corner of Cherry and Seventh Streets is the former site of the **Masonic Temple** (1897), an ornate 4-story Romaneque stone building designed by architect Samuel M. Patton. ⑱ Originally planned as the site of the local Mountain City Club, that private organization occupied the building only briefly (if at all), and in 1900 the structure (pictured on page 62) was dedicated as the headquarters of the local Masonic Order. During the widening of Cherry Street in 1930, it became necessary to slice approximately 20 feet off of the front of the building. As early as 1954, moreover, discussion began as to the possible replacement of the building with a newer structure, and in 1960 the building was torn down. Although the site was intended to function as a temporary parking lot until the Masons could construct a new temple on the lot, this plan was not carried out, and the corner spot continues to be used for parking purposes at the present time.

Across Seventh Street, at the northeast corner of Cherry and Seventh Streets where currently sits a county parking garage, is the former site of the **Temple Court** building, a 6-story red sandstone office building built around 1900. ⑲ Early on, this building was advertised as "the only exclusive lawyer's office building in the South." Following a fire in 1947, the ornate building was renovated and reopened (1948) as the new, shorter (5-story) Jackson Building. In 1976, the building was torn down in order to make way for parking facilities for the new Hamilton County Justice Building nearby.

Also replaced by that development was **Turner Hall**, a meeting hall (618 Cherry Street) erected in the 1880s by the German "Van Turin Society," or Turner Club, which was founded in Chattanooga in 1868. The building, (right) which was designed by architect James C. Edwards, was constructed of brick, with large stone arches along the front of the structure. In 1936, Albert Schickling opened the popular Rathskellar Restaurant (meaning "meeting place") in the building, replacing an earlier restaurant which had been closed by Prohibition. This German beer hall, which was decorated with furnishings from the defunct Chattanooga Brewery, closed in 1970 after Schickling's retirement, and the building was soon torn down (1973) after several fires had gutted its interior.

Further down Cherry Street is the site of the former **Jacob Kunz** residence (614 Cherry Street), which was located in a grove of trees set back from the street at this location. A native of Switzerland who became a long-time grocer and baker in early Chattanooga, Kunz was a Union supporter who sent a substitute to fight in the Union army in his place during the Civil War. Ironically, when razing the antebellum house in 1925 in order to build 2 large town homes on the property, workmen found a large stash of Confederate money behind the hearth, reportedly placed there by Kunz on behalf of a soldier who never came back to claim it. Today, the former Kunz residence is the site of the Hamilton County Justice Building complex.

*To return to the beginning of the tour of Irish Hill, turn east onto Seventh Street and proceed along McCallie Avenue to Lindsay Street. **Note:** if you are touring the area by automobile, both Seventh Street and McCallie Avenue are one-way streets; you will wish to consult the map for an alternate route.*

Big Nine

The tour of the Big Nine explores the portion of the downtown area in the vicinity of East Martin Luther King Jr. Boulevard. Originally, the portion of this street west of Georgia Avenue was known as James Street, named for minister Jesse J. James (1805-1856), who moved to Chattanooga in the 1850s and established a large farm south of the city limits; the east part of the street was called Branham Street, named for an early resident who owned a large parcel of land southeast of the original town limits. On the heels of the Civil War, moreover, the area was the site of a number of African-American cabins which became known as "Scruggs Town," so named after a one-armed African-American businessman who owned many of the houses in this area. Subsequently, however, the entire street was labeled Ninth Street, colloquially known to local residents as "The Big Nine," and it became the center of African-American life in Chattanooga for several decades.

As a result of increasing traffic and congestion, during the 1950s Ninth Street was widened from 65 to 92 feet in order to accommodate 4 rather than 2 lanes of traffic. At that time, a number of original buildings in this area, some predating the Civil War, were torn down. In addition, in ensuing years the road was transformed to a one-way street; while this development served to facilitate travel between the downtown core and outlying suburban neighborhoods, the transformation of the Big Nine to a travel corridor had a negative impact upon the neighborhood atmosphere of the surrounding area. In 1982, the street was renamed Martin Luther King Jr. Boulevard, and in 1984 the area, listed as the M.L. King Boulevard Historic District, was added to the National Register of Historic Places. Today, the redevelopment of the Big Nine area, spurred by the construction of facilities for the University of Tennessee at Chattanooga along the street, continues. Along with the current plan to re-introduce 2-way traffic to MLK Jr. Blvd., this development should serve to revitalize the neighborhood ambience of the area in the near future.

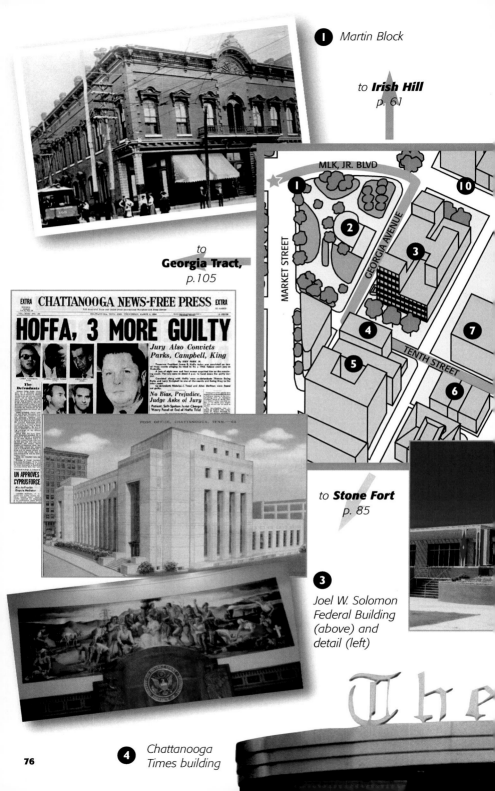

1 Martin Block

to **Irish Hill**
p. 61

MLK, JR. BLVD

MARKET STREET

GEORGIA AVENUE

TENTH STREET

1

2

3

4

5

6

7

10

to
Georgia Tract,
p.105

EXTRA CHATTANOOGA NEWS-FREE PRESS EXTRA

HOFFA, 3 MORE GUILTY

Jury Also Convicts Parks, Campbell, King

UN APPROVES
CYPRUS FORCE

POST OFFICE, CHATTANOOGA, TENN.—64

to **Stone Fort**
p. 85

3

Joel W. Solomon
Federal Building
(above) and
detail (left)

The

4 Chattanooga
Times building

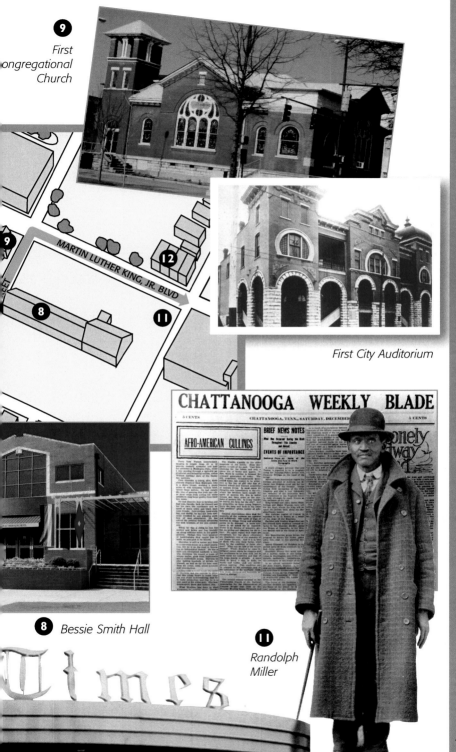

9 First Congregational Church

First City Auditorium

CHATTANOOGA WEEKLY BLADE

AFRO-AMERICAN CULLINGS

8 Bessie Smith Hall

11 Randolph Miller

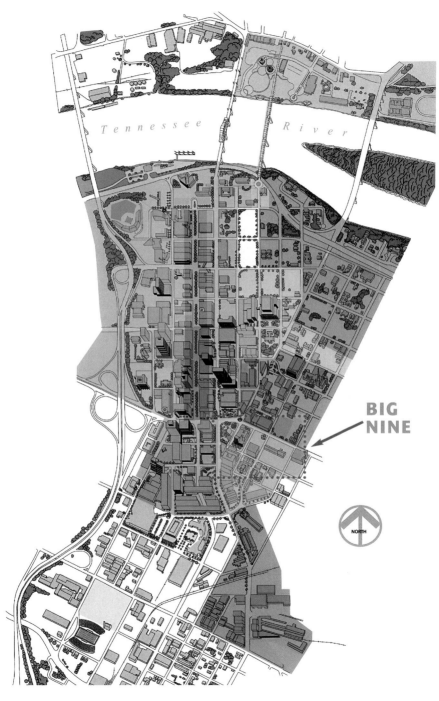

T e n n e s s e e   *R i v e r*

BIG
NINE

NORTH

The tour of the Big Nine begins at the southeast corner of Martin Luther King Jr. Boulevard and Georgia Avenue. ❶ Constructed in 1876, the 3-story brick **Martin Block** (below) was built at

this spot to accommodate the Martin brothers wholesale grocery. Located on the first floor of the building at one time was the Chattanooga National Bank, which was chartered in 1887. The focal point of the Martin Block, however, was the Rossmore Hotel (also known at one time as the "Williams House"), which was founded by Abner L. Ross and occupied the second and third floors of this building. In the 1890s, this hotel advertised its hospitality and services with the slogan "Meet Me at the Rossmore," in ads featuring a bear and alligator (representing the North and South) meeting and shaking hands. The building, which was purchased from the John S. Martin family by the First Federal Savings & Loan Bank for $125,000 in 1946, fell to the wrecking ball during the widening of Ninth Street in the early 1950s.

Nearby, located in a row of buildings erected along Georgia Avenue to the south of the Martin Block, was the **Dixie Theater,** which was opened by Frank Dowler, Jr., in 1938. Operating the movie house for more than 20 years, Dowler closed the theater in 1960, citing the increasing prevalence of sex in movies, as well as the migration of patrons away from the downtown area. After remaining idle for several years, in 1970 the building reopened briefly as the Midtown Cinemas, with 2 theaters seating 220 patrons each. In the mid-1970s, however, the building was torn down as part of the initiative to create the Miller Park, below.

The block bounded by MLK Jr. Blvd., Georgia Avenue, Market Street, and Tenth Street is known as **Miller Park** (1976). ❷ Following World War II, Colonel Harrison Gill proposed that a war memorial park be created in the block across the street from the federal building, occupied at that time by a number of low 2- and 3-story brick buildings. Although a study

was conducted in 1964 to determine the feasibility of doing so, the project was scrapped after it was concluded that the property could not be acquired at that time. In 1974, however, Mayor Robert Kirk Walker announced that this block would be purchased and razed, at a cost of $1.5 million, in order to develop a downtown park. Due to complications associated with the purchasing of the northern portion of the block occupied by the First Federal Bank, the first phase of the park was focused upon the southern section of the block and included plans for an 8-foot waterfall, reflection pool, and concert shell. While early plans also contemplated the permanent closure of Georgia Avenue between MLK Jr. Blvd. and Tenth Street, this portion of the proposal was not implemented. Named for the grandparents of local attorney and park proponent Burkett Miller, the first phase of Miller Park was dedicated on December 8, 1976.

As for the northern portion of the block, when negotiations with the First Federal Bank stalled in 1974, the Downtown Park Commission asked the city to condemn the property and force the bank to move; eventually, however, the bank agreed to sell the property for $750,000 and relocate its operations. This area was then reserved for a second phase of the park in 1977. Though a number of supporters envisioned retaining the building as an arts center (a proposal which was retained in plans for the park as late as 1976), in the end the structure was razed in order to create a "plaza" at the north end of the block. This portion of the park, much of which is raised above street level, was planned to be "more urban" than the first phase of the park, and includes a flag plaza placed on a patchwork of brick and limestone accented with plantings and benches. Today, the park continues to host several annual festivals and serves as a welcome green space in the downtown area.

From this corner, proceed east on MLK Jr. Blvd., turning right on Georgia Avenue. On your left is the **Joel W. Solomon Federal Building** (910 Georgia Avenue). ❸ This site was originally occupied by the Chattanooga Southern Railroad depot and several local businesses. One company which was located at this spot was the Davenport Hosiery Mill, which was founded at the close of World War I and produced, among other items, the popular "Humming Bird" brand of seamless silk hose; a pioneer in the production of nylon stockings, this business eventually closed in 1961. This block also housed the Chattanooga Transfer

Company, which opened in 1865; this household-moving business, which evolved from a simple operation moving goods in a wagon from the wharf at the river, eventually came to be known as the Chattanooga Transfer and Storage Company.

In the early 1930s, these buildings were razed, and in their place was built the $1 million Federal Building (above and on page 76), the last major Chattanooga work designed by architect R.H. Hunt. This Art Deco building is composed of Georgia white marble, with large corner pylons and aluminum grilled windows. The interior walls are of Tennessee and Missouri marble and contain the fossil remains of numerous bryozoans, coral, and cephalopods. One of the courtrooms is finished entirely in myrtle and features the New Deal-era "Allegory of Chattanooga", pictured on page 76 (1937), a large oil-on-canvas mural depicting the history of the city from the time of the Cherokee Indians to the advent of the Tennessee Valley Authority (TVA). Created by Sarasota, Florida, artist Hilton Leech, this 5-by-17 foot mural was commissioned by the Section of Fine Arts of the United States Treasury and installed in the courtroom in June 1937. The first floor of the building, moreover, contains The Mail Carrier, an 8-foot tall aluminum-and-marble sculpture added to the building in 1938. Designed by New York sculptor Leopold Scholz, who also designed the statues of John Sevier and Andrew Jackson which represent Tennessee in the Statuary Hall of the Capitol in Washington, D.C., the sculpture bears the famous inscription attributed to Herodotus: "Neither snow, nor rain, nor heat, nor gloom of night stays these couriers from the swift completion of their appointed rounds."

Chosen by the American Institute of Architects as one of the 150 best buildings constructed in the United States since 1918, the building was part of a photography exhibit displayed throughout the United States and Europe. Its artistic and historic importance were noted in the application for inclusion of the building on

the National Register of Historic Places (1980), which stated that "its exterior is clad with smooth materials for sleek lines; it has vertical bays of windows providing an emphasis on verticality; it has a flat parapet roof; it has rectilinear bands of ornamentation in the form of integrated, low-relief sculpted stone panels; and it has ornamental doorways." Currently, plans are in the works for construction of a new, larger courthouse elsewhere in the downtown area, at which time it is expected that the federal bankruptcy court and other governmental offices will move to this historic structure.

Several significant and interesting legal trials have taken place in the courtrooms of the historic Federal Building. In 1911, the trial of *United States v. Forty Barrels and Twenty Kegs of Coca-Cola* took place here. In the early years of its production, rumors spread that Coca-Cola was a health hazard and that it contained alcohol, cocaine, or other harmful substances. Coca-Cola countered by advertising that the product was guaranteed by the Pure Food and Drug Act and that Nap Lajoie, "the greatest ball player in the world" (a .338 lifetime batter who was inducted into the Baseball Hall of Fame in 1937) drank it regularly. The controversy came to a head when several cases of Coca-Cola were seized by government officials in Chattanooga, claiming that the product was harmful. While prosecution witnesses in the subsequent trial claimed that Coke kept boys awake at night and led to "wild, nocturnal freaks . . . violations of college rules and female improprieties and even immoralities" at a girls' school, the trial resulted in a verdict in favor of the company; following a subsequent appeal, the case was settled out of court in 1917.

In 1936, a suit referred to as the *"Nineteen Companies"* (or *"Eighteen Companies,"* after one withdrew) or, in the alternative, the TEPCO case, was filed by a local power company challenging the existence of the Tennessee Valley Authority, alleging that the prime focus of the TVA was competing with private enterprises to produce electric power, and not flood control or any other goal affecting the public interest. Following a trial here, in 1938 a verdict was rendered in favor of TVA, the highest constitutional judgment rendered with regard to the agency. This decision solidified and, to some degree, legitimized the federal agency and its objectives during its early years.

Finally, in 1964 Teamsters boss James R. "Jimmy" Hoffa was tried in Chattanooga for jury-

HOFFA, 3 MORE GUILTY

Jury Also Convicts Parks, Campbell, King

No Bias, Prejudice, Judge Asks of Jury

Paychecks to Show

tampering: it was charged that Hoffa had engaged in jury-tampering at a trial held in Nashville to determine whether he had shared in a $1 million payoff from a Michigan trucking company in exchange for labor peace. Hoffa and his legal team came to Chattanooga, maintaining their headquarters on the ninth floor of the Hotel Patten, while the jury was housed on the tenth floor of the nearby Read House. It is said that Hoffa's legal team used listening devices to monitor deliberations from the Hotel Patten during the trial. Hoffa also gave a rallying speech to a crowd of Teamsters at the Tivoli Theater, proclaiming that "hundreds of federal agents are in Chattanooga...spying on our attorneys and stealing our records." Although Hoffa referred to the trial as a "railroad job," he was found guilty and sentenced to 8 years in prison (as reflected in the newspaper headline above and on page 76), along with a $10,000 fine. This decision was affirmed by the court of appeals and the Supreme Court, and Hoffa was incarcerated from 1967 until 1971, when his sentence was reduced for good behavior by President Richard M. Nixon.

Continue along Georgia Avenue to Tenth Street. In 1899, newspaperman and developer J.B. Pound erected a permanent headquarters for his *Chattanooga News* at the southeast corner of Georgia Avenue and Tenth Street. ❹ The 2-story building, which produced a local afternoon newspaper, included a tall, pitched roof and a circular tower at the street corner; the structure also had large plate glass windows so that passersby could stop and look in to see the presses turning out the newspaper. After 1908, when Pound constructed the new Pound Building to house the newspaper offices, the building was taken over by James Inman Carter and his sons, who operated a business buying large lots of merchandise from distressed merchants and then selling them to businesses for use as advertising sales. As for the newspaper itself, after being purchased by George F. Milton, C.B. Johnson, and Walter Johnson, in 1939 the business was acquired by Roy McDonald, who merged it with his *Chattanooga Free-Press*

(1933) to form the *Chattanooga News-Free Press*. The paper then entered into a joint-publication agreement with the *Chattanooga Times* in 1942 due to war-related shortages in manpower and materials, at which time the two papers moved into this new, Art Deco building. This arrangement lasted until 1966; another joint publication agreement was temporarily begun in 1980, and in 1999 the two papers merged into the *Chattanooga Times-Free Press*. Today the building is occupied by a variety of businesses.

Next door to this structure on Georgia Avenue is the **Lupton Building** (1010 Georgia Avenue), erected in 1910. ❺ After being occupied by the TVA for approximately 30 years, in 1981 this tower was sold to a Panamanian corporation, and in 1997 it was purchased for $106,000 for use as a personal storage business.

From this spot, turn left and proceed east along Tenth Street. Located at the southeast corner of Tenth and Columbia Streets ❻ is the former **Colonial Hotel**, a 32-bedroom hotel with 5 guest baths which was erected by Leis Albert Hitzfeld in 1914. Most recently housing the Choo-Choo Deli, the building is currently being renovated for use as a 16-room bed-and-breakfast inn, the Stone Fort Inn.

Across Tenth Street, at the northwest corner of Tenth and Lindsay Streets, is the 6-story Minnesota granite **Emerson Building** (1956), named for Charles F. Emerson, a member of the board of directors of the Stone Fort Land Company for a number of years. ❼ After acquiring the properties of the Cumberland Telephone Company (1926), the Southern Bell Telephone Company built this modern structure, which was designed to handle the increase in telephone subscribers in Chattanooga at that time (20,000). This facility also eliminated the "Number, please" method of connection and allowed a new dial system to be utilized. In the 1970s, the company was succeeded by South Central Bell, and additional floors were built, enabling the building to reach its current height of 6 stories.

From this spot, proceed to Lindsay Street and turn left, toward the southeast corner of MLK Jr. Blvd. and Lindsay Street. ❽ This corner is the site of the **Bessie Smith Hall,** which houses the Chattanooga African-American Museum (200 MLK Jr. Boulevard). Originally a brick warehouse building, this 1-story brick structure (pictured on pages 76-77 and 82) was renovated in 1983 for use as a museum and perform-mance hall. The museum houses a variety of displays, including a replica of an African village, an Ethiopian temple, displays concerning antebellum slavery, and historical information about the African-American community in Chattanooga.

Previously, the lawn in front of the Bessie Smith Hall was the site of a series of 2- and 3-story brick buildings, including the **Martin Hotel,** which was established in 1924 to serve African-American patrons. This hotel, commemorated by a historic marker at the corner of MLK Jr. Blvd. and Lindsay Street, became a significant magnet for visiting African-American figures, including Mahalia Jackson, Ella Fitzgerald, Nat King Cole, Lena Horne, Cab Calloway, Satchel Paige, and Willie Mays. After greeting visitors for 60 years, the widening of Ninth Street in 1954, as well as the transformation of the Big Nine to a one-way boulevard, eventually forced the Martin Hotel and a number of other businesses in this area to close their doors. The building was subsequently torn down in 1985.

Across Lindsay Street, at the southwest corner of MLK Jr. Blvd. and Lindsay Street, is the **First Congregational Church,** organized in 1867 by E.O. Tade, an African-American business leader who owned a large parcel of land near Fort Wood. ❾ Tade sold a number of lots in the area between downtown Chattanooga and Fort Wood to African-American residents at low prices and on easy terms, and the area became known as "Tadetown" as a result. In 1904, the current brick church building (lower right) was erected at this site. The foundation of the church is comprised of cut stone taken from the Stone Fort, and the building features large stained-glass windows and a square bell tower. A taller tower at the southeast corner of the building was removed in later years due to structural problems. In the 1970s, the building ceased to be used as a church, although it continues to stand as a memorial to E.O. Tade and his efforts on behalf of African-American residents of Chattanooga.

To the west of this church building, located midway between Lindsay Street and Georgia Avenue on the south side of MLK Jr. Blvd., is the site of the **First City Auditorium** (1897).

Composed of brick with large stone arches along the front facade, the auditorium (below) seated 5,000 patrons, who entered the building via exterior stairwells leading to the second story of the theater. The building was destroyed by fire in 1916, after which it was replaced by the nearby Soldiers & Sailors Memorial Auditorium in 1922.

Also near the First Congregational Church, between Lindsay Street and Georgia Avenue along MLK Jr. Blvd., was the **Howard Free School**. The first school superintendent in Hamilton County was E.O. Tade, who came to Chattanooga from Memphis in 1865 through the American Missionary Association to establish a freedmen's school and thereafter came to be referred to as the "Moses of the Colored People." A building for the freedman's school was completed in this area by 1871, at a cost of more than $10,000. Titled the "Howard Free School," the facility was named for General Oliver Otis Howard, a Civil War soldier and commissioner of the Freedmen's Bureau. The school later moved to a new building at East

Eighth and Douglas Streets, and in 1883 the Howard High School (which is still in operation today) evolved from this early educational institution.

Across MLK Jr. Blvd. from this spot are 2 small 2-story brick buildings (111-113 and 115 MLK Jr. Blvd.) erected circa 1902, ❿ which are representative of the commercial structures built along MLK Jr. Blvd. around the turn of the century. Next door to these buildings, at the northwest corner of MLK Jr. Blvd. and Lindsay Street, is the **Volunteer Parking Garage**, a parking facility with spots for 400 cars which opened in 1928. Costing $500,000 to complete and referred to as "a highly innovative structure for its day," this 4-story, 110,000 square-foot garage was designed by Louis Bull and constructed of white brick with terra cotta trim. As was noted in the application for the inclusion of this structure on the National Register of Historic Places in 1978 (as part of the Patten Parkway Historic District), it was noted that "Volunteer's parking garage is an early example of a modern parking garage and therefore reflects the increasing need in the 1920s to cope with the growing influences of the automobile industry." In addition to parking facilities, the building housed a print shop and a service station. In the late 1920s, the garage served as the Chattanooga bus terminal, and a dozen intercity bus lines operated from this location; in 1931, however, the need for additional bus space motivated the construction of a new bus terminal at Market and Tenth Streets. Today the structure continues to operate as a parking facility for the nearby Volunteer Building and other businesses.

From this spot, proceed east along MLK Jr. Blvd. to the southwest corner of MLK Jr. Blvd. and Houston Street. ⓫ At this corner is an historic marker commemorating the career of **Randolph Miller** (above), a former slave who arrived in Chattanooga with Major General William T. Sherman's Union army in 1864. After learning the printing trade from Adolph Ochs at the *Chattanooga Times*, in 1899 Miller launched *The Blade*, (pictured on page 77) a newspaper which was characterized by a "picturesque and forceful style of writing." Operating for approximately 12 years, *The Blade* served as an important social critique and aided in the creation of a cohesive African-American community in Chattanooga. Miller, whose personal trademark was "a high silk hat always worn at a rakish angle," voiced his opposition to the Jim Crow system of racial segregation from an early date, and on July 5, 1905, he launched a boycott of the segregated streetcar system in Chattanooga. On July 16, 1905, a

"hack line," or jitney taxi service, was organized with "three vehicles of sorry appearance" to serve African-American residents. Miller's efforts were opposed by the streetcar system as an unlicensed taxi service, and an attempt by 9 African-American businessmen to obtain a charter for the Transfer Omnibus Motor Car Company, capitalized at $10,000, subsequently failed. This obstacle, however, served to point a finger at the Jim Crow social system existing at that time in the South, and it did not stop Miller, who wrote, "They have taken our part of the library; they have moved our school to the frog pond; they have passed the Jim Crow law; they have knocked us out of the jury box; they have played the devil generally, and what in thunder more will they do no one knows." Randolph Miller's career serves as an important example of the educated critique of social segregation which surfaced in Chattanooga at the turn of the century.

Across MLK Jr. Blvd., at the northwest corner of MLK Jr. Blvd. and Houston Street, is a row of 2-story brick business and apartment buildings erected circa 1894. ⓬ As was indicated in the application for inclusion of these buildings on the National Register of Historic Places in 1984 (as part of the MLK Jr. Blvd. Historic District), "Capital in the black community was scarce and this fact is apparent in the plain architectural style of the commercial buildings" in this vicinity. In the area situated to the rear of these buildings was the Civil War-era **Battery Taft,** a line of cannon established on the west side of Ninth Street (MLK Jr. Blvd.) between Lindsay and Houston Streets. Named for Colonel J.B. Taft (73rd Pennsylvania Infantry), who was killed at the battle of Missionary Ridge on November 25, 1863, this battery was intended to link Fort Jones and Fort Sherman, portions of the defensive lines surrounding the city during the Union occupation of Chattanooga.

Also near these buildings, at a spot on B (now Houston) Street between Eighth and Ninth Streets, was a 10-room antebellum house erected by the Catholic Church and occupied by the family of Andrew Warren, an Irishman who came to Chattanooga along with the Nashville & Chattanooga Railroad. During the Civil War, the home became a **Union Hideout** where Warren, a Northern sympathizer, occasionally hid other Union supporters in the attic. Though the structure no longer stands, this site is a testament to the varied allegiances of Chattanooga citizens during the conflict.

Finally, near this spot, in the vicinity of Eighth and Mabel Streets, is the former site of **Battery Ervin** (also referred to as Battery Erwin), which was established on the highest point of the hill in this area during the Civil War. Named for Major S.C. Ervin, a member of the Sixth Regiment of the Ohio Volunteer Infantry who was killed at the battle of Missionary Ridge on November 25, 1863, this site was occupied by a battery of field cannon trained to the east for the purpose of protecting Chattanooga from attack by Confederate forces.

To return to the start of the tour, return west along Martin Luther King Jr. Boulevard to Market Street.

Stone Fort

The area known as the Stone Fort is the former site of a 40-50 foot-high limestone outcropping bordered by Market, King, and Ninth Streets and the Western & Atlantic Railroad tracks to the south. Following the completion of the Nashville & Chattanooga railroad in 1854, this property was purchased by an eccentric hermit named Daniel Hogan who came to Chattanooga along with the railroad. Although the hill was deemed too rugged and steep to be of any value, Hogan erected a quarry and lime kiln on the property. A frugal individual, he lived in a shack built from second-hand lumber, wore a U.S. Army overcoat he purchased at a "fire sale" at the close of the Civil War, and cooked his meals over the fire from the kiln; his only luxury was a silk hat which he reportedly wore wherever he went. Some of the stone quarried by Hogan was carried to the corner of Eighth and Lindsay Streets for construction of the Saints Peter and Paul Catholic Church; in preparation for the siege of Chattanooga, however, the stones were confiscated by the Union army and carried back to the hill to be used in fortifications – thus giving the area the name "Stone Fort."

A favorite "trysting" place during the 1880s, the Stone Fort was continually quarried for stone throughout the latter half of the nineteenth century. A full-scale plan to dismantle the hill arose in 1886 when the Stone Fort Land Company was organized by a group of Cincinnati investors. Though it was initially organized for the purpose of erecting housing for immigrants, the Stone Fort Land Company never erected a single house, instead coming to develop much of the commercial space in downtown Chattanooga. In 1903, tracks were lain on the east side of the hill for the Southern Railway, and the portion of the hill fronting on Market Street was then graded. Subsequently, the entire hill was dismantled and developed. Stone from the hill was used for construction of various structures, including the First National Bank, the foundation of the First Congregational Church, and the walls surrounding the Hamilton County Courthouse and the campus of the University of Tennessee at Chattanooga. Today, the Stone Fort area contains a number of historic buildings which were constructed after the rocky hill was leveled, as significant downtown growth took place in Chattanooga at the turn of the twentieth century.

1 Plaza Hotel

to
Big Nine
p. 75

to
Georgia Tract
p. 105

2 Hotel Patten

J.B. Pound

to
Stanton Addition
p. 93

86

4 Custom House

5 Pound Building

6 Chattanooga Municipal Building

STONE FORT

NORTH

Tennessee River

The tour of the Stone Fort begins at the triangular block bounded by Market and Tenth Streets and Georgia Avenue, at the site of the **Plaza Hotel** building (1006 Market Street). ❶ This 4-story brick building was originally erected in

1893 by the Southern Express Company upon the announcement that Chattanooga would become that company's headquarters (which were previously located in Augusta, Georgia, and Memphis, Tennessee). In 1919, local developer J.B. Pound acquired the building and reopened it as the Patten Annex, a small, 75-room addition to the Hotel Patten next door. In 1935, a hotel company owned by Paul N. McQuiddy bought the building and renamed it the Plaza Hotel. This new enterprise, which was advertised as a modern, fireproof hotel conveniently located across Market Street from the bus terminal, offered rooms at $1.50 and up. During its use as a hotel, the original building was supplemented with a narrow addition and upper deck, which housed the new "Triangle Grill" (as seen in the postcard above). The hotel again changed hands in 1969, and in 1978 the site was renovated for use as a business building; a restaurant, the Pickle Barrel, continues to operate in the narrow first-floor lobby of the building today.

One important figure in the development of the Stone Fort area, who was mentioned above and referred to throughout this tour, was newspaperman Jerome Balaam "J.B." Pound, who came to Chattanooga after selling his *Macon News* paper to begin the *Chattanooga Evening News*, which published its first issue on July 1, 1888. Pound later added the *Knoxville Morning Tribune*, *Knoxville Sentinel*, and *Memphis Morning News* to his newspaper group. Shifting his interests at the turn of the century, Pound sold his newspaper businesses and began building hotels. He was instrumental in the development of Eleventh Street (which until 1926 dead-ended at Market Street), and a number of buildings in this area were either built by

Pound or placed at their current locations as the result of his influence and efforts. In addition to those in Chattanooga, he owned the DeSoto Hotel and Hotel Savannah in Savannah, Georgia, and the Seminole Hotel in Jacksonville, Florida; he also built the Ansley Hotel in Atlanta and the Hotel Henry Watterson in Lousiville, Kentucky.

Another of Pound's projects was the **Hotel Patten** (1908) located at the northeast corner of Market and Eleventh Streets (1 East Eleventh Street). ❷ Designed to rival the Read House, this $2 million fireproof hotel was conceived by Pound, financed by Chattanoogan Z.C. Patten, and designed by Atlanta architect W.T. Downing. The 12-story building is composed of granite, steel, and copper and has a lobby of white marble; a "European plan" hotel, it was opened with 254 rooms for guests. Over the years, the hotel was the site of several Chattanooga milestones. In 1914, a group of local drivers organized the Chattanooga Automobile Club to promote improved roads in the area. Joining with northern driving enthusiasts, they proposed the creation of a road linking Detroit and Miami, and in 1915 a meeting led by local judge Michael M. Allison took place at the Hotel Patten to organize the "Dixie Highway Association" with the slogan "We all live on the same street." The Dixie Highway was subsequently completed in 1927, carrying innumerable travelers through Chattanooga on their way to the beaches of Florida and helping to spur the status of Chattanooga as a tourist destination.

In addition to this development, soon after the first radio program was transmitted in Chattanooga on April 13, 1925, Pound offered the hotel as the headquarters for the local WDOD ("Dynamo of Dixie") radio station, which took up residence in the attic of the hotel on August 13, 1925, as can be seen in the above postcard; two transmitting towers were placed on the roof, and broadcasts of the 500-watt station began from this location. After 70 years in business, in 1978 the

the building was closed as a hotel and, following an extensive renovation, reopened as a residential retirement facility for the elderly, a use it continues to serve today.

Continuing his development of Eleventh Street, in 1907 J.B. Pound opened the **Eastern Hotel** directly across Eleventh Street from the Hotel Patten, at the southeast corner of Market and Eleventh Streets. ❸ The hotel, which advertised rooms with a bath for 75 cents to $1.50 per day, had 66 hotel rooms and 6 first-floor retail spaces. The building was subsequently torn down in 1951, and the 82,000 square-foot Edney Building (1953) was erected in its place by a Florida corporation headed by R.H. Edney. The current 9-story structure is the product of a subsequent 2-story addition to the original, 7-story building which took place in 1959. The Edney Building, which underwent a substantial $3.2 million renovation in 1988, is currently leased to the Tennessee Valley Authority for use as office space.

From this corner, head east along Eleventh Street to the northwest corner of Eleventh and Lindsay Streets. ❹ Erected at this spot in 1893, the Richardsonian Romanesque **Custom House**, designed of rough and smooth stone, was built to house the federal post office and other U.S. government offices. As can be seen in the photograph below (and on page 87), originally the roof was of a greater pitch than it is at this time. Though part of the original design, the 1-story north wing was not added until 10 years after the remainder of the structure. By the early 1930s, overcrowding led the federal government to conclude that a new, larger building was necessary, a decision which led to the construction of the Joel W. Solomon Federal Building nearby. Currently, the building, which was added to the National Register of Historic Places in 1973, houses the United States Bankruptcy Courts and other governmental offices; it is proposed, however, that

these offices will be relocated to the current federal building in the near future, upon completion of a new federal building elsewhere in downtown Chattanooga. It remains to be seen what use this building will serve in the future.

Across Eleventh Street, at the southwest corner of East Eleventh and Lindsay Streets, ❺ is the former site of the **Pound Building** (1906), named for its owner, J.B. Pound. The architect of the building was R.H. Hunt, and the builder was Chattanoogan Joe Trimby. Originally, the building was intended to be 4 or 5 stories high, but Pound decided to "go on up" after reaching that level; when finished, the 8-story building was referred to as "Chattanooga's first skyscraper" (at least until the James Building was erected the following year). The masonry structure, built of brick and wood, was once said by Ripley to be the tallest structure in the world erected without steel; it was, in fact, the tallest such building in the South. The walls at the base of the building were 6 bricks thick, the interior was composed of oak and poplar, each room was fitted with gas and electric fixtures, and electrical elevators were installed in the building. The 29,000 square-foot building first housed the *Chattanooga News* offices and several other businesses, though the *News* moved out of the building in 1920 after constructing a new building on East Tenth Street. In the 1940s, the Tennessee Valley Authority took over the building, performing a $70,000 renovation. By the

1980s, however, the Pound Building, which was listed on the National Register of Historic Buildings (1988), had sat vacant for a number of years. Many viewed the building as unsafe, claiming that it swayed in the wind and often had to be evacuated in high winds. The city then began to contemplate the creation of a park on this site, which was adjacent to the new Warehouse Row development, and the building was torn down. During demolition of the building, it was debated as to whether to save the ornate archway as an entrance to the Warehouse Row park and shops; eventually, the arch, along with its sandstone base and

glass fanlight, was saved from the demolition, although it was not placed at the park.

Near this spot, at the northeast corner of Eleventh and Lindsay Streets, ❻ is the **Chattanooga Municipal Building** (1908), which currently houses City Hall and administrative offices for the city of Chattanooga. When it was announced at the turn of the century that the city was considering the construction of a new municipal building, J.B. Pound and several other prominent citizens lobbied to have the building placed on the expanding Eleventh Street. Following a special election, the present site won approval, and this building (pictured below and on page 87) was placed on the site. The 3-story structure, which is listed on the National Register of Historic Places (1980), is composed of Indiana Bedford limestone, with Corinthian half-columns and granite entry steps. The interior lobby, moreover, features marble tile floors and ornamental columns.

Adjacent to this structure is the **Fleetwood Building** (below), a tall brick building built by Henry King which formerly housed one of the largest coffee roasting and importing plants in the South. Recently, a group of Knoxville developers announced that they had purchased an option on this group of buildings for the purpose of undertaking an $8 million renovation project to develop the block into retail space with residential loft apartments.

From the corner of Eleventh and Lindsay Streets, head south to Market Street. ❽ Here, at the northeast corner of Market and Twelfth Streets, is the site of **Fort Jones**, a fortification erected during the Civil War. During the federal occupation of Chattanooga in 1864-1865, the rocky knoll on which these buildings now stand was utilized as a federal gun emplacement known as Battery Hazen. In 1864, the site was renamed "Redoubt Jones" in honor of Captain William G. Jones (Tenth U.S. Infantry and acting colonel for the 36th Regiment of Volunteers), who was killed at the battle of Chickamauga in September 1863. On the western slope of the hill, somewhere near this spot was erected a federal guard post intended to ensure the security of the railyards during the federal occupation of the town.

From this point, the tour turns south (right) onto Lindsay Street. If you wish to further investigate Eleventh Street, however, at the southeast corner of King and Lindsay Streets is the **Schubert Theater building**, ❼ which was founded by J.B. Pound and named for the Schubert Brothers, who were involved in the production of theater attractions at that time. In 1906, popular French actress Sarah Bernhardt was invited to lay the cornerstone for the theater; though large crowds gathered at the site for this occasion, the actress never left her hotel, instead sending the crowd a note of apology which the mayor could not understand, as it was written in French. The theater (which was also known as the Albert Theater at one time) opened in 1908, hosting primarily vaudeville comedies. Though the theater building (above right) remains today, it was subsequently acquired by the Loveman's department store for use as a warehouse, and little remains to reference its theater past.

Turn right onto Market Street. On the right at this point is a series of buildings known collectively as **Warehouse Row** (1118-1148 Market Street). ❾ The creation of the Stone Fort Block at the turn of the century enabled many merchants to move into large quarters near the railroad complex, which was also in constant need of additional warehouse space. These 8 buildings were erected circa 1900 by various merchants and wholesale companies; importantly, freight lines were located at the back doors of these buildings to provide a convenient link to the railroads. The first occupant of Warehouse Row was the Trotter Brothers wholesale grocery business (1904), which moved into a 5-story building designed by Atlanta architect W.T. Downing for the Stone Fort Land Company (1132-1136 Market Street). This building was described at the time as "one of the most complete business houses ever erected in Chattanooga, with every modern facility," including "electric elevators, automatic fire extinguishers and every modern appliance that will facilitate the transaction of a great business." In discussing the decision to locate at this site, W.H. Trotter explained that the Market Street frontage and railroad access made the spot "the legitimate location of the future jobbing business." Other initial businesses located in Warehouse Row were the Stagmaier & Fletcher wholesale grocery business (1124-1130) and the Tom Fritts Hardware and Archer Paper Company businesses (1114-1120), which opened in 1906-1907. A second phase of construction in 1909-1911 resulted in the completion of the James Supply Company (1118 Market Street), Mills & Lupton supply company (1146), Knox-Thomas-Spears Company (1140-1142), and Betterton-England Shoe Company (1144) buildings. In particular, the Stagmaier and Fletcher building (1124-1130 Market Street) was creatively designed, constructed in a "V" shape in order to conform to the pattern of Market Street and create a uniform facade throughout Warehouse Row.

These buildings, which are now listed on the National Register of Historic Places (1980) and provide the only remaining example of row warehouses in the city of Chattanooga, sat largely empty as railroad traffic declined in the latter half of the twentieth century. In 1985, however, a plan was proposed to create a $35 million "Warehouse Row historic district and shopping center" at this location. The project was temporarily delayed when the Department of the Interior rejected portions of the plan in connection with a request to award historic designation to the property (a proposed walkway across Market Street to the TVA Building and an atrium connecting separate portions of the warehouse structures were removed from the plan, though the atrium was later added anyway). The 323,000 square-foot Warehouse Row complex was finally opened in 1989, a move which was seen as "a commitment to the future vitality of the downtown at a time when most retail stores were relocating to the suburbs." This project has since been labeled as a fine example of the "smart growth" features of historic preservation, green space (a 1-acre public park is located on the east side of the row), and public/private economic partnership in development. Today, a variety of retail stores and offices are located throughout Warehouse Row and the adjacent Freight Depot.

Continue north to Eleventh Street, returning to the beginning of the Stone Fort tour. In the years following the Civil War, Chattanooga became a significant industrial center – a New South industrial leader which was referred to as the "Dynamo of Dixie." This industrial development, however, had a high environmental price, as recognized very early by one traveler, who remarked, "One cannot repress a fear that some day all [its] natural beauties will be hidden by the smoke from the five hundred chimneys which will be created in honor of the god Iron. For it is to be a town of rolling-mills and furnaces, giant in its traffic, like Pittsburgh and St. Louis, and inhabited by thousands of hard-handed, brawny armed artisans." Eventually, this prediction came true: in 1969, Chattanooga was found to have the worst particulate air pollution in the United States. In an effort to correct this problem, the city and county enacted the Chattanooga Air Pollution Control Ordinance (which would become a model for the Federal Clean Air Act of 1970) and created an Air Pollution Control Board, and in October 1972 Chattanooga celebrated "Clean Air Week" by receiving the annual National Air Pollution Control Association award. Chattanooga's turnaround was one of the first steps in the redevelopment of the downtown core, and the city's environmental efforts continue today; in 2000, in fact, Chattanooga was named one of Environmental News Network's Top 10 "Most Environmentally Friendly Cities."

To return to the beginning of the Stone Fort tour, proceed north on Market Street to Eleventh Street.

Stanton Addition

The area south of Twelfth Street was not within the original town limits of the town of Chattanooga, and the few early settlers who had homes in this area were considered to be living "out in the country." In 1868, however, "carpetbagger" John C. Stanton arrived from Boston, initiating a railroad venture intended to consolidate the Wills Valley and Northeast & Southwest Alabama railroads (the Alabama & Chattanooga Railroad), with the goal of extending the rail line to Meridian, Mississippi. To enhance this development, Stanton built a large hotel, the Stanton House, which became the focal point of this area and anchored the early development of the southern part of town. To influence the growth of this section, Stanton also convinced the city to relocate the post office to Market and King Streets, despite complaints that the new location was too far from the center of town.

Although Stanton's railroad venture failed by 1871, his enthusiasm was infectious, and the 1870s came to be referred to as the "Stanton Times," an early financial boom founded upon credit and financial speculation. Following the national financial panic of 1873, however, this brief period of intense growth ended in the "most extensive crop of litigation which Chattanooga ever harvested," as well as Stanton's eventual departure from town.

Despite the failure of the Alabama & Chattanooga Railroad, substantial growth occurred within the Stanton Addition between 1880 and 1900, and a number of railroad facilities were established to handle freight and passengers for the various lines in and out of Chattanooga. The seminal event in the development of this area, however, was the opening of the landmark Terminal Station in 1909, which then created a pressing need for additional hotels and other railroad-oriented businesses in the area. Although passenger rail travel was eventually eclipsed by the automobile and airplane in the latter half of the twentieth century, the "Stanton Addition" continues to be a vibrant part of downtown Chattanooga today. In 1992, an 8-block area roughly covering this tract was listed on the National Register of Historic Places as the "Market and Main Streets Historic District." Numerous renovation projects in this "Southside" area, moreover, have led to the creation of new restaurants, retail shops, businesses, and residential opportunities, and the Stanton Addition continues to grow and develop today.

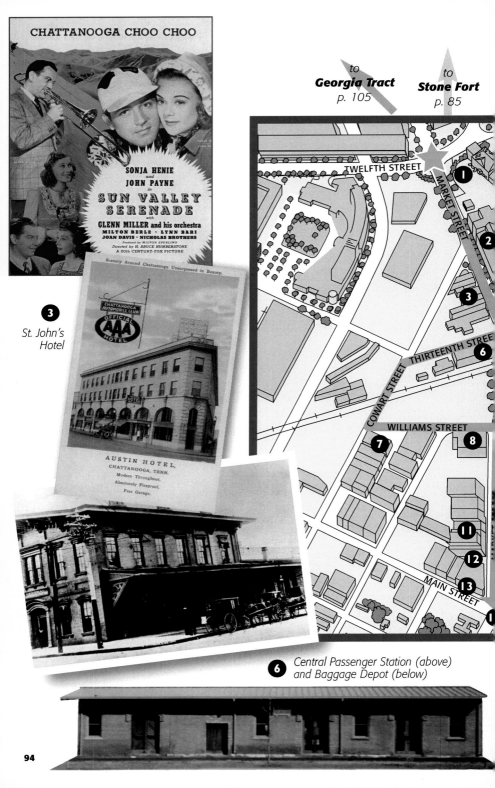

CHATTANOOGA CHOO CHOO

SONJA HENIE and **JOHN PAYNE** in

SUN VALLEY SERENADE

with

GLENN MILLER and his orchestra

MILTON BERLE · LYNN BARI
JOAN DAVIS · NICHOLAS BROTHERS

Produced by MILTON SPERLING
Directed by H. BRUCE HUMBERSTONE
A 20th CENTURY-FOX PICTURE

to
Georgia Tract
p. 105

to
Stone Fort
p. 85

TWELFTH STREET

MARKET STREET

1

2

3

THIRTEENTH STREET

COWART STREET

6

WILLIAMS STREET

7

8

11

12

MAIN STREET

13

3
*St. John's
Hotel*

Scenery Around Chattanooga Unsurpassed in Beauty.

CHATTANOOGA
AUTOMOBILE CLUB
AAA
OFFICIAL
HOTEL

AUSTIN HOTEL,
CHATTANOOGA, TENN.
Modern Throughout,
Absolutely Fireproof,
Free Garage.

6 *Central Passenger Station (above)
and Baggage Depot (below)*

3 *1200 Block of Market Street*

[85]

THE MOST COMFORTABLE RESORT IN THE SOUTH.

STANTON HOUSE,
CHATTANOOGA, TENNESSEE.

This spacious Hotel is most elegantly furnished, has perfect ventilation, commodious grounds, courteous attention, and the table is at all times supplied with the best the market affords. The scenery from the Stanton House is simply grand. The cloud-capped peak of

"OLD LOOKOUT" MOUNTAIN.

Towering 2,000 feet above the plain, stands a tireless sentinel, keeping a faithful watch over the inhabitants of Chattanooga. A fine carriage drive takes the tourist to the top, where the scenery is grand beyond description. The traveler can view

SIX DIFFERENT STATES FROM THE TOP OF 'LOOKOUT.'

To the east, in full view from the verandah of the Stanton House, lies the Battle-ground of Mission Ridge, with its line of redoubts and fortifications still extant, the National Cemetery lying in the rear; the renowned Battle-field of Chickamauga only seven miles distant.

The Climate of Chattanooga is Surpassed by None Other. The air is healthful and invigorating. During the hot sultry months, the rooms of the Stanton House are always kept cool by a pleasant breeze ever present in the valley.

FREE BUS TO AND FROM ALL TRAINS.

COMMODIOUS SAMPLE ROOMS FOR COMMERCIAL TRAVELERS, NEAR THE DEPOT.

By strict personal attention to the wants of guests, we endeavor to make all feel at home. Come and see us. For particulars address

GOODNOW & CO.,
CHATTANOOGA, TENN.

General John T. Wilder

10 *Terminal Station / Chattanooga Choo Choo*

CHATTANOOGA CHOO-CHOO

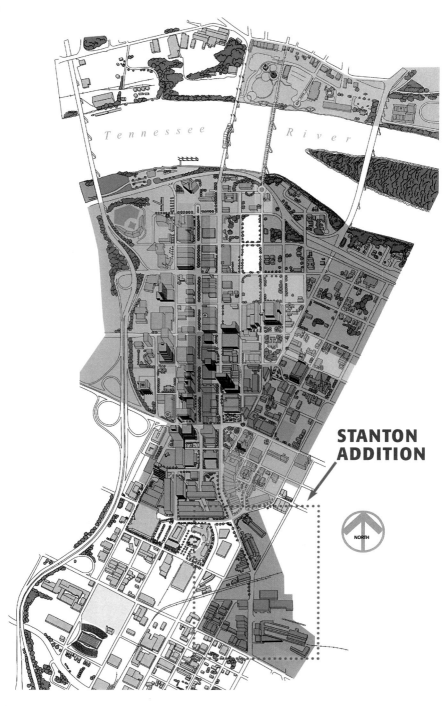

T e n n e s s e e   *R i v e r*

**STANTON
ADDITION**

NORTH

The tour of the Southside area begins at the southeast corner of Market and Twelfth Streets, across from Warehouse Row. ❶ At this location is the **Southern Railway Freight Depot** (1206 Market Street). Originally constructed in 1871 as an iron foundry, the building was purchased by the Eastern Kentucky & Georgia Railroad in 1894 for use as a freight depot; in 1901, this railroad was subsumed within the Southern Railway system. Following the departure of the railroads in the latter half of the twentieth century, the old depot building fell into disuse, becoming the site of John's Railroad Salvage by the early 1980s. It subsequently underwent a $4 million renovation to become the first phase of the Warehouse Row project. Designated a National Historic Landmark and placed on the National Register of Historic Places in 1983, the building today houses a variety of retail shops and business tenants. Interestingly, in keeping with the "railroad-themed" Freight Depot development, the drive-through bank branch located next to the depot, which was originally built by the First Federal Savings & Loan, was also designed to resemble a depot building.

The Freight Depot was the site of the beginning of one of the most interesting legal cases of the segregation era, now known as the **Scottsboro Boys Trial.** On March 25, 1932, a group of 9 African-American boys, 4 of whom were from Chattanooga, emerged from a hobo camp near Chattanooga and jumped aboard a Southern Railway freight train en route from Chattanooga to Memphis. When the train stopped in Paint Rock, Alabama, two white girls claimed that they had been raped by the youths. A brief trial before an all-white jury in Alabama resulted in death sentences for 8 of the defendants – partly because 4 of the boys began accusing one another during the trial — with the ninth ending in a mistrial. Following several appeals, the International Labor Defense, the legal arm of the U.S. Communist Party, obtained a reversal from the U.S. Supreme Court, which concluded in a landmark decision that the boys had been denied fair representation and due process. Although one of the girls later recanted her story, a second trial also ended in guilty verdicts; during this second trial, noted New York attorney Samuel Leibowitz, who represented the defendants, endured cross-burnings, death threats, and attempts by the prosecutor to advise the jury that they should show "that Alabama justice can't be bought with Jew money from New York!" After additional legal wrangling and a third guilty verdict, a fourth and final trial began in 1936; although five of the defendants were again found guilty, the charges against the remaining 4 were dropped. Four of the 5 convicted defendants were released between 1943 and 1946, and the last remaining prisoner escaped in 1950 and fled to Michigan, which then refused to return him to Alabama. In 1976, Alabama Governor George Wallace pardoned the last living Scottsboro Boy, Clarence Norris, who died in 1989 at age 76.

Next door to the Freight Depot is the **Hamilton County Development Resource Center,** or "One-Stop Shop" (2002), an 85,000 square-foot structure built as part of a $96 million package to boost the Southside area. ❷ This center was established to house a number of local governmental and development offices which had previously been spread out throughout the city.

From this spot, proceed south along Market Street. This portion of Market Street (between MLK Jr. Blvd. and Main Street) was first "paved" in 1915 with wood blocks, at a then-substantial cost of $58,833.05.

Over time, this section of Market Street has been the subject of several discussions concerning the redevelopment of downtown Chattanooga. Following the creation of the Chattanooga Choo-Choo complex, for example, it was suggested in 1982 that this portion of Market Street be renamed "Choo-Choo Boulevard," and identified by special train-shaped street signs along the road. Another recurring theme has been the extension of a fixed-line trolley from the Chattanooga Choo-Choo along Market Street to Martin Luther King Jr. Blvd., a proposal which has resurfaced several times since initially being introduced in the 1970s.

On the right side of the street across from the Development Resource Center, in the **1200 Block of Market Street**, is a row of 2- and 3-story brick buildings built on the former sites of saloons, barbershops, restaurants, and boarding rooms which were originally established to serve railroad patrons and employees. ❸ By the 1920s, these buildings came to house a number of wholesale businesses, and today this row of buildings houses several retail shops, restaurants, and loft apartments.

The buildings which currently house **Porker's Barbecue Restaurant** (1251-1253 Market Street) and **Mom's Italian Villa** (1257 Market Street) are 2-story brick Italianate structures originally built circa 1910 as commercial buildings tied to the bustling railroad activities in Chattanooga. The building at 1251 Market Street is characterized by a decorative pressed metal cornice with modillion brackets, and the storefront at 1253 Market Street features cast-iron columns which were manufactured by the local Cahill Iron Works. Mom's Italian Villa, which was first operated as the "Walnut Inn" in the nearby St. John's Hotel, later relocated to its current location, which also features interesting cast-iron columns similar to those at 1253 Market Street.

Further down the street, located at **1263 Market Street** is a 2-story brick building erected circa 1910, which has a decorative stone-and-brick band along the cornice. This structure (pictured on pages 95 and 97) includes a side entrance to the second floor, which has served as boarding rooms as well as commercial and apartment space over the years. Next door (**1265 Market Street**) is a 3-story brick structure with a similar band of patterned stone and brick, as well as cast-iron columns forged at the Cahill Iron Works.

The structure at 1269 Market Street is the former **Graham Wholesale Building** (circa 1890). This 3-story Victorian commercial building (also pictured on pages 95 and 97) is constructed of brick, with a decorative cornice, raised parapet with stone finials, and semi-elliptical arched area. This building is the last remaining structure in this block which pre-dates the nearby Terminal Station.

Next door to the Graham Wholesale Building, at the southwest corner lot currently occupied by the Firestone Tire and Auto Store (1271 Market Street), is the location of the former **Milner Hotel** (also known as the "Ford Hotel" at one point). Erected in the railyards area to house

visitors arriving in Chattanooga by train, this 3-story, 80-room hotel became outdated and unnecessary as rail travel was replaced by the automobile in the latter half of the twentieth century; it was purchased by the Stone Fort Land Company for $69,000 and torn down in 1960.

To the rear of the above row of buildings was located another important early enterprise, the **Union Stockyards** (1872), erected by A.J. Wisdom and O.P. Foust in the vicinity of the railyards. In 1885, this business expanded with the addition of 6 cottages and a 2-story, 12-room boarding house adjoining the stockyards along Hooke (Thirteenth) Street. Following the deaths of Wisdom and Foust in the 1890s, however, the stockyards were slowly broken up; part of the site was acquired by the Krystal Ice Company in 1909 (later succeeded by the Atlantic Ice and Coal Corporation in 1914), and another portion became the Cloverleaf Dairy. Today, few remnants of this early Chattanooga enterprise exist.

Across Market Street from the Milner Hotel, at the northeast corner of Market and King Streets, is the **St. John's Hotel** (1916). ❹ In an effort to influence the development of the area surrounding his new Stanton House hotel, J.C. Stanton convinced the city that the portion of Market Street between Ninth Street (MLK Jr. Blvd.) and Main Street should run in front of his hotel, a move which required the street to veer

AUSTIN HOTEL,
CHATTANOOGA, TENN.
Modern Throughout.
Absolutely Fireproof.
Free Garage.

to the east, thereby creating a series of triangular blocks along Market Street. In 1871, Stanton convinced the post office to move to a building he erected on this triangular lot (the only brownstone structure located on Market Street at the time). The post office was later moved from this spot in 1875 due to customer complaints that it was too far from town. The original post office building here was then remodeled by H.F. Parrish and became the May Hotel. In 1913, this hotel (also known at one point as the Ronnhers Hotel) was torn down, and in 1916 the 76-room Ellis Hotel, owned by Victor and Gus Ellis, opened at this spot. This

24,000 square-foot Victorian building is composed of terra cotta and brick, and the interior features elaborate marble and plaster work and wrought iron railings along the interior stairwells. From 1922-1930, the hotel was operated as the Austin Hotel (as is seen in the postcard on pages 94 and 98), after which it reverted to the Ellis Hotel name until 1933, when it became the Gilbert-Ellis Hotel. In 1967, the name was again changed, this time to the St. John's Hotel. In 1971, the building was purchased for $200,000 and converted into low-income apartments. By 1983, however, the building was vacated, and it was acquired by the city at auction for $76,000. Although demolition was originally considered for the building, in 1995 renovations overseen by the local Cornerstones historic preservation organization were undertaken, and although the remainder of the deteriorating block was cleared in the 1990s, the St. John's Hotel building reopened for business in 1999. Though it is no longer a hotel, the renovated structure contains several retail shops and businesses (anchored by an upscale restaurant in the former lobby at the south end of the building), and plans are in the works for apartments in the upper stories of the building.

Across King Street from the St. John's Hotel, at the southeast corner of King and Market Streets, ❺ is the former site of the **Chattanooga Foundry and Machine Works**, an important early Chattanooga iron foundry. Founded in 1850 by a number of early financial supporters of Chattanooga, the East Tennessee Iron Manufacturing Company was taken over by Englishman Thomas Webster in 1857, after which the business was renamed. The foundry, which was constructed on a 6-acre spot at this location in 1853 and initially produced freight cars and other railroad machinery, housed the first coke furnace erected in Chattanooga and some of the earliest coke ovens built in the State of Tennessee. After the Union artillery bombardment of Chattanooga in 1862, the foundry was put into service day and night forging munitions for the South, and several cannon produced there were used by the Confederate army in the subsequent siege of Chattanooga in 1863 (including the "Lady Lilla," a cannon named for Webster's daughter which was captured by the federal army at the battle of Missionary Ridge). Though the foundry was destroyed by the Union army during its occupation of the city, Webster returned after the war and rebuilt the business; he was forced to do so again after a fire destroyed the facility in 1867.

Although the company also weathered the 1873 financial crisis, Webster eventually decided to close the business in 1874. The site subsequently housed the Henry Clay Evans & Co. Anchor Flouring Mills, today few remnants are left of this significant early Chattanooga enterprise.

Across Market Street from this site, at the southwest corner of Market and Thirteenth Streets, is the **Southern Railway Building** (1301 Market Street). ❻ Due to increased crowding at exist-

ing railroad facilities by the 1880s, on September 16, 1888, the Cincinnati Southern and Alabama Great Southern railroads (collectively known as the Queen and Crescent Route) opened the Central Passenger Station at this spot, utilizing an existing building erected in 1871 as a freight station for the Alabama Great Southern Railroad. To the left (south) of the depot (pictured on page 94) was an iron shed spanning 5 tracks which provided shelter for passengers. Subsequently, the railroad network, which came to be known as the "Southern Railway," took over the Memphis & Charleston and the East Tennessee, Virginia, & Georgia railroads; this growth and consolidation led to a pressing need for additional space, and in 1906 the Southern Railway began construction of a new Terminal Station to replace the Central Passenger Station. The old depot building was then used to store grain, hay, and wheat. In a later effort to consolidate the numerous employees working at various locations throughout the city, in 1922 the Southern Railway razed the old Central Passenger Station and at a cost of $150,000 erected the current 3-story brick building, which features a Classical entryway with columns and a pediment. This 40,000 square-foot building (above) served as the offices of the railroad for several decades; following the closure of the company's offices here, however, the building sat vacant until it was given to the City of Chattanooga. In 2000, the property was sold for $300,000 to a Florida development company, which undertook a $2.6 million renovation of the building, which now houses offices for Chattanooga Neighborhood Enterprise (CNE) and 20 "loft-like" apartment spaces.

Behind the Southern Railway Building is the oldest building still standing in downtown Chattanooga, the former **Baggage Depot** for the Queen & Crescent Route. Dating to circa 1860, this small structure (pictured on page 94) was part of the original freight depot constructed by the railroad at the southwest corner of Market and Thirteenth Streets. Currently, this 1-story brick building, which was subsequently occupied by the "George J. Haley & Co. Paper Cutting" company and other small businesses, is in the process of renovation for retail and/or commercial purposes.

From the baggage depot, turn left onto Cowart Street. The land in this general vicinity, between the Nashville & Chattanooga Railroad facilities (north) and Main Street (south), was originally the farm of pioneer Rush Montgomery, referred to as "**Oakwood**." Built by early Ross's Landing resident Thomas Crutchfield, the brick colonial home on the property had a large, columned front porch and rich mahogany trim on the interior. After the home was acquired by Judge Robert Hooke, a small brick office was built next door for use in Hooke's duties as division superintendent of the N&C Railroad. Two nearby streets were originally named for the owners of this home: Montgomery (Main) Street and Hooke (Thirteenth) Street. While the house survived initial orders by the approaching federal army to destroy the majority of the homes immediately south of Chattanooga in 1863, following the battles of Chattanooga an African-American regiment was assigned to the grounds; part of the house was torn away, and breastworks and rifle pits were dug into the yards and gardens throughout the property. Judge Hooke then decided to move to a new location on some property he owned on McCallie Avenue east of town; however, he found that a number of soldiers had been buried on that property. Although he petitioned to have the bodies removed, he was instead given $9,000 for the land, which later became part of a National Cemetery to honor the soldiers killed in the war.

Despite its relative distance from the river, the Stanton Addition was not immune to flooding, and several major floods inundated this area prior to the completion of the Chickamauga Dam upriver in 1940. During the 1886 flood, for instance, floodwaters inundated the streets and lower floors of buildings throughout this area. In an effort to survey the damage and rescue any stranded residents, a party set out in a small boat; arriving in this vicinity, near the corner of Cowart and Main Streets (to the south), they saw saloon owner Billy Barlow sitting in a second-story window with a large jug next to him. Pulling up to the building, the boatmen were given "pretty fair quantity of white corn whiskey" in exchange for their rescue efforts.

From this spot, proceed to the northeast corner of Cowart and Williams (Fourteenth) Streets, ❼ where is located the **Southside Grill** (1400 Cowart Street), a fine dining establishment opened in a brick commercial building erected circa 1907 to house the Armour meat packing plant.

Turn left onto Williams Street. Labeled "one of the first privately-financed buildings to go up from scratch in the Southside in years," the 2-story, 7,000 square-foot structure located at **1400 Williams Street** was designed by architect Louis Wamp and erected in 2000, at a cost of approximately $700,000. Next door, the 2-story brick industrial/commercial building at **1401-1407 Williams Street**, erected circa 1900, features a corner entrance, iron circular support beams, and faux key stones above the windows; it is currently utilized as retail space.

Continue to the southwest corner of Market and Williams Streets. ❽ The completion of the Terminal Station in 1909 created the immediate need for hotel facilities in the area south of Ninth Street, and numerous hotels opened their doors in this area in the early years of the twentieth century. As a result, as one 1911 article recognized, "Chattanooga's wonderful growth during recent years is shown more emphatically by the improvement of hotel facilities than in nearly any other phase of the city development." Citing the need for a "class hotel" in Chattanooga, in 1911 E.R. Betterton and J.O. Martin opened the $100,000 **Grand Hotel** (1400 Market Street), a 5-story hotel with 102 rooms (50 of which had novel "shower baths"), a 40-seat dining room, 60-seat grill, billiard room, bar, and tobacconist. The building itself was constructed of brick trimmed with Darlington ooltic limestone, and the street sides of the building had large plate glass windows in the lobby. Built in a time when dangerous hotel fires were quite common, the Grand Hotel had large signs placed on the roof of the building and above the front door noting that it was "fire proof." As with other hotels in this area, the growth of automobile travel spelled the end of the road for the Grand Hotel in the latter part of the twentieth century, and in 1975 it was announced that the building had been purchased for $100,000 to be transformed into a large indoor shopping mall. As part of this plan, the building was accented with red-and-white striped awnings and iron grillwork on the windows, and each floor was designed with a specific theme – including the Mexican Village, Wharfside, French Quarter, Western Store, and Hawaiian Village. Though this $650,000 project opened briefly with 17 shops, it passed into receivership later in 1975, and the building was sold at auction in 1976. Subsequent plans to reopen in 1977 failed, and despite a $9 million bond to assist in creating a 50-suite motel at the site in 1985, no action was taken. As a result, in the ensuing years the 48,000 square-foot building became "a haven for derelicts and vagrants." In 1995, however, the hotel, which was referred to at that time as "an eyesore to visitors we're encouraging to come to Chattanooga," was purchased for $200,000 and renovated by Chattanooga Neighborhood Enterprise (CNE). In 1997, the building reopened with 4,500 square-feet of ground floor retail space and 36 apartments.

Next door to the Grand Hotel (**1407 Market Street**) is a small 2-story Italianate structure which dates to approximately 1887, at which time it opened as a saloon for visitors and railroad workers. In 1917, the building was temporarily operated as the parcel post subsidiary, and today it continues to function as a retail business.

Continue south down Market Street. On the left, near the present-day CARTA bus barns (1398 Market Street), is the site where former Union general and Chattanooga mayor (1872) John T. Wilder, who had been involved in the shelling of Chattanooga from the north side of the river in 1863 and for whom Wilder Tower at the Chickamauga battlefield is named, planned along with several others to construct the **Wilder Opera House** during the real estate boom of 1887-1888. ❾ Deciding that Chattanooga needed a fine opera house, Wilder (above) hired workmen to begin constructing

such a building immediately north of the Stanton House. Although a fine stone wall was quickly completed, work was stopped when hints arose that the boom might be ending, and all that was left was a wall which collected rainwater and became a stagnant pool. When a prominent visitor came to visit from Knoxville to evaluate Chattanooga's progress, Wilder gave him a tour of the city; when they came to the site of the unfinished opera house, Wilder quickly concocted a long discussion of a structure across the street, hoping the visitor would not notice the unsightly pond. The visitor, however, had been told about the spot, and when a group of Chattanoogans later asked him what he thought of the town, he replied, "Seeing has convinced me that we in Knoxville are a little slipshod, and now and then neglect a good many things that ought to be attended to. But here, you people are certainly wide awake to every interest, and encourage every enterprise to the uttermost. You even put fine, expensive stone walls around your frog ponds." Though it was never finished, the Wilder Opera House remains a humorous story of the real estate boom and its aftermath in Chattanooga.

Immediately south of the CARTA bus barn is the **Chattanooga Choo-Choo** convention center and hotel (1400 Market Street). ❿ Arriving from Boston in 1868, John C. Stanton purchased (on credit) 69 1/2 acres of land south of town at this spot, which he subdivided and sold as the Stanton Addition (or Stanton Town). As the keystone of this development, in 1870 he built the Stanton House (first called the Lookout Hotel), a $100,000, 5-story hotel with mansard roof, balconies, observatory, bathrooms on every floor (a luxury at the time), and the first telephone in Chattanooga. Though the hotel was the social center of Chattanooga for a period of time, (as reflected in the advertise-

ment on page 95), the area never became the apex of town as Stanton had hoped, and by 1892 the hotel had been seized by the sheriff for outstanding debts. In 1900, businessman Z.C. Patten purchased the building, referred to as "one of the best-known hotels in the South," for $25,000. In 1905, he sold the property to the Southern Railway for $75,000, and the hotel was razed in 1906 for construction of a new passenger terminal to replace the nearby Central Passenger Station.

The new Terminal Station (pictured on pages 95 and 101) was designed by New York architect Don Barber. The building is a combination of an exterior design which received a prestigious award from the Beaux Arts Institute in Paris and an interior modeled after the fashionable National Park Bank of New York. Designed to impress visitors to Chattanooga, the $400,000 station features outer walls of dark red vitrified brick with terra cotta trim; the 85-foot front arch was at the time of construction the largest brick arch ever constructed. After a court battle attempting to force the railroad to build overpasses at several crossings delayed the opening of the completed building, 48 trains entered the station on opening day in 1909. The Terminal Station continued to greet passengers until 1970, when increasing auto and air travel sealed the fate of the passenger railroad industry; on August 11, 1970, the *Birmingham Special* became the last train to arrive at the station, and demolition was expected. However, a group of investors purchased the site, which opened in 1973 as the Chattanooga Choo-Choo (named after the 1941 Glenn Miller song, above) as a 30-acre vacation complex with shops, gardens (including an All-American Rose Selection garden), gazebos, fountains, a convention center, and an ice rink. The complex also has a fixed-line trolley which was originally built in 1920 for use on Canal Street in New Orleans. As for the Choo-Choo itself, the wood-burning locomotive (pictured on page 95), which is similar to the first train to arrive in Chattanooga from Cincinnati in 1880, was last used in the 1940s by the Smoky Mountain Railroad. Today, the renovated Choo-Choo,

CHATTANOOGA CHOO CHOO

SONJA HENIE and JOHN PAYNE
SUN VALLEY SERENADE
GLENN MILLER and his orchestra
MILTON BERLE · LYNN BARI
JOHN PAYNE · NICHOLAS BROTHERS

which was placed on the National Register of Historic Places in 1973, remains a popular local tourist attraction, hotel (a new Holiday Inn is located on the premises), and spot for conventions.

When visiting the Chattanooga Choo-Choo, note the interesting statue which greets visitors at the rear of the station. Presumed by some visitors to be an image of J.C. Stanton, in actuality the statue is of an unknown individual and is not intended to represent anyone in particular.

Also, located to the rear of the Stanton House, in the vicinity of the current Holiday Inn hotel, was Chattanooga's first baseball field, which was later dismantled when the Terminal Station was built. Businessman O.B. Andrews then obtained the franchise for the Chattanooga Lookouts team in 1909, after which "Andrews Field" (later Engel Stadium) was built on East Third Street for the local minor league franchise. Today, the Chattanooga Lookouts continue to represent Chattanooga today at the downtown BellSouth Park.

From the Chattanooga Choo-Choo, visitors may take 30-minute horse-drawn carriage rides for a tour of the downtown area; similar tours begin at the Tennessee Aquarium near the riverfront. For more information, contact Chattanooga Horse Trams at 265-6544.

Immediately south of the Terminal Station is the **Terminal Hotel** (1470 Market Street), which opened near the time the Terminal Station itself began operation (circa 1909). Originally separated from the Terminal Station by Hotel Street, this 3-story brick structure (also known as the Stong Building) is a very narrow triangular building which housed a hotel, cafe, and pool room for visitors. The short-lived hotel was defunct by 1930, and after having been occupied by various businesses and residential tenants over the years, today the building sits vacant and awaiting restoration.

From the front of the Chattanooga Choo-Choo complex, cross to the west side of Market Street. ⓫ This stretch of property was sparsely developed in the years prior to the construction of the Terminal Station, and as late as 1885 the street included only vacant lots, the Cleage Brothers Cotton Warehouse, and a single saloon. By 1900, however, the announcement that a railroad terminal would be built across the street led to a demand for additional hotel facilities, and the **Tourist Hotel** was soon erected across the street from the station (1427 Market Street). This conveniently-located 50-room hotel charged 75 cents to $1 per day and included a restaurant which could seat 75 people.

Like the former Tourist Hotel location, the majority of the buildings on the west side of Market Street at this spot are vacant at the present time. In the first half of the twentieth century, however, this portion of Market Street was the site of several hotels and eateries for railroad patrons and workers. The majority of these buildings, which were erected between 1900 and 1930, have been altered with new facades in recent years. For instance, the Art Deco-influenced building at **1437-1439 Market Street**, which was erected circa 1930, replaced a brick structure which housed the Redmon Hotel in the 1910s and the Farley Hotel and Union Restaurant in the 1920s.

In addition, located at 1443 Market Street is the **Ellis Restaurant** building. Opened at the turn of the century by cafe owner Gus Ellis at 838 Market Street, the restaurant was relocated to this building circa 1930, where it remained for a number of years, until the number of railroad passengers decreased with the advent of the automobile. This now-vacant 1-story brick building, which dates to approximately 1920, is highlighted by an Art Deco neon sign with decorative metal frogs and advertisements for steak and seafood. The restaurant was advertised as "Chattanooga's most popular and up-to-date cafe, and it is reported that during World War II the line of soldiers waiting to get in the restaurant would extend along the block to the Grand Hotel. By 1979, however, Elllis' death and the closing of the Terminal Station led to the restaurant to close as well.

Next door to this restaurant building is the former **St. George Hotel** (1449 Market Street). Opened in 1917 as the Hotel Glenn, by 1930 the 60-room building had changed names, to the Hotel Walden (also listed at times as the Walden Hotel), and in 1948 the building became the St. George Hotel. Gus Ellis, who was involved with the nearby Ellis Hotel and Ellis Restaurant, was also associated with this hotel. The 4-story building is composed of pale brick, with small, multi-pane metal windows; the rooms on the upper floor look into a large courtyard to the rear of the building. Currently vacant, this structure, which is listed as one of the most "endangered" historic properties in Chattanooga, is awaiting renovation; with the continuing development of the Southside area,

it is anticipated that rejuvenation of the former hotel is not far away.

Past the St. George Hotel (**1465 Market Street**) is a 2-story brick commercial building erected circa 1900, the first floor of which has been modified and enclosed with wood. **⑫**

Next door to this small structure, at the northwest corner of Market and Main Streets, is the site of a former branch of the **South Chattanooga Savings Bank** (1889), an early bank which later evolved into the Hamilton National Bank in 1929. **⑬** The 2-story Neoclassical building at this site (1467 Market Street), which was constructed circa 1900, features a curved storefront accented with stone Corinthian pilasters, as well as a corner entrance highlighted with a triangular pediment and decorative stone cornice with dentils. After a $50,000 renovation of the building was undertaken by the First National Bank in or around 1929, the building was acquired by the Clark Brothers Furniture Store, a use which continues today (although at the present time the renovation of the building for residential purposes is in the discussion process).

From this point, continue south to **Main Street**. **⑭** The southern boundary of the Southside area, this road was originally called Montgomery Street, named for pioneer Benjamin Rush Montgomery, whose property the street passed. Considered far out in the country for a number of years, in 1853-1854 this area became part of Chattanooga after the town limits were extended 1/2 mile on the east and south, to Montgomery Avenue and East End (now Central Avenue); residents in the annexed areas were temporarily exempted from city taxes, so long as their property remained in woodland or farmland. In the 1870s, the condition of Main Street was so poor that alderman James R. Harris proposed changing the name of Montgomery Avenue to Mason & Dixon's Line, because "south of it they did not get their fair share of appropriations." In 1928, the city limits were extended past Main Street, and a shanty town in that area referred to as "No Man's Land" was taken down so that Market Street could be extended to Twenty-Third Street. This enabled development of the area at Market and Main Streets, which today is itself undergoing considerable renovation along with the Southside area.

Main Street was also the southern terminus of the first streetcar operation in Chattanooga. In November 1872, (after an earlier enterprise in

1867 had failed), the first streetcars began operating on a track along Market Street which linked the river to Main Street. This business, the Chattanooga & Lookout Street Railroad Company, dissolved in April 1873 after the city imposed a schedule of pro-rata annual taxes on streetcars. Subsequently, Atlanta resident A.J. "Fatty" Harris, backed by Chattanooga investors, formed the Chattanooga Street Railroad Company in 1874 along the same line. Using a 12 foot-long, mule-drawn New York City streetcar and traveling over parallel T-rails along the street, the line opened on September 4, 1875. A turntable was located at the wharf, and the first streetcar barn was located at the south end of the line, near this spot. Although the initial success of the business enabled the company to replace the mule with a pair of fine carriage horses, the 400-pound Harris drank up most of these early profits (it is said that Harris congratulated himself by buying a drink each time the streetcar went by). Coupled with the uneven tracks and long delays associated with the streetcars, Harris' financial mismanagement caused the enterprise to lose money; it was then purchased for $2,750 by several local businessmen fronted by A.J. Wisdom, although these individuals also failed to turn a profit. It was not until 1881, when J.H. Warner purchased the line and relocated it to Broad Street, that the Chattanooga streetcar system became a reliable means of transportation.

To return to the beginning of the tour,

proceed north on Market street to the corner

of Market and Twelfth Streets.

Georgia Tract

The Georgia Tract (along with the Ross's Landing area) anchored the early development of Chattanooga. The single most significant event in the early history of Chattanooga was the 1839 announcement that the town would serve as the northern terminus of the Western & Atlantic Railroad, to be built from Atlanta north to the Tennessee River. The potential impact of the railroad upon the town was not lost upon Chattanoogans; when the 1837 financial panic threatened the future of the rail line, one citizen wrote that "if Georgia fails to finish the road or to make the appropriation for its completion all is flat in Chattanooga." The 137-mile W&A Railroad was eventually completed in 1850, followed by the Nashville & Chattanooga (1854) and Memphis & Charleston (1858) Railroads. With the completion of additional rail lines during the antebellum period, it could be said that "Chattanooga's rail connections reached south, north, east, and west, giving it a strategic position equaled by few internal towns in the country."

During the initial sale of lots in Chattanooga in 1839, the State of Georgia acquired a 20-acre tract south of Ninth Street for its railroad yards and facilities. Soon, the area was filled with rail lines and industrial structures serving the railroad, and as additional railroads came to Chattanooga the concentration of railroad facilities attracted industry, warehouses, and hotels nearby.

The purchase of this land by the State of Georgia was often a topic of humor. At one time, bronze markers were imbedded in the street marking the property as that of the State of Georgia, and in 1947 one Georgia governor remarked, "There has been a great deal of controversy throughout the years as to whether Chattanooga really belongs to Georgia rather than Tennessee . . . I took Mayor [Hugh P.] Wasson in when I arrived here and welcomed him as the mayor of the second largest city in Georgia. There is no longer need for the cities of Savannah, Macon, and Augusta to be fighting over which is the second largest city in Georgia because that is the city of Chattanooga, Georgia."

As railroad travel dwindled in the latter half of the twentieth century, the State of Georgia announced the sale of this property to the Stone Fort Land Company in 1972 for $445,000. Since that date, substantial changes have taken place in the Georgia tract; once covered with rail lines and railroad facilities, today tall buildings and parks stand where once passengers and goods streamed into the Gateway to the South on a daily basis.

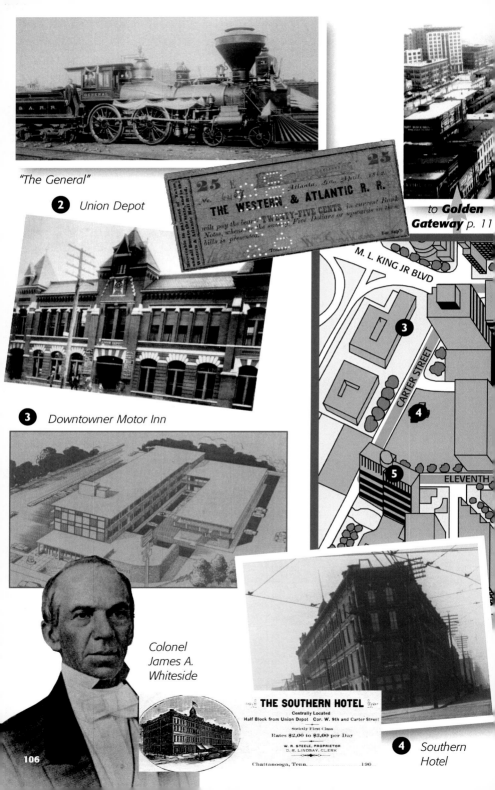

"The General"

2 Union Depot

THE WESTERN & ATLANTIC R. R.

25 — 25

to **Golden Gateway** p. 11

M. L. KING JR BLVD

CARTER STREET

ELEVENTH

3 Downtowner Motor Inn

Colonel James A. Whiteside

THE SOUTHERN HOTEL
Centrally Located
Half Block from Union Depot   Cor. W. 9th and Carter Street
Strictly First Class
Rates $2.00 to $3.00 per Day
W. R. STEELE, PROPRIETOR
D. R. LINDSAY, CLERK
Chattanooga, Tenn.   190

4 Southern Hotel

Railroad
enue p.155   *to Market*
              Center p.167

to
Big
Nine
p. 75

to
Stone
Fort
p. 85

MARKET STREET

TENTH STREET

BROAD STREET

9 Western & Atlantic
Passenger Depot

8 Car Sheds

Looking North on Market Street, Chattanooga, Tennessee

to **Stanton**
Addition *p. 93*

**GEORGIA
TRACT**

NORTH

The tour of the Georgia Tract begins at the corner of Martin Luther King Jr. Boulevard and Broad Street. ❶ The portion of Broad Street to the south of MLK Jr. Blvd., now referred to as **South Broad Street**, was originally called

Whiteside Street, named in honor of early Chattanooga promoter James A. Whiteside (below), whose enthusiasm and efforts were instrumental in attracting the railroads to Chattanooga. At one point, in fact, Whiteside rode his horse from Ross's Landing to Milledgeville, Georgia, and back in order to appear before the Georgia state legislature to

discuss the advantages of locating the northern terminus of the W&A railroad in Chattanooga.

Originally, a number of buildings owned by the State of Georgia blocked access to South Broad Street at this point, and Broad Street effectively ended at Ninth Street (MLK Jr. Blvd.); the State of Georgia refused to alter this arrangement or permit the development of the area. For a number of years, a water fountain maintained by the Women's Christian Temperance Union (W.C.T.U.) was placed in the center of this intersection, as seen in the photograph above and on pages 106-107. This situation became a bone of contention between Chattanooga and Georgia, especially with increased expansion in the early decades of the twentieth century following the introduction of the automobile. As a result, several lawsuits were filed between the city of Chattanooga and the State of Georgia concerning this issue, though none was able to fully resolve the matter. On the evening of May 6, 1926, therefore, Chattanooga city officials and workmen simply knocked down the structures blocking Broad Street. Having thus symbolically "opened" Broad Street, a Stutz limousine was driven through the hole, while the Elks Junior Band

played the tune "Marching Through Georgia." This change (and the development of South Broad Street through the Georgia Tract) was later recognized in a formal legal agreement between the city, the State of Georgia, and the lessee of the railroad (the Nashville, Chattanooga & St. Louis Railroad) in 1927.

At the southwest corner of MLK Jr. Blvd. and Broad Street is the former site of the historic **Union Depot**. ❷ By the early 1880s, the increasing volume of railroad traffic in and out

of Chattanooga created a pressing need for new passenger facilities in the town, and Colonel W.C. Smith of Nashville designed the $38,000 Union Depot, which opened on July 1, 1882. The "talk of the town," this fine brick building (above), which was attached to the older car sheds (pictured on page 107) to the rear, featured stone accents and a West Virginia slate roof; the double walnut doors on the front of the building opened into high-ceilinged rooms of ash, walnut, and white pine. The 65-by-16 foot entrance corridor was lain in mosaic tile; while the remaining floors were originally simple wooden plank floors, in 1900 these were replaced with fine Georgia marble. Immediately west of the Union Depot, approximately where the tall Tallan Building now sits, a freight depot designed in a similar style to the Union Depot and opened at the same time (1882) was constructed by the Nashville, Chattanooga, & St. Louis Railway.

For several decades, the Union Depot housed the historic locomotive **The General**, pictured on pages 106 and 110) which had participated in the "Great Locomotive Chase" led by Andrews' Raiders during the Civil War. In April 1862, several Union spies, led by civilian James J. Andrews, seized a train at Big Shanty, Georgia, and proceeded north, cutting telegraph wires, tearing up tracks, and attempting to burn bridges. The saboteurs were pursued by the conductor of the train, who chased them on foot, by pole car, and by switch engine before obtaining a second locomotive, the *Texas*, with which to chase the Raiders. After the *General* ran out of fuel, the Raiders were forced to flee on foot, and all 22 men were eventually captured and taken to Chattanooga; 8 of the men were hanged in Atlanta after a trial for espionage. In 1891, the engine (still bearing bullet holes received in the course of the locomotive chase) was placed on exhibit in the station, where it remained until 1961. At that time, the train's owner, the L&N Railroad, removed the locomotive for a "temporary" tour of the country in conjunction with the centennial anniversary of the Civil War; at the conclusion of this tour, however, it was announced that the train would be permanently relocated to Kennesaw, Georgia, where the locomotive chase had begun. Outraged, Chattanooga city officials

seized the train as it passed through Chattanooga on its way to Kennesaw in 1967. However, an ensuing legal battle ended with a ruling in favor of the State of Georgia, and the *General* left Chattanooga permanently. The locomotive remains on display in Kennesaw today.

The Union Depot itself, a vibrant symbol of the city's role as a rail center in the New South, was dramatically affected by the increasing reliance upon automobile and air travel in the latter half of the twentieth century. By 1970, few trains carried passengers to or from Chattanooga, and on May 1, 1971, the locomotive *Georgian* made its last-scheduled run from the Union Depot, which was then closed to rail traffic. On March 21, 1973, the station, which was listed on the National Register of Historic Places (1973), was razed in conjunction with the commercial development of the former Georgia tract. As part of the subsequent downtown building boom of the late 1970s, in 1978 the Krystal Company erected an 11-story office building of white concrete accented by solar bronze glass (to your left), and in 1982 the adjacent 178,000 square-foot Tallan Building (to your right) was opened on the site of the former freight depot next door to the Union Depot.

From this point, proceed west to Carter Street and turn left. At the southwest corner of MLK Jr. Blvd. and Carter Street is a tangible symbol of the rise of the automobile and development of the freeway system in Chattanooga, the current

Days Inn Hotel (901 Carter Street). ❸ Fueled by the construction of the adjacent freeway interchange at Ninth Street, this motel was constructed in 1965 as the **Downtowner Motor Inn** (above). Ironically, the building was erected virtually next door to the Union Depot, which eventually suffered its demise in part as the result of the increasing use of automobile travel.

Continue south along Carter Street. Following the Cherokee Removal in 1838, several investment companies were formed for the purpose of speculation in the land located in present-day Chattanooga. One of these groups was called the **Hines Company** and included several prominent citizens of Milledgeville, Georgia; this group purchased several parcels of land in the southern portion of town, and a number of the streets in this area were named for these early investors and developers. For instance, Carter Street was named for Milledgeville resident Farish Carter, and Boyce Street (renamed South Chestnut Street in 1912, despite protests by some residents who disliked replacing the names of early pioneers with "common" street names) was named for early investor Ker Boyce, of Charleston, South Carolina; each of these individuals was also involved in the founding of the East Tennessee Iron Manufacturing Company (1850), an important early Chattanooga enterprise. Originally, South Chestnut Street split off to the east of Carter Street at Ninth Street; following the development of the former railroad yards in the early 1970s, however, the portion of South Chestnut Street between Ninth and Eleventh Streets became the site of commercial construction and no longer exists.

Following the Civil War, this area became a particularly rough area referred to as **Sutlertown.** Characterized by crudely-built shanties and storefronts lining the streets, Sutlertown attracted a variety of speculators and drifters, earning a reputation as a dangerous place to venture after dark. On the east side of this street (to your left), moreover, once stood a crude wooden building which was erected by the federal army during its occupation of Chattanooga in 1865; it was then purchased by an entrepreneur in the government sale conducted after the war and transformed into a hotel, the Burns House. It was eventually torn down in 1881.

Near this spot, grocer W.O. Peeples erected a 4-story brick hotel and business building in 1881 on a triangular block bounded by Carter, Chestnut, and Ninth Streets. ❹ Referred to as the **Peoples Block** (or, alternately, the Peeple's Block), the 140-room hotel was designed by architect James C. Edwards. Initially, the hotel portion was leased to Frederick Voigt and

opened as the Palace Hotel; this short-lived endeavor, however, was soon replaced by the "Southern Hotel," pictured above and on page 106. Also located in this building were 8 first-floor business offices, one of which housed the first automobile dealership in Chattanooga, the Chattanooga Automobile Company. Opened by Charles and Joseph C. Forstner in 1905, this dealership "sold, bought and rented new and second-hand automobiles," operated "the only garage in Chattanooga," and included a "fully-equipped machine shop." In 1907, the building was purchased for $50,000 by the Southern Express Company for use as additional office space, though it was subsequently torn down.

Continue along Carter Street, past Eleventh Street. Much of the area in this vicinity was originally owned by local railroad advocate James A. Whiteside, who in 1852-1853 sold a portion of his land to the Nashville & Chattanooga Railroad to erect a freight depot (1854). In 1855, the State of Georgia sold 8.79 acres of its 20 acre-plot to the N&C Railroad for use as railyards, thus adding to the number of rail facilities in this area. With the 1882 construction of the Union Depot, the original N&C depot in this

vicinity was rented out for non-railroad purposes, and it was torn down in 1885. Today, this property is part of the site of the **Chattanooga Convention Center**. ❺ Initially opened in 1985, the Convention Center is currently in the process of undertaking a $56 million addition intended to increase the size of the facility from 113,000 to 298,000 square feet; this expanded facility is expected to be completed in 2003. Across Carter Street from the Trade Center is the Siskin Institute, a 64,000 square-foot educational facility which opened in 2002.

At this point, turn left onto Eleventh Street and proceed east to Broad Street. Originally overlain with numerous rail lines, in 1926 Eleventh Street was "opened" between Market and Broad Street, and in the 1970s the street was extended to the west, to Carter Street. On your right, at the southwest corner of Broad and Eleventh Streets, is the 2-story headquarters of the Tennessee-American Water Company, opened at a cost of $500,000 in 1978.

Looking south from the corner of Broad and Eleventh Streets, the large structure at the south end of the Georgia Tract is occupied by the **Tennessee Valley Authority**. ❻ For a number of years, the expanding operations of the TVA had required the agency to occupy offices in numerous locations throughout the downtown area; in 1979, however, it was announced that operations would be consolidated into this single $140 million complex, the largest single development in the history of the downtown area. Covering 2 city blocks, the separate portions of the 1.149 million square-foot complex are connected by a walkway over South Broad Street. Planned as a solar heating model for the nation, the building is topped with a number of black solar panels, which required the 5-story building to have a sixth story on the north side to accommodate the equipment needed for the system. The immense 5-building project was completed in 1985, at a final cost of nearly $200 million. Beyond the TVA complex are two additional streets which were originally named for early investors in the East Tennessee Iron Manufacturing Company: Cravens Street (now Twelfth Street) was named for ironmaster Robert Cravens; and Hooke Street (now Thirteenth Street) was named for Judge Robert Hooke. Like South Chestnut Street, these streets were subsequently renamed in 1912.

From this corner, head north along Broad Street. Immediately north of the TVA complex, in the block bounded by Market, Broad, Tenth, and Eleventh Streets, is the **Civic Forum,** ❼

and Eleventh Streets, is the **Civic Forum,** ❼ which was constructed in 1979 to house a variety of civic and governmental enterprises.

On your left is the **Chattanooga-Hamilton County Bicentennial Library** (1976), located in the block bounded by Broad, Carter, Tenth, and Eleventh Streets. ❽ Designed by Alan Derthick and Carroll Henley, this modern 5-story building is composed of precast, warm-tone concrete panels and houses the collections maintained by the library since it was founded in 1900. In April 2001, the original fountain at the main entrance to the library was replaced with a new fountain designed by

sculptor Jim Collins to represent stacks of opened books. The resulting work, entitled "Volumes," is constructed of 12-gauge stainless steel and sits amidst 5 fountains. The sculpture includes "three books standing on end, with one falling onto an open book that it resting on four horizontally stacked books," as well as two 4-foot stainless steel compact discs, which reflect "the importance of technology in the modern library."

The library is constructed on the site of the **Car Sheds**, an early railroad facility erected in 1857-1858 by Western & Atlantic Chief Engineer Eugene LeHardy pursuant to an agreement between the W&A, Nashville & Chattanooga, and Memphis & Charleston Railroads to construct a depot for the joint use of the railroads. Designed to resemble the W&A depot on State Square in Atlanta, the 100-by-304 foot sheds (pictured above and on page 107) were composed of limestone from a Chickamauga quarry and Chattanooga brick, with large stone pillars along the bases. Two 24 1/2-foot arches at each end of the shed allowed 4 tracks to enter the building, with 2 tracks passing through each entryway. The shed was set back 100 feet from Ninth Street, thus allowing locomotives to pass completely through the building in order to prevent smoke from filling the station. The roof was supported by single bowstring spans and covered in tin, with a 6-by-16 foot ventilator

along the center spine of the roof. Due to limited space, waiting rooms were first located at the nearby Burns House. During the Civil War, the car sheds were utilized as a Confederate hospital facility after the battles of Stone's River, Chickamauga, and Chattanooga; wounded and dying soldiers were placed on sheets from the nearby Crutchfield House, which were stuffed with leaves to make crude mattresses. In 1882, the car sheds were updated with the addition of the Union Depot to the front of the building. At some point prior to 1911, the original roof was replaced with an asphalt covering after high winds blew it off, and 285 feet of the shed was burned by fire, after which it was rebuilt to be 424 feet long. In 1926, after Broad Street was extended past the structure, the rear 300 feet (all but 124 feet) were removed, and three 1,000-foot-long butterfly sheds were substituted at the rear of the building. The car sheds fell into disuse in the latter half of the twentieth century, and the *Georgian* locomotive eventually paid its last visit to the facility in 1971. The property was then sold to the Stone Fort Land Company in 1972, and the structure was torn down by the company to create space for commercial construction in the former Georgia Tract.

Head north to MLK Jr. Blvd. and turn right, proceeding to the southwest corner of MLK Jr. Blvd. and Market Street. ❾ The vacant block at this location, bounded by Market, Broad, Ninth, and Tenth Streets, was originally the site of a number of brick business buildings, most of which were affiliated with the railroads and some of which were built prior to the Civil War. In June 1978, the city of Chattanooga acquired the block from the State of Georgia for $460,000. A subsequent plan (1983) by banker Jake Butcher to construct a 28-story tower for his United American Bank collapsed along with the bank itself, and since that time the block has been colloquially referred to as the "Butcher Block." A subsequent proposal by a South Carolina developer to build a $28 million office tower (1988) and a recent proposal by a local real estate development firm to erect an 11-story, 142,000 square-foot office building (1998) at the spot were likewise unsuccessful. In 2000, however, it was announced that the city of Chattanooga and the Electric Power Board would trade properties – the EPB building at Sixth and Market Streets for the Butcher Block. To that end, the EPB is currently in the process of constructing a 120,000 square foot, 8-story structure and parking garage, designed by local architects Franklin & Associates, on this spot which has eluded development for so many years.

At the southeast corner of this block was one of the most distinctive buildings in early downtown Chattanooga, the **Western & Atlantic Passenger Terminal** (pictured below and on page 107). This early building (1851) was a 2-story combination passenger and freight depot; the first story had a passenger area and offices for freight operations, while the small, square (40-by-40 foot) upper floor held additional offices for the passenger depot. To the rear of the structure was a crude transfer shed (14-by-700 feet long) built of planks and covered with shingles. During the Civil War, the structure was used as a bunkhouse by Confederate forces,

and both armies utilized the facility as a commissary. Though it survived the Civil War, after the Union Depot was opened in 1882 the terminal was no longer needed as a rail facility. One section was used as a Postal Telegraph office until 1902, and the remainder was rented out to merchants, who established businesses along Market Street within the building. Subsequently, the 1-story portion of the building along Market Street (40-by-235 feet long) was dismantled and replaced with a series of 12 one-story commercial buildings, while the remaining section of the terminal operated for years as the "Chattanooga Steak House." Despite the historic status of the building, however, the widening of Ninth Street eventually spelled the end for the W&A Terminal, which was completely leveled by 1957.

Near this spot were the antebellum offices of **A.S. Johnston & Company**. Though Tennessee was a slaveholding state prior to the Civil War and a number of local residents did possess slaves during the antebellum period, on the whole east Tennessee was not a large plantation area. Only one private "dealer in Negroes" appears to have operated in the town – A.S. Johnston & Company, which was located at this spot.

At Market Street, turn right and proceed south toward Tenth Street. On the right (west) side of Market Street is the former site of the **Rogers**

Theater, ❿ a $310,000 first-run movie theater opened in 1950 in one of the buildings which replaced the southern portion of the W&A Terminal. This theater (pictured below and on page 107) was named for Emmett R. Rogers, a local resident who, during his involvement in the movie business, "introduced into the South the first poster work in theater lobbies; the first pretentious

lobby displays and theater fronts; the first uniformed ushers; and made the first use of pipe organs, pit orchestras and stage presentations keyed to the then silent pictures." Upon the opening of the theater, Rogers received congratulatory letters from, among others, Ginger Rogers, Alan Ladd, Cecil B. Demille, Charlton Heston, Bing Crosby, and Bob Hope. Featuring a 35-by-71/2 foot marquee and a circular glass box office, this theater was modern in design and technology. To increase ticket sales, costumed characters greeted patrons, and movie stars such as Audie Murphy and Keenan Wynn personally promoted their films at the theater. The building was subsequently renovated in 1969, at which time the number of seats was reduced from 1,257 to 814. That year, a brief controversy erupted when the American Legion protested the showing of the movie "Che,"

depicting the life of the Cuban revolutionary figure, at the theater. Referred to as the "Pride of Chattanooga" the Rogers Theater greeted moviegoers for 25 years, until closing in 1976. The distinctive theater marquee was removed in 1980, and the building was destroyed soon thereafter.

To return to the beginning of the tour of the Georgia Tract, return to MLK Jr. Blvd., turn left, and proceed to Broad Street.

Golden Gateway

One of the most significant changes to the urban fabric of downtown Chattanooga was the Golden Gateway Redevelopment Project of the 1950s and 1960s. Implemented in conjunction with the construction of the freeway on the west side of downtown, the "Golden Gateway" project was intended to create new commercial growth, attract industry, and replace deteriorating residential areas with new, progressive developments. Covering 403 acres on the western fringe of the downtown area, the project was aided by a $20 million federal grant (1958) which made possible the massive changes envisioned by city planners.

Epitomized by the leveling of Cameron Hill and the construction of the freeway and Olgiati Bridge, the Golden Gateway project completely altered the west side of downtown Chattanooga. All in all, the project resulted in the destruction of 1,170 structures and the removal of 1,400 families from the area. Critics of the project cited the destruction of several historic buildings in the area, and the fact that a majority of the residents displaced by this development were African-American led many to refer to the project as "Negro removal" rather than urban renewal.

The long-term success of the Golden Gateway project is debatable. Despite this development, the population in the central business district continued to decrease in ensuing years, from 8.9 persons per acre in 1960 to 4.3 by 1980, and as shoppers were drawn to new suburban developments, downtown Chattanooga saw many businesses leave the downtown core during this period. With the 1990s redevelopment of the riverfront and the Southside area, however, the possibility for renewed growth in the city center and, consequently, the Golden Gateway area has become a topic of renewed discussion and planning.

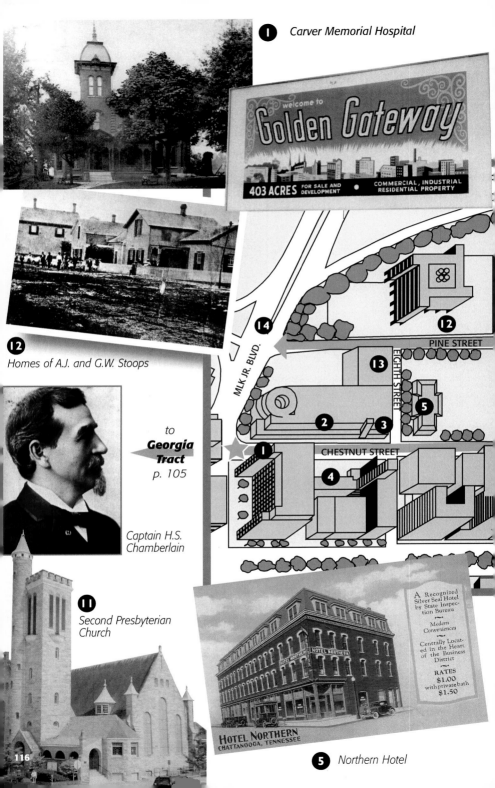

1 Carver Memorial Hospital

welcome to **Golden Gateway**
403 ACRES FOR SALE AND DEVELOPMENT • COMMERCIAL, INDUSTRIAL RESIDENTIAL PROPERTY

12 Homes of A.J. and G.W. Stoops

Captain H.S. Chamberlain

to **Georgia Tract** p. 105

to **Georgia Tract** p. 105

MLK JR. BLVD.

PINE STREET

EIGHTH STREET

CHESTNUT STREET

14
12
13
5
2
3
1
4

11 Second Presbyterian Church

HOTEL NORTHERN
CHATTANOOGA, TENNESSEE

A Recognized Silver Seal Hotel by State Inspection Bureau

Modern Conveniences

Centrally Located in the Heart of the Business District

RATES $1.00 with private bath $1.50

5 Northern Hotel

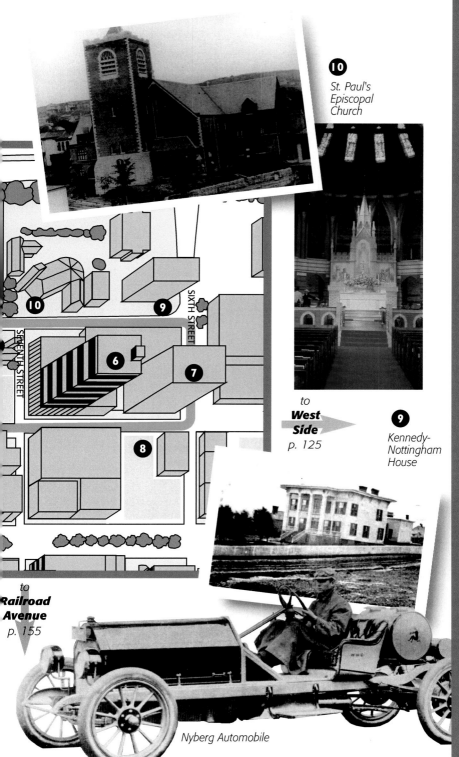

10
St. Paul's
Episcopal
Church

to
**West
Side**
p. 125

9
Kennedy-
Nottingham
House

to
**Railroad
Avenue**
p. 155

Nyberg Automobile

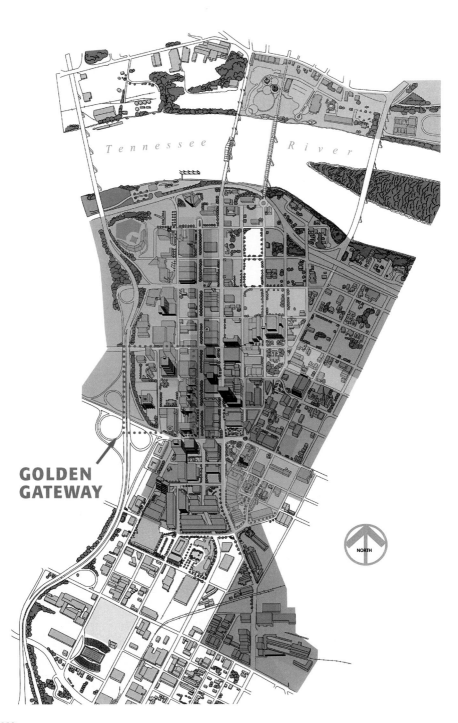

T e n n e s s e e   R i v e r

**GOLDEN
GATEWAY**

NORTH

The tour of the Golden Gateway begins at the northwest corner of Chestnut Street and MLK Jr. Blvd. ❶ To the west of this spot is a freeway interchange constructed in the 1960s at Ninth Street (MLK Jr. Blvd.). Immediately west of this freeway overpass is a historic plaque marking the site of the now-demolished **Carver**

Memorial Hospital, also known as the Carlile-Divine Residence. A former jeweler, Philadelphia native Thomas J. Carlile came to Chattanooga during the Civil War to assume the position of Provost Marshal for the Union army. Later becoming the purchasing agent and secretary for the Stanton railroad, Carlile constructed a 2-story Victorian mansion on an entire block at West Ninth Street, at the foot of Cameron Hill. This home (above) was brick trimmed with stone, with a small side porch and a large capped tower. Carlile later became mayor of the city of Chattanooga, a post which he occupied at the time of the 1878 Yellow Fever epidemic; despite retreating to the Natural Bridge Hotel on Lookout Mountain at the beginning of the epidemic, Carlile died of the fever on October 29, 1878, after spending time in the city to address relief efforts. He lies buried in the Citizens' Cemetery, along with numerous other victims of the epidemic.

The 2-story house was then occupied by John L. Divine, a former apprentice of tailor (and future United States President) Andrew Johnson in Greeneville, Tennessee. During an overnight stay in Ross's Landing in January 1838, Divine's wallet was stolen; deferring his journey long enough to earn money to pay for his prior night's lodging, he eventually decided to stay in the town, where he became a successful merchant. Divine served as a local guide for the Confederate army during the Civil War; though he was imprisoned in the local military prison following the battle, his friend William Crutchfield secured his release from General George H. Thomas. He subsequently moved to this home after Carlile died of Yellow Fever in 1878. Following Divine's death in 1892, the

home was temporarily used as the West-Ellis Sanitarium, affording 16 rooms for patients. In 1947, the house became the Carver Memorial Hospital, the first municipal hospital in the South completely staffed with African-American doctors and nurses. The building continued to be used as a hospital until 1962, when the house was torn down as part of the Golden Gateway urban renewal project, and today no trace exists of this early Chattanooga residence.

Return to the southwest corner of Chestnut Street and MLK Jr. Blvd. The advent of the automobile, as demonstrated by the construction of the freeway in this area, had a dramatic effect on downtown Chattanooga in the latter half of the twentieth century. One fine example of the influence of the automobile is the Citi Park parking garage, erected at this site in 1969. ❷ This block previously housed the **Chamberlain Building** (823-829 Chestnut Street), a 3-story building erected by Captain H.S. Chamberlain (below) in 1902. After serving as the post quartermaster for the Union army in Knoxville, Tennessee, during the Civil War, Chamberlain moved to Chattanooga in 1871 to operate the Roane Iron Works. His industrial expertise also fueled his involvement with the Citico Furnace Company and the Southern Iron Company,

experiences which led him to be named in an 1880s *New York Tribune* list of the "seven millionaires of Chattanooga." The building, which was designed by George Q. Adams and Charles E. Bearden, was composed of buff-colored brick adorned with ornately carved stonework. Referred to in 1902 as "the first 'good' office building here," this structure featured an innovative interior design which included a large open-court lobby 3 stories high topped with a skylight, so that offices within the building overlooked the well-lit lobby area. In 1954, it was announced that this building would be razed and replaced with a 2-story parking deck, which now sits on the site.

To the north, the property at the southwest corner of Chestnut and Eighth Streets, ❸ which was originally the site of the Chickamauga Stable Company, was later occupied by a 2-story brick building which became the **W.H.**

Burk auto garage and dealership operated by W.H. Burk after the turn of the century. Said to be the first Chattanoogan to own an automobile, Burk was "regarded as an expert when it comes to high-grade, complicated repairing." In 1934, the garage (below) was labeled "unserviceable," and razed, and today the site is also occupied by the Citi Park structure.

Though it did not occupy this site, between 1911 and 1912 Chattanooga was the site of one auto manufacturer – the **"Nyberg,"** named for Swedish native Henry Nyberg, who began his auto manufacturing company with financial backing from local entrepreneur Charles E. James. The Nyberg was produced in the Ridgedale area of Chattanooga; only a few hundred of the cars, including the $2,400 "Dixie Special" pictured above and on page 117, were produced before the company went bankrupt. Nevertheless, this business is an important relic of Chattanooga's early involvement in the automobile industry at the turn of the century.

Across the street from the Citi Park is the Read House hotel. The pink-toned building to the left (north) of the hotel is the **Read House Motor Inn**, now referred to as the "Read House Manor." ❹ Around the turn of the century, the quarter-block site adjoining the Read House was the site of one of the many local projects started by the entrepreneurial Stoops brothers: at this spot, a roller coaster was constructed, featuring ordinary wooden benches on which patrons sat "rather sidewise" clutching the backs of their seats as the ride, propelled by its own momentum, teetered and tottered over the street below. Despite its initial success, several injuries suffered by riders forced the roller coaster to close after 2 seasons. Thereafter, in 1917 this spot was the site of a "Turkish bath"

which likely served patrons of the Read House next door. Anticipating an increase in interstate travel and tourism, in 1962 an older section of the Read House hotel was torn down and replaced with this $1.5 million, 3-story "Read House Motor Inn," featuring modern rooms, indoor parking, and a swimming pool. A brochure from the late 1970s indicates the continued emphasis on this location as a convenient spot for tourists stopping over in Chattanooga, noting that the hotel is "only one block from [the] Interstate."

North of the Read House Motor Inn, at the southeast corner of Chestnut and Eighth Streets, is the AmSouth Bank Building, which is discussed in greater detail in the Railroad Avenue section on page 165.

From this point, cross Eighth Street. At the northwest corner of Eighth and Chestnut Streets ❺ is the former site of the **Northern Hotel** (below). Erected in 1886 by A.J. Hulse, the Northern was the second-largest hotel in Chattanooga (after the Read House) until the construction of the Hotel Patten. Advertised as "a recognized Silver Seal hotel by State Inspection Bureau," the hotel charged $1 per day without bath, and $1.50 with private bath. In 1908, a fourth floor was added to the hotel, which included several first-floor offices and 64 guest rooms. In 1957, the hotel was purchased by the Stone Fort Land Company for $120,000;

HOTEL NORTHERN
CHATTANOOGA, TENNESSEE

one of the first casualties of the West Side redevelopment program, in 1958 the hotel was torn down by the Stone Fort Land Company, which announced its intention to construct a multistory office building at the site, until which time a parking lot would be placed at that location.

Currently on a portion of the site of the Northern Hotel is the **Mountain City Club** (729 Chestnut Street). Organized in 1889 after merging with the Cobweb Club (1887), the Mountain City Club had over 200 members by 1890. After occupying several temporary locations, around 1900 the membership purchased

a lot on Chestnut Street between Seventh and Eighth Streets and constructed a 2-story colonial building (above) with a large columned front porch, plate-glass windows, stone foundation, and stone entrance steps. In 1974, the current 2-story, 24,000 square-foot Williamsburg-styled clubhouse was built immediately south of the former building, which was then dismantled and removed.

From this spot, continue to Seventh Street. On your left, at the northwest corner of Chestnut and Seventh Streets, is the **Republic Center**, ❻ also referred to as the Bank of America Building (and originally the Commerce Union Bank, or "CUB," building). This 21-story, 270,000-square foot building was built by Chattanoogan Franklin Haney in 1975 and is currently occupied by private offices, as well as the private Walden Club.

Continue down Chestnut Street. On your left, at the southwest corner of Chestnut and Sixth Streets, ❼ is the **Chestnut Tower** (605 Chestnut Street), a 17-story building which was completed in 1978. Originally planned as a possible site for TVA to consolidate its local offices, this tower was constructed in an innovative fashion: the building was completed in several stages, allowing it to be partially occupied (and therefore generate income) before it was totally completed. Owner Franklin Haney also built a 300-car parking garage across the street. Initially, Haney intended to connect the building to the Commerce Union Bank building next door by elevated walkways, though this portion of the project was not completed. In 1994, the green trim on the building's exterior was added as part of a renovation intended to add "pizzazz" to the building, which continues to be utilized as private office space at the present time.

Across Chestnut Street, at the southeast corner of Chestnut and Sixth Streets, ❽ is an historic marker commemorating the life of G.W. Franklin, an early African-American businessman who came to Chattanooga from Quitman,

Georgia, and eventually operated a blacksmith shop, wood-and-coal yard, hack (taxi) line, and undertaking business at this location (610 Chestnut Street). Franklin advertised his business with the claim that "I own and operate the only colored undertaking and embalming establishment in Chattanooga, Tennessee. With an elegant hearse, team, etc., can furnish coffins, caskets, and robes of all grades and prices." Franklin served as an honorary pallbearer for early African-American activist Booker T. Washington, and he also conducted the funeral of Mrs. Washington, both of whom were friends of the Franklin family.

At Sixth Street, turn left and proceed to the southwest corner of Sixth and Pine Streets. ❾ At this corner is the site of the **Kennedy-Nottingham House**, one of the oldest and finest antebellum homes in Chattanooga. Built in the 1840s by W.F. Ragsdale, a merchant, Confederate soldier, and mayor of Chattanooga (1854), the house featured Ionic columns, a front door of cathedral stained glass, and carved walnut mantels with elaborate tiling (one room in particular depicted scenes from Shakespeare's plays). The home, (pictured below and on page 117) which was reached by a stately approach lined with cedar trees, was

sold to Dr. William E. Kennedy in 1859 for $5,000 and then underwent a rapid succession of owners, including J.C. Warner (for whom Warner Park in Nashville is named), former Union general and Signal Mountain promoter Timothy R. Stanley, and 4 Chattanooga mayors. During the Civil War, the home was the headquarters of Major Generals D.H. Hill (C.S.A.), J.M. Palmer (U.S.A.), and James B. McPherson. McPherson's remains were returned to the home to lay in state for 2 days after his death at the battle of Peachtree Creek, Georgia, on July 22, 1864; an immense American flag was hung across the front of the house at that time.

In 1866, the home was purchased by W.P Rathburn for $5,000. The mansion later survived a fire in 1882 which almost required its destruction, and it was subsequently inherited by Mrs. C.C. Nottingham, the daughter of Mr./Mrs. Rathburn (and great-granddaughter of Revolutionary War General Joseph Whiton, whose sword hung over the library mantel). Although the Nottinghams subsequently drafted a joint will devising the property "to the City of Chattanooga for public park purposes," the Depression caused the loss of the family fortune; the house passed into receivership in 1938, and the personal items within the home were auctioned off in 1940. Although the West Side Improvement League and Cameron Hill Garden Club petitioned for preservation of the home as part of a public park and businessman E.Y. Chapin offered $10,000 to purchase the house and do the same, these plans were rejected, and the city sold the house to the Cosmopolitan Funeral Home for $80,000. In 1959, the property was sold for $110,000 to the Chattanooga Housing Authority as part of the West Side Redevelopment Project; despite vigorous protests, the home (one of 4 remaining antebellum houses in the city at the time) was razed, and the Saint Barnabus Apartments, a senior living center, were built on the site.

From this spot, head south along Pine Street. On the right, where Seventh Street dead-ends into Pine Street, ⑩ is the **St. Paul's Episcopal Church** (305 West Seventh Street). The first service of the Episcopal Church in Chattanooga was held in 1852, on the second floor of a warehouse at Market and Fourth Streets. When the city was incorporated in 1851, the authority of the city commissioners to grant property for church lots expired, and as such the church arrived too late to receive a granted lot similar to that received by other churches. In 1853, the 10-family congregation selected the name "St. Paul's Episcopal Church" at the home of James A. Whiteside, and afterwards Whiteside donated a lot on Chestnut Street for construction of a small frame church building. Several years later,

a new brick church with a belfry and white picket fence was built on Chestnut Street between Eighth and Ninth Streets. The church was aided during the Civil War by the efforts of Dr. C.T. Quintard, who raised money to improve the furnishings of the church. Though the building was damaged during the war after being used as a hospital and warehouse, the congregation received a $3,640 payment from the federal government to refurbish the building, and full services resumed on Easter 1867.

The church lot was sold in 1885 for $20,000, and the current Romanesque Revival church building, designed by New York architect W. Halsey Wood, was erected at this spot in 1888 for less than $50,000. In designing this building, (pictured left and on page 117) which is modeled after a typical English village parish church, Wood was inspired by an abbey he had seen on his native Isle of Mann. Rising above the asymmetrical structure is a distinctive 4-story brick tower. The current colonnade at the front of the building, moreover, was erected in 1968. The interior has been mostly unchanged since 1888; the ornate Italian altar was donated by Mrs. William Yonge and Miss Catherine Humphreys, and the current pipe organ was installed in 1950. Located in the St. George's Chapel in a niche along the east wall of the church, moreover, is the original carved wooden altar which graced the first St. Paul's Church building. The building was added to the National Register of Historic Places in 1978.

Across the street, at the southeast corner of Pine and Seventh Streets, ⑪ is the **Second Presbyterian Church** (700 Pine Street). Founded on September 3, 1871, and led by Rev. W.J. Trimble, a former Union army chaplain, the church was initially housed at several temporary  locations. The current Victorian Romanesque building, designed by R.H. Hunt, was erected in 1891 (it is the oldest remaining Hunt design located in Chattanooga). The beautiful sandstone building (pictured above and on page 116), which features a tall belfry and adjoining tower, is listed on the National Register of

Historic Places (1980). Immediately south of the stone church building is the 2-story brick-and-limestone Founders Memorial Hall, which also continues to serve the congregation.

From this spot, proceed south to the southwest corner of Pine and Eighth Streets, **⑫** the site of the **Blue Cross-Blue Shield of Tennessee Building**. Previously, this block was occupied by several frame houses erected by the Stoops Brothers, Andrew Jackson Stoops and George Washington Stoops, who arrived in Chattanooga in 1870 to supply the eating houses associated with the J.C. Stanton railroad venture. The Stoops brothers were born in Pittsburgh and spent time in Missouri and Ohio before coming to Chattanooga; during the Civil War, A.J. Stoops was a boat builder and operated a federal gunboat on the Mississippi River, while G.W. Stoops was known locally for having shaken hands with Lincoln on the way to the 1860 presidential inauguration. After the failure of the Stanton railroad, the Stoops brothers

operated a restaurant in the Western & Atlantic passenger terminal at Ninth and Market Streets. They then moved their business to the new Union Depot in the 1880s, also operating a series of interesting ventures in town – including a skating rink, roller coaster, the James Hall theater, and the Florentine Hotel. Around 1875, the Stoops brothers erected three 1-story frame houses on this block (above), where they lived for a number of years.

Although these early houses were long gone by that time, in 1967 the Tennessee Hospital Service placed a $317,000 bid on this block in anticipation of future expansion of the Chattanooga office of Blue Cross/Blue Shield of Tennessee, which had occupied 4 different locations since its arrival in Chattanooga in 1945. Originally planned to be built of "either anodized aluminum and marble or precast concrete with nonglare black glass," the Blue Cross-Blue Shield Building (1971) is a 10-story, 200,000 square-foot structure with a reflective glass exterior, an open, 10-story lobby, 4 glass "bubble" elevators, and a 2-story underground parking garage. Designed by noted Atlanta architect John Portman, the building was selected as one of a handful of "Offices of the Year" in 1972. The building continues to house the local headquarters for BlueCross/Blue Shield of Tennessee today.

Across Pine Street previously sat another early log cabin erected by a pioneer resident of Chattanooga. **⑬** Known as "**The Cabins**," this 2-story log cabin was erected in the early days of the Ross's Landing settlement by Thomas Crutchfield, Sr., near the Crutchfield House hotel. The "dogtrot" home had rooms on either side of a middle hallway, and a kitchen and dining room were located to the rear of the structure. Originally, several outlying slave cabins also stood in this area, thus giving the property its name. Continuing downtown development claimed last section of this residence in 1923, at which time the cabins were replaced by a Standard Oil filling station. Today, this site is part of the Citi Park structure.

Continue south to the corner of Pine Street and MLK Jr. Blvd. **⑭** In the 1970s, a Flag Plaza was proposed at this corner as part of a planned development to emphasize the "market center" of the downtown area. This plaza was intended to "provide a positive sense of arrival to those entering Downtown from the Interstate via Ninth Street" at this location. The plaza continues to serve this purpose today, welcoming visitors to downtown Chattanooga.

To return to the start of the tour, turn left on MLK Jr. Blvd. and proceed to the corner of that street and Chestnut Street.

The western boundary of the original town limits of Chattanooga was Cameron Hill, a 370-foot outcropping which is one of the more distinctive natural features in the downtown area. The hill is named for artist James Cameron, who was given this hillside property in the 1850s in exchange for several paintings he crafted for James A. Whiteside, who had originally purchased the land following the Cherokee Removal. Following the Civil War, Cameron Hill was developed for residential housing, and by the turn of the century the West Side was a crowded residential area.

By the 1950s and 1960s, suburban flight led to the creation of the "Golden Gateway," a project designed to create new residential, commercial, and industrial opportunities on the West Side, which was a largely African-American neighborhood with many substandard houses and poor areas. As part of this plan, mayor Rudy Olgiati called for the construction of a freeway across the west side of downtown and a new bridge connecting downtown to the north side of the Tennessee River. It was determined that a great amount of fill dirt would be needed for the construction of this bridge, and 160 feet were removed from the top of Cameron Hill in 1962. Several stately homes on the hill were dismantled, and all traces of those early neighborhoods were eradicated. A subsequent city directory listed the addresses in the former East Terrace neighborhood as "all torn down." Today, however, the West Side is witnessing renewed development, including new museums, theaters, and hotels which opened in the wake of the Tennessee Aquarium in 1992.

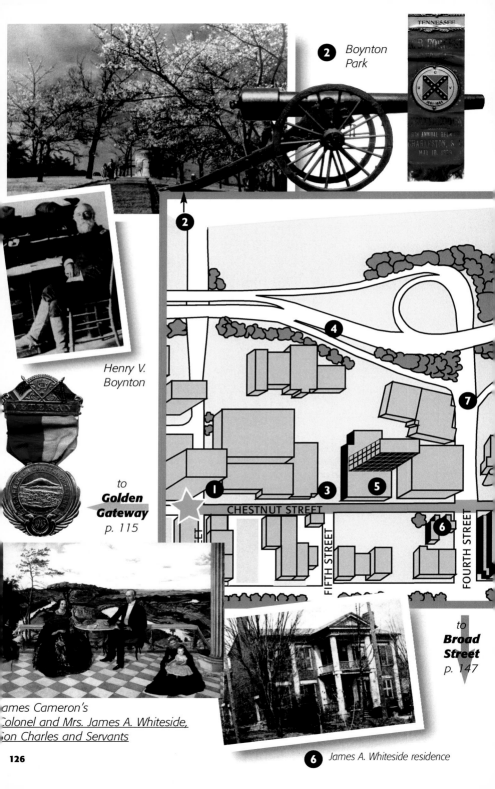

② Boynton
Park

TENNESSEE

Henry V.
Boynton

VETERAN

to
**Golden
Gateway**
p. 115

2

4

7

1

3

5

CHESTNUT STREET

FIFTH STREET

6

FOURTH STREET

to
**Broad
Street**
p. 147

James Cameron's
*Colonel and Mrs. James A. Whiteside,
Son Charles and Servants*

⑥ James A. Whiteside residence

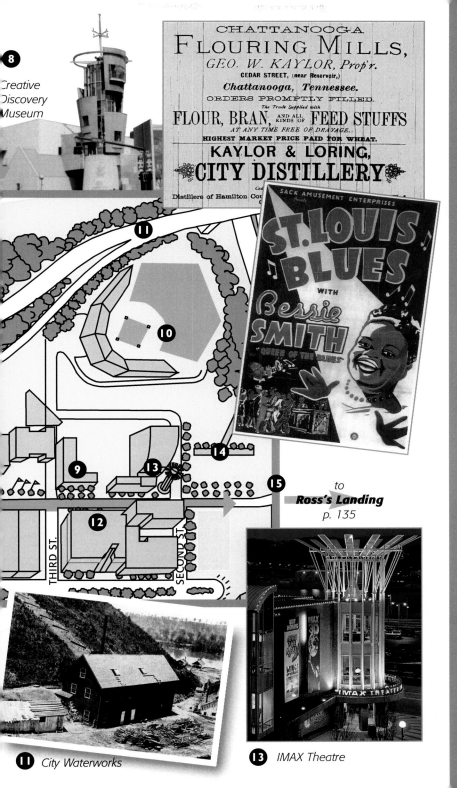

8 Creative Discovery Museum

CHATTANOOGA
FLOURING MILLS,
GEO. W. KAYLOR, Prop'r.
CEDAR STREET, (near Reservoir,)
Chattanooga, Tennessee.
ORDERS PROMPTLY FILLED.
The Trade Supplied with
FLOUR, BRAN, AND ALL KINDS OF FEED STUFFS
AT ANY TIME FREE OF DRAYAGE.
HIGHEST MARKET PRICE PAID FOR WHEAT.
KAYLOR & LORING,
CITY DISTILLERY
Distillers of Hamilton Cou

SACK AMUSEMENT ENTERPRISES
Presents
ST. LOUIS BLUES
WITH
Bessie SMITH
"QUEEN OF THE BLUES"

to
Ross's Landing
p. 135

THIRD ST.

SECOND ST.

11 City Waterworks

13 IMAX Theatre

127

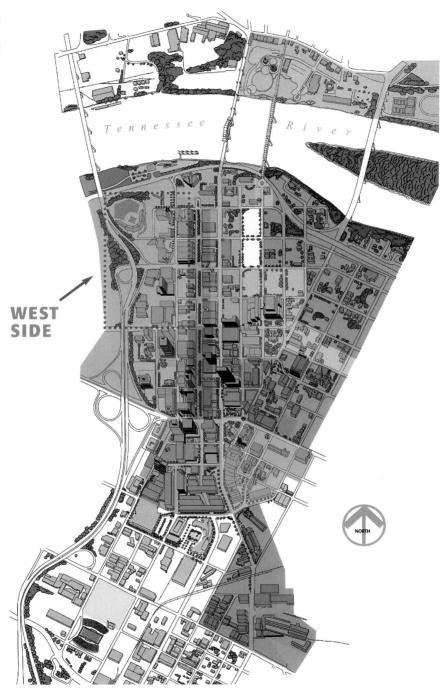

WEST
SIDE

Tennessee River

NORTH

The tour of the West Side begins at the northwest corner of Chestnut and Sixth Streets, ❶ at the **IBM Building** (535 Chestnut Street), which was completed in 1969 by local developer Franklin Haney. Haney was largely responsible for developing a number of buildings in this vicinity in the years following the Golden Gateway urban renewal project, many designed for occupation by the Tennessee Valley Authority and large businesses locating in Chattanooga.

If you wish to visit **Cameron Hill,** ❷ turn left on Sixth Street; approximately one-quarter mile to the west, you will see a sign on your right marking the road leading to the top of the hill. At one time, Cameron Hill was a 370-foot tall hill which stood above the Tennessee River on the west side of downtown Chattanooga. Following the Cherokee Removal, most of the hill was purchased by early Chattanooga developer James A. Whiteside. The hill is named for James Cameron, a painter who was given a portion of the outcropping by Whiteside in exchange for a painting which Cameron made of the Whiteside family; this painting, which today hangs in the Hunter Museum of American Art, is reproduced on page 126. Although Cameron left town during the Civil War, his wife remained for a period of time, eventually receiving $30,000 in payment for

timber cut on the property by the federal army during its occupation of the city. Cameron Hill was occupied by both armies at various times during the Civil War, as it was a prime spot for the placement of artillery batteries. The hill was also used as a relay station for signals received from Signal Point, and the first shell fired into

Chattanooga in 1862 is said to have landed without exploding in the mud there; this shell was kept in the collection of a local historical museum for a number of years after the war.

Along the top of Cameron Hill sat the western defensive lines of the Union army, erected during the occupation of the city in 1864-1865. Just south of Sixth Street, on the top of the hill, was Fort Mihalotzy, named for Colonel Geza Mihalotzy (Twenty-Fourth Regiment of Illinois Volunteers), killed near Dalton, Georgia, on February 25, 1864. This fort was manned with 4 siege guns and 4 light cannon. Near that spot, on the western edge of the hill, was Redoubt Coolidge, named in honor of Major Sidney Coolidge (Sixteenth U.S. Infantry), who was killed at the battle of Chickamauga on September 19, 1863. At the crest of the hill, moreover, was Fort Cameron, a battery of 100-pound Parrot guns which was named for artist

James Cameron.

Following the Civil War, Ms. Cameron sold off her land in small parcels over a period of time. The Chattanooga Land Company was subsequently organized to create a residential neighborhood atop the hill; this enterprise was disbanded in 1888, although 3 lots were set aside for any company which would establish a park, hotels, and incline on the hill. In fact, in 1889 a new incline was constructed to the top of Cameron Hill, leading to a pagoda with dining hall, ball room, and observatory at the crest of the hill (as can be seen in the picture to the left). Frank P. Marquet then announced his intention to build a concert hall and beer parlor on the hill; although this enterprise was abandoned by May 1890, concerts did begin on land leased from the city on the top of the hill.

Financial problems plagued the incline running up Fourth Street to the summit of the hill, which was torn away in 1894 and replaced by electric trolleys until paved roads were lain to the top of the hill. The pavilion at the top, which had been converted into a mini-theater in 1891, also fell into disuse; after a plan to move the Chattanooga Cyclorama (one of several similar Civil War attractions in operation across the country) to this location fell through, the pago-

frame, an unique plan to construct a suspension bridge with trams carrying passengers across the river to Stringer's Ridge (1893) from the hill fell through. Despite these disappointments, however, Cameron Hill soon became a fashionable residential area, particularly along the east terrace of the hill, which looked out over the downtown skyline, and numerous fine residences dotted the lower slopes of the hill by the late 1890s.

As the various ribbons and medals on page 126 indicate, Cameron Hill was also the site of important military reunions in the years following the Civil War. The first meeting of the Society of the Army of the Cumberland south of the Mason-Dixon line occurred in Chattanooga in September 1881. The day before the meeting was to commence, President James A. Garfield, himself a Union veteran who had been stationed in Chattanooga during the Civil War, was assassinated; a requiem service was then held at the crest of Cameron Hill for the fallen president. Cameron Hill was also the site of the first general Confederate Reunion ever held in the country, on July 3-5, 1890; General John B. Gordon was the commander of the United Confederate Veterans at the meeting, and, in a gesture demonstrating the reconciliatory nature of the gathering, the opening address was made by a former Union soldier, Mayor John A. Hart.

In 1895, the federal government created the Chickamauga & Chattanooga National Military Park, a project which was driven largely by the efforts of the founder and president of the Chickamauga Park Commission, **Gen. Henry V. Boynton** (pictured above and on page 126), who had served as a lieutenant-colonel with the 35th Ohio Infantry during the Civil War, was wounded at the battle of Missionary Ridge, and received the Congressional Medal for Gallantry. In 1888, Boynton began publishing letters urging that the Chattanooga battlefields be preserved and marked. For his efforts, Boynton was given a 225-piece chest of sterling silver by the Chattanooga community during the grand opening of the park, at ceremonies officiated by

Vice-President Adlai E. Stevenson. While Cameron Hill was not originally included as part of the military park, local citizens hearing of Boynton's death in 1905, decided to erect a park in his honor at that location; to that end, the city purchased the northern summit of the hill from the Southern Land & Loan Company, erected a pavilion at the highest point of the hill (below), and requested that the federal government provide cannon to adorn the park where it overlooked the city of Chattanooga.

As a result of the urban renewal initiative of the 1950s and 1960s, approximately 160 feet was shaved off of the top of Cameron Hill. This plan required the demolition of the bandstand erected at the top of the hill, which had been used as a community gathering place and the site for Liberty Bond sales during war times. The cannon and plaques placed throughout Boynton Park were removed in 1959. In 1967, plans began to surface for the creation of a new, smaller version of Boynton Park at the top of the hill; this park, with low brick walls reminiscent of the angled ramparts of a Civil War fort, overlooks the city of Chattanooga, and the cannon and plaques which were removed from the original park have been returned to this location.

As referenced above, the "Golden Gateway" project required the top of Cameron Hill to be shaved off and used for fill dirt in the construction of the Olgiati Bridge across the Tennessee River. This plan received strong support from Mayor Peter R. "Rudy" Oligiati, who referred to the project as a "surgeon's blade, removing a malignancy that was past responding to other treatment." The $15 million project, however, was opposed by several groups, including U.S. Grant III, local historian Zella Armstrong, and a group entitled "Let's Keep Tennessee Green." Alternative plans, including creating a national park at the site and bringing in engineers to propose alternate ideas, were not adopted, though in 1957 Mayor Olgiati promised that the site would not be completely leveled, as only a "bit" would be taken from the top for the freeway project. Additional protests that the urban renewal plan would require the destruction of a number of fine mansions upon Cameron Hill were disregarded due to the scattered nature of the "rehabitable" homes in the area, as well as the steep grades and poor streets throughout

the Cameron Hill neighborhood. A lawsuit filed by a group of Chattanooga citizens was then dismissed by the Tennessee Supreme Court, on grounds that "[c]itizens cannot be allowed to interfere with the legally exercised discretions of public officials, no matter how violently they may disagree." Although Mayor Olgiati subsequently changed his opinion about this plan due to political pressures, in July 1962 the top of the hill was removed, and the fine homes along the top of the hill were razed. In 1966, the creation of new "garden apartment" development was proposed as a possibility for the newly-shortened hill; this plan came to fruition with the Cameron Hill Apartments in the early 1970s, which remain at this historic site today.

Returning to Chestnut Street, to the north of the IBM Building (at the southwest corner of Chestnut and Fifth Streets), ❸ is a parking lot which was formerly the site of another Golden Gateway project, a 6,360 square-foot stucco **Greyhound Bus Station** constructed at this location, which was torn down in the 1990s.

From this spot, continue north on Chestnut Street. West of Fifth Street, approximately where the freeway sits today, is the site of the antebellum residence of **James A. Whiteside**, attorney and early Chattanooga promoter whose efforts earned him the nickname "Old Man Chattanooga." ❹ This 2-story house, the first brick residence built in Chattanooga, was erected by builder George Dabney in 1840 using bricks from the Thomas Crutchfield brickyard near the river. As can be seen in the photograph above, the home had chimneys on either side of the building, and 2 tall columns graced the front facade of the building, enclosing porches on the first and second stories. An early owner of much of Cameron Hill, Whiteside died in 1861, and during the Civil War his family was forced to evacuate Chattanooga and go north to Louisville, where they were imprisoned for a time. Forced to sell many of the family's possessions for only $3,000, Ms. Whiteside nevertheless kept James Cameron's painting of her

family (page 126) with her, stowing the frame in a loft in the rafters of the carriage house, where it was found intact after the war. Numerous lawsuits concerning the lands owned by the Whitesides greeted the family upon their return to town, a problem which was exacerbated by the fact that many records had been lost and destroyed during the war. The house was eventually torn down in the early 1920s and replaced by the Breckenridge Apartments, which were in turn razed during the Golden Gateway development.

From this spot, cross Fifth Street. North of Fifth Street, on the left (west) side of Chestnut Street, ❺ is the **Clarion Hotel** (407 Chestnut Street), which originally opened in 1974 as "Chattanooga's hotel for business" and continues in operation today.

Across the street, at the southeast corner of Chestnut and Fifth Streets, is the former **Second District School**, also referred to as the "Chestnut Street School" (400 Chestnut Street). ❻ This 2-story, turn-of-the-century brick building closed in 1927, after which the Chattanooga Vocational School founded by industrial arts teacher Otis Clifford Kirkman was placed at the site (1928). The name of the school was changed to the Kirkman Vocational School after Kirkman's death (1943), and later to the Kirkman Technical High School. The institution moved from this site in 1939, and in 1985 the building was converted for use as the Chattanooga Regional History Museum. The museum features a permanent exhibit tracing the history and development of Chattanooga entitled "Chattanooga: Its Land, Rivers and People," a companion film entitled "Marks on the Land," and a number of temporary exhibits concerning subjects such as the Tennessee Valley Authority, company towns in the Tennessee Valley, and the Civil War in Chattanooga.

Cross Fourth Street. To your left is another entrance to the freeway, ❼ designed during the urban renewal of the West Side as an entrance to the "Market Center" area of the downtown core. In the vicinity of this freeway overpass is the spot where **Bessie Smith**, the "Empress of the Blues," was born in 1898 (though other sources say 1894, 1895, or 1900). After losing both of her parents, Smith began singing in the streets of Chattanooga, accompanied by her brother on guitar. Legend has it that Smith later entered into the tutelage of Gertrude "Ma" Rainey, the mother of all blues singers and the leader of the Rabbit Foot Minstrels, who helped to develop the young singer's talent and style. She moved to Philadelphia in 1922, and in 1923 she made her first recording, "Downhearted Blues," for Columbia Records in New York City. The top-paid black entertainer of her time, Smith earned

$1,500 a week during the 1920s, when she was billed as the "greatest blues singer of all time." Smith was injured in a car crash in 1937 on her way to Memphis for a show, and she died soon afterward in a hospital in Clarksdale, Mississippi. Today, Bessie Smith is celebrated annually at the "Bessie Smith Strut," a popular part of the city-wide Riverbend Festival which takes place on MLK Jr. Blvd., in the vicinity of the Chattanooga African-American Museum and Bessie Smith Performance Hall. The home where Smith lived during her childhood, located in an area near here known as "Blue Goose Hollow," was likely torn down at the time of the urban renewal which created the freeway at this spot.

At the northwest corner of Chestnut and Fourth Streets is the **Creative Discovery Museum** (321 Chestnut Street), ❽ which opened in 1995 after evolving from a planned children's wing of the local Hunter Art Museum to become "a multi-disciplinary educational institution for young people." Designed by the Lee H. Skolnick Architecture + Design Partnership in New York, the whimsical building (pictured right and on page 127) was intended to be "rich in imagery, exciting to the eye, welcoming to the visitor and friendly to the child." The 42,000 square-foot, 2-story building features an Artist's Studio, Musician's Workshop, Field Scientist's

Laboratory, Inventor's Workshop, Optics Tower and a "Little Yellow House" play space. Also sparking children's interests are a 2-story kinetic water sculpture, a 120-seat theater, special exhibits gallery, and a birthday party room. In 2002, a $2 million renovation of the museum was begun, with the intention of creating a river play area where children can "captain a riverboat, climb among the treetops and change a river's current."

Next door to the Creative Discovery Museum is the **Hilton Garden Hotel** (311 Chestnut Street), erected in 2001. At the northwest corner of Chestnut and Third Streets, moreover, is the **Residence Inn by Marriott** (215 Chestnut Street). ❾ In 1939, the Kirkman Vocational School, which was renamed the Kirkman Technical High School in 1958, moved from the corner of Chestnut and Fourth Streets (page 131) to a 3-story brick building at this site. In 1950, the growing school acquired the former Stein Construction Company buildings on either side of Second Street, and in 1955 the school also purchased and remodeled the adjacent Freeman Pontiac Company building at the northwest corner of Chestnut and Third Streets. Added to the school's facilities in the 1960s, moreover, were a new gymnasium, auditorium, and football field, made possible by the Golden Gateway Development of the west side, which opened up large areas to development and enabled the school to expand. In 1996, the Kirkman school buildings were torn down to make way for the current 4-story, 76-suite stone-and-brick hotel constructed at this spot. Envisioned as a way in which to "help extend downtown activity from 8am to midnight, increase foot traffic and add more residents," this hotel opened in July 1996 to coincide with the Summer Olympics in Atlanta, Georgia.

To the left (west), up Third Street from Chestnut Street, is the 6,160-seat **BellSouth Park** (2000), ❿ home to the Chattanooga Lookouts minor league (AA) baseball team. Previously utilized as the Kirkman Technical High School football field and referred to as "Hawk Hill" (so named for the school's mascot), this spot was originally known as "Reservoir Hill." The first cemetery in Chattanooga is reported to have been located on the east flank of this hill. During the initial artillery battle at Chattanooga in June 1862, moreover, Reservoir Hill was occupied by the Lookout Battery (CSA), which was shelled from across the river by federal forces under the command of Brigadier General James Negley. During the federal occupation of Chattanooga in 1864-1865, a defensive work known as Redoubt Carpenter was established on Reservoir Hill; the crest of the hill was enclosed with earthworks, and 5 light guns and 1 seacoast cannon were placed at this location, named for Major Stephen D. Carpenter, who died in the battle of Stone's River on December 31, 1862.

The original name "Reservoir Hill," however, was derived from a use for this site which arose after the battle. Initially, early Chattanooga residents obtained fresh water from wells dug throughout the downtown area, as well as the river itself. However, the increased population associated with the federal occupation made it necessary to locate a source for fresh, potable water. Thus, a flouring mill was converted for use as a water pumping station (as shown in the photograph on page 127). Water was drawn from the Tennessee River and pumped to storage tanks located on Reservoir Hill, and 6-inch metal pipes carried the water down Sixth Street to Market Street, at which point water lines were installed for a mile to the north and south. By 1865, additional tanks were placed at this location and on Cameron Hill, in order to ensure the availability of sufficient quantities of water. Following the war, the waterworks, which has been referred to as "the germ of the post-war water company of the town," was sold to private investors and renamed the "Lookout Water Company." Following consolidation of this enterprise with a similar company into the City Water Company (1887), the waterworks were moved in 1888 to a new location on the Tennessee River at Citico Creek. Reservoir Hill was then subdivided into residential lots, and Second, Cedar, and Poplar Streets were extended into this new "Reservoir Hill Addition," which attracted numerous working-class residents.

To the west of this spot, ⓫ between Reservoir Hill and Cameron Hill (where today the freeway prepares to cross the Tennessee River) was previously a deep ravine known as "Stillhouse Hollow." This spot was the early site of a 4-story brick flouring mill and distillery owned by onetime Chattanooga mayor (1858) W.S. Bell. The distillery, which produced 300 gallons of white corn whiskey per day for sale at 30 cents a gallon, was sold on the eve of the Civil War by Bell, who went to Memphis, joined the Confederate army as a surgeon, and was subsequently killed by a stray cannonball while standing on the deck of a Mississippi River steamboat. During the federal occupation of the city, the distillery

was torn down by the federal army, and its bricks were used for chimneys in soldiers' tents.

Nearby, New York native Daniel Kaylor founded the Chattanooga Steam Flouring Mill (1866). Later taken over by his son George, the mill produced 50 barrels of flour daily and had 10 employees by 1876. Another of Daniel Kaylor's sons, Harry, opened the Kaylor Distillery (1876) near the original Bell distillery site to produce corn and rye whiskey. This business, which produced 100 barrels of whiskey per day, was taken over in 1879 by J.B. Gilkerson. An early advertisement for these businesses is shown below and on page 127. Interestingly, the city granted an exception to a law forbidding hogs to roam loose in the city limits for this enterprise, and pigs were allowed to fatten on discarded corn and rye mash used in the distillery process – after which they were sent to a near-

by slaughterhouse.

Today, Stillhouse Hollow is the site of the **Olgiati Bridge**. During the mid-twentieth century, increased automobile traffic led to growing roadway problems in Chattanooga, and at one point it was suggested that the city might need to request the army to construct temporary pontoon bridges across the river in order to allay the problems associated with temporary closures of the Market and Walnut Street Bridges. The State of Tennessee approved construction of a new bridge in 1950, but it took several years to complete; in fact, it eventually became necessary to seek federal aid for the project, and the bridge was eventually built as part of the nation's interstate system. Originally referred to as the Pine Street Bridge, the structure was finally designed to connect Cedar Street on the south with Cherokee Boulevard on the opposite bank, and the tentative name was changed to the "Cedar Street Bridge." On November 20, 1959, this $7 million "footlog" across the river was opened, at which time it was formally labeled the "Olgiati Bridge," in honor of Mayor Peter R. "Rudy" Olgiati, whose urban renewal of the West Side was said to have "altered the face and heart" of Chattanooga. Currently, the Olgiati Bridge is in the process of being widened from 4 to 8 lanes.

Returning to the bottom of Reservoir Hill, across the street from the Residence Inn is the **Bijou Theater**, ⑫ which sits on the former site of the turn-of-the-century Chattanooga Brewery. These structures are discussed in greater detail on page 153.

Next door to the Bijou Theater is a **Courtyard by Marriott** hotel (200 Chestnut Street), constructed at the southeast corner of Chestnut and Second Streets in 2001.

Across Chestnut Street, at the southwest corner of Chestnut and Second Streets, ⑬ is the **IMAX Theater** (201 Chestnut Street). Designed by Tuck-Hinton of Nashville, Tennessee, this 6-story building opened in 1996 to exhibit large-format, 3-D IMAX films. Part of the Tennessee Aquarium complex, the 406-seat theater "combines brilliant images which fill a viewer's peripheral vision, superb sound and theatre geometry which gives everyone the best seat in the house."

Across Second Street, at the northwest corner of Chestnut and Second Streets, is a large parking lot which was previously the site of the **American Manufacturing Company**. ⑭ During the Civil War, this entire area was part of a large corral complex established by the Union army in the area bounded by Third Street, the river, Railroad Avenue (Broad Street), and Pine Street. Large encampments of soldiers also clustered around this area during the federal occupation of the city. After the war, the area developed as a business area near the wharf and the Tennessee River. One business that located in this area was the Chattanooga Buckle Company, which manufactured harness and saddle hardware. In 1898, this business was purchased by William M. Weber and James B. Robinson, who renamed it the American

Manufacturing Company. Around 1906, the business moved to this site, in the block bounded by Pine, Second, Water, and Chestnut Streets, building a sprawling concrete facility with a metal roof. Though destroyed in 1910 by fire, the business was soon rebuilt at a cost of $30,000; a second fire destroyed the building on May 14, 1919, largely due to a mixup in telegraphic signals which delayed the fire department's response to the blaze. The business was again rebuilt, and the company eventually diversified, spinning off the Cumberland Case Company, which manufactured milk bottle delivery cases (1937). In 1985, the business moved from this location, complaining that the old spot was an "industrial island" in a run-down part of town. The property was then purchased by Quadel Riverfront Associates Ltd. in 1984, and the buildings, with the exception of the old smoke stack in the center of the parking lot, were torn down as part of the Tennessee Aquarium project.

To the north of this spot, where Chestnut Street dead-ends into Riverfront Parkway at the river, ⑮ was the old **Chestnut Street Bridge**, a timber bridge 12-feet wide and 200-feet long erected during the antebellum period in order to cross a deep ravine between First and Second Streets on Chestnut Street. In the 1850s, the city enacted an ordinance prohibiting people from driving horses or vehicles over the bridge faster than at a walk, with the penalty being a 1-dollar fine, or 5 lashes for a slave. The bridge was subsequently demolished, and over the years the ravine was filled in; no trace exists of this early bridge today.

The beginning of the West Side tour is located four blocks to the south, at the corner of Chestnut and Sixth Streets.

Ross's Landing is the historic center of Chattanooga and the oldest inhabited section of the city. Chattanooga was founded on the banks of the Tennessee River, the main artery coursing through the Tennessee Valley and "the only available natural path leading through the mountains north and south, from the Virginia Line to the Muscle Shoals, a distance of about three hundred miles." With deep water immediately off of the banks and nearby bluffs which were not flooded by the river, this spot was, as early settler John P. Long declared, "the best landing from the headwaters to this point," and "the first high ground and suitable harbor above the mountains." In addition, this point was a convenient stop-over point above the snags, whirls, and sucks of the Tennessee river gorge, a 26-mile stretch through a narrow river canyon immediately downriver.

Recognizing these advantages, in 1815 John Ross established a ferry, landing, and warehouse at this spot, which then became known as "Ross's Landing." Located at the northern edge of the Cherokee Nation, Ross's Landing served to connect the United States to Indian territory. The landing was also an important link between the river and the trading post of Scottish trader John McDonald (Ross's grandfather) at Rossville, Georgia.

Following the Cherokee Removal of 1838, the area was opened to land speculation. Sensing the same opportunities which Ross had foreseen, settlers poured into the area, leading one early resident to remark that the town "had become the greatest landing and depot on the river for the produce of East Tennessee." Or, as John P. Long boldly proclaimed, "Here is the gate through which the highway of nations must pass."

Originally, Ross's Landing was the center of residential and commercial life in Chattanooga. As business came to be focused upon the riverfront, however, houses were placed back from the water (and the fog and clouds of mosquitoes which gathered there). Over time, therefore, the property adjacent to the river was increasingly occupied by warehouses and industrial buildings serving the river trade. As river commerce slowed in the twentieth century, many of these buildings were eventually abandoned. In 1992, however, the construction of the Tennessee Aquarium fostered the redevelopment of Ross's Landing; today, this area serves as a key piece of the downtown redevelopment project.

Shipyards

"Cherokee" by Bud Hartmann

14 Advertisement for Loomis & Hart Company

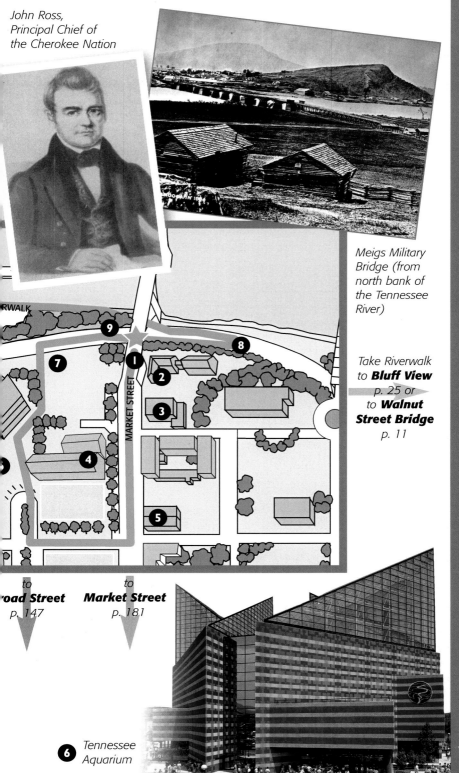

John Ross,
Principal Chief of
the Cherokee Nation

Meigs Military
Bridge (from
north bank of
the Tennessee
River)

Take Riverwalk
to **Bluff View**
p. 25 or
to **Walnut
Street Bridge**
p. 11

RWALK

9

7

1

2

8

MARKET STREET

3

4

5

to
oad Street
p. 147

to
Market Street
p. 181

6 Tennessee
Aquarium

137

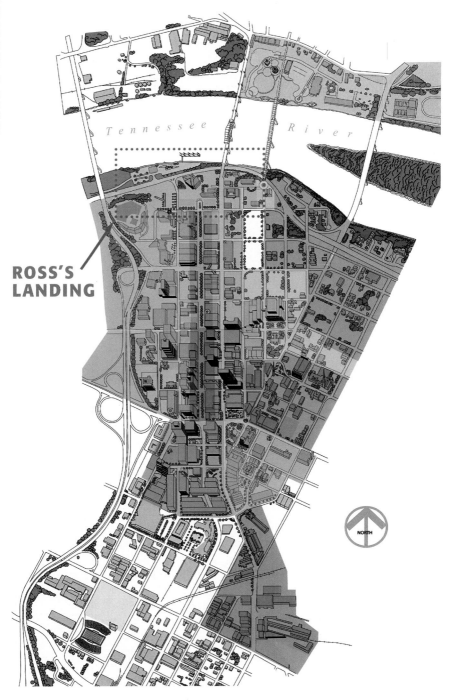

ROSS'S LANDING

Tennessee River

NORTH

The tour of Ross's Landing begins on Market Street, at the southern end of the **Market Street Bridge.** ❶ At the beginning of the twentieth century, only the Walnut Street Bridge (to the east) spanned the Tennessee River at Chattanooga. Ongoing repairs to that structure, the growth of the Hill City (North Chattanooga) and Riverview neighborhoods on the north bank of the river, and the increasing volume of automobile travel in and out of the town created the need for an additional span across the river. In 1911, Congress approved the construction of 2 bridges into Chattanooga: one from Sixth Street west to Moccasin Bend, and one either above or below the Walnut Street bridge. Interest soon focused upon the latter plan, although discussion continued as to exactly where to place the new bridge. Despite the requirement that part of the city wharf be destroyed in its construction, a site at Market Street was eventually selected due to the fact that the busy addresses of that street were "the ultimate destination of nine-tenths of the people from the north side of the river who visit the city of Chattanooga on business." Construction of the structure was approved by Congress on October 6, 1913. Due to the lower maintenance costs as compared to steel, a concrete design was preferred by the local bridge committee; the only engineer who proposed a completely concrete structure was New Yorker Benjamin H. Davis, and his design was therefore accepted. Following the approval of this design, construction of the Market Street Bridge began in November 1914.

Due to the relatively low spot where the bridge connected to Market Street, it became necessary to construct a drawspan to allow for passage under the bridge by steamboats and other large river craft. A number of obstacles, including underground cavities and a lack of solid footing in the riverbed, as well as the unpredictable nature of the river itself, slowed construction of the bridge; as such, costs continually escalated, and following its completion the bridge was commonly referred to as the "Million Dollar Bridge." Work was slowed in 1915 due to river flooding, and the *Chattanooga Times* reported on December 20, 1915, that "Span No. 3 on the Market Street Bridge went out yesterday morning Dec. 19, 1915, at 8:30 in a 38-foot stage flood. Falsework and forms reinforced ready for pouring of concrete were swept 10 miles down the river." Despite these difficulties and delays, the bridge was eventually completed and was opened on November 17, 1917. The Market

Street Bridge (also referred to as the "Chief John Ross Bridge") is today recognized as the largest bascule bridge in the United States, and the third-largest in the world.

Near the Market Street Bridge are the remnants of the first bridge to span the Tennessee River at Chattanooga, the **Meigs Military Bridge** (pictured below). Using timber from the north side of the river, in 1865 the federal army constructed the Meigs Military Bridge to replace the

various pontoon bridges which crossed the river at Chattanooga during the Civil War. Named for the quartermaster general of the army, the structure was often referred to as "Meigs Folly" because of its cost – $75,000 (especially given the fact that the bridge was always intended to be a temporary structure). The 1,000-foot long wooden-plank bridge sat on wooden piers filled with stone, ore, and cinder which were spaced 90 feet apart; a drawbridge was included in the spans near the south riverbank. One amusing incident occurred during construction of the bridge: in completing work on the drawbridge, engineers telegraphed Cincinnati to request 4 steamboat capstans, a type of hoist or windlass; several days later, four steamboat *captains* arrived, wondering why they had been rushed to Chattanooga! A dance was planned to celebrate the completion of the bridge, but the frivolity ended when the structure began to sway with the music. Following the war, the Meigs Military Bridge was given to the city, which prepared a toll schedule as follows:

A single person on foot 3 cents or 5 cents round trip

A man and horse 10 cents each way

A vehicle drawn by horse, mule, or oxen 10 cents

A vehicle drawn by 2 horses, mules, or oxen 15 cents

A vehicle drawn by 4 horses, mules, or oxen 25 cents

A Mrs. Cowart claimed rent for the northern bank of the river where the end of the bridge sat, and the bridge was subsequently leased to James R. Slayton, who complained about this rent, given the high cost of keeping the bridge in repair. In 1866, the city proposed auctioning the bridge for scrap, as it was "in a dangerous unsafe condition, and liable to fall at any time." However, the 1867 flood took care of this problem. As the waters of the river steadily rose, citizens gathered to watch the bridge, commenting that it would certainly be washed away when the water reached the deck of the bridge. Indeed, the bridge was torn away and destroyed by the flood. Prior to the construction of the Hales Bar dam, at low water one could still see portions of the old piers in the water. Today, however, no visible remnant of this wartime structure exists.

To the right (east) of the Market Street Bridge ❷ are the **Riverset Apartments** (2 Market Street), erected in 1994 as "the first new downtown housing in 20 years." Previously, this property was the site of the White Oak Distillery, operated by E.R. Betterton on a large lot east of Market Street and north of First Street. Prohibition ended this business in 1913, and in 1919 the Ancient Arabic Order of the Nobles of the Mystic Shrine of North America (the "Shriners") bought the distillery warehouse, renovating the structure for a new Alhambra Shrine Temple. This building was dedicated in 1921 and used until 1966 when, due to impingement by the Riverfront Parkway, the Shriners elected to move to a new location on East Brainerd Road (1970). In the 1970s, the building was put to use as the River's Edge restaurant and the Greater Chattanooga Music Hall. After standing vacant for a number of years, in 1974 a plan arose to tear down the building and erect a 5-story, $3.6 million "River Bluff" office and condominium complex, to be built on First Street between Market and Walnut Streets. However, a petition to close part of First Street for this project was denied in July 1974, and the project never got off the ground. In the late 1980s, however, the Shrine temple was torn down, and in 1994 the current apartments were erected as an early part of the riverfront redevelopment project.

From this spot, head south down Market Street. In the early decades of the twentieth century, the south landing of the Market Street Bridge became the site of a number of **laundries**, all of which were erected within a 1-block area. ❸ These businesses arose in this area in an effort to capitalize on the growing traffic between the downtown core and the residential neighborhoods across the river. At 18-26 Market Street was the Crown Laundry (1915),

and further down the street, at 122-124 Market Street, was Mertins French Dry Cleaning Company (1910). Due to competition, changing patterns of business, and city growth, these businesses eventually folded. The Crown laundry went out of business in 1945, and the Mertins laundry closed in 1958. The 2-story brick cleaning plant of the Crown laundry, however, was purchased by the Miller Brothers Company for use as a bulk storage building, and it still stands at this location today.

Nearby, the west side of Market Street between the river and Second Street is the current site of the **Tennessee Aquarium Visitors' Center** and food court. ❹ Along this block, at 103 Market Street, is the former site of the Extract Wool & Merino Company, a textile company which was founded in Chattanooga in 1901. In 1903, 3 adjoining lots were purchased, and a massive 3-story plant was erected, into which the company moved in 1904. Several enterprises subsequently occupied this row of buildings after the dissolution of the Extract Wool & Merino Company in 1929, including the 1928 Plymouth Laundry (103-107 Market Street) owned by John P. Brown. Like other laundries in the area, in 1972 this laundry closed, "a victim of the introduction of home laundry equipment, synthetic and permanent press fabrics, and coin-operated laundries." The building was then torn down. Currently, plans are existing for the construction of a new, $30 million Aquarium expansion (2005), including a 75,000-gallon saltwater tank and roof garden focusing upon aquatic life in the Gulf of Mexico.

Also at 103 Market Street was a notorious early tavern which today serves as a reminder of the rough nature of the riverfront during the early years of Chattanooga's development. Here, William Pettibone maintained a saloon which was labeled in the 1880 city directory as the "Cincinnati Lager Beer Parlor." It was remarked that this was a wild area after dark, and "cutting and shooting affrays at Pettibone's saloon were common."

Another enterprise located in this block was the Noland Company, which opened in 1930 near this spot (115 Market Street) to sell plumbing, heating, and air conditioning equipment in a 4-story building also built by the Extract Wool & Merino Company. In 1937, a renovation of this site included mounting a new black marble facade on the Market Street front, with "Noland" in art-deco lettering. In 1957, the Market Street property was closed, and the expanding company moved to a new location. In 1960, the building was purchased by the American Manufacturing Company and used for storage. In 1989, the building was demolished as part of the construction of the Tennessee Aquarium development, and the current visitors' center complex was subsequently built on the site.

From this site, head north to the northeast corner of Market and Second Streets. ❺ The 2-story brick building at this spot (**138 Market Street**) was erected in 1876 by Clement Clay Shelton, who arrived in Chattanooga in 1871. Shelton, who lived in a house on the back side of the property, became an innovator in the roller process of flour-making, and the flour mill he erected at this location, the Shelton Grain & Feed Company, turned out approximately 150 barrels of flour per day. After housing a number of businesses in subsequent years, including the Chattanooga Dry Cleaning Company, a feed-and-seed business, a tire company, a printer, Bennett's Auto Transmission Service, and (in the 1980s) an interesting enterprise

known as "Competition Cars of Chattanooga," today the structure houses several restaurants.

From this corner, turn right onto Second Street. On your right is the centerpiece of the riverfront area, the **Tennessee Aquarium**, a $45 million, 130,000 square-foot project which opened in May 1992. ❻ The structure (above), which is as tall as a 12-story building, was designed by Peter Chermayeff of Cambridge Seven & Associates in Cambridge, Massachusetts, after receiving funding from private and public sources in Chattanooga. With the mission of "fostering the understanding, celebration and conservation of aquatic environments of the world through excellence in education, husbandry, exhibitry and community relations," the Aquarium houses 24 exhibits in 450,000 gallons of water. These exhibits include such permanent residents as giant catfish, alligator

snapping turtles, red piranha, beluga sturgeon, green moray eels, and great barracuda. The Aquarium has also housed special exhibits, including "Jellies: Phantoms of the Deep," "Venom: Striking Beauties," and "Seahorses: Beyond Imagination." The park-like area surrounding the Aquarium, moreover, includes fountains, street vendors, mini-arboretums, and a stream which cascades through the site, inviting children of all ages to play.

Facing the Aquarium, bear right (east) along the side of the Aquarium structure. Here, the path becomes part of the Tennessee Riverwalk; follow the elevated pathway (not the stairs) which winds along the side of the Aquarium building. In this area is a large stone block placed at what is believed to be the original site of **Ross's Landing**, ❼ the spot where Chattanooga was born. The founder of Chattanooga, John Ross (below), was born in 1790 in Turkeytown, Alabama. Both his father and grandfather were Scottish traders who lived among the Cherokee, and Ross was in fact one-eighth Cherokee and seven-eighths Scottish. His Cherokee name was "Gu'wisguwi," the name of a rare migratory bird of large size and grayish plumage which is said to be found at remote edges of the Cherokee country. In 1813-1814, Ross fought against the Creek Indians under General Andrew Jackson at the Battle of Horseshoe Bend, Alabama. In 1815, Ross and his brother, Lewis, established Ross's Landing as a stopover for traders bringing goods down the Tennessee River; the small frontier operation included a ferry, landing, and warehouse. In 1817, a missionary described this frontier outpost as a "kind of shanty for goods and a log hut for the ferryman. All, all the region within  the sight of Lookout's summit was then a wilderness, with here and there and Indian cabin and 'truck patch.'" The property was subsequently sold in 1826 to Pleasant H. Butler and Methodist minister Nicholas Dalton Scales, after Ross moved to the headwaters of the Coosa River near Rome, Georgia. From 1828 until the removal of the Cherokee from their eastern lands, Ross served as Principal Chief of the Eastern Cherokees, and between 1838 and 1866 he was Principal Chief of the Cherokee Nation. He died in 1866, in Washington, D.C.

Continue walking away from the Aquarium (east) along the Riverwalk, passing under the Market Street and Walnut Street bridges. ❽ From beneath the Walnut Street Bridge, you can ascend the stairs to your right to the bridge itself (page 11), which crosses the Tennessee River at this spot. If you wish, you can proceed to the Bluff View area (page 25) by continuing to your right (east) along the winding path in that direction. To continue the Ross's Landing tour, however, turn left and follow the Riverwalk as it parallels the Tennessee River toward the west.

The road which runs between the Aquarium and the Tennessee River is known as **Riverfront Parkway.** ❾ In 1915, a portion of this road, labeled Riverside Drive, was constructed along the river heading east from downtown. As part of the urban renewal of the 1960s, this road was extended; requiring the demolition of several old homes and the relocation of 250 families, the road was completed in 1973 at a total cost of $7.8 million. In 1974, the "Riverfront Parkway" was completed to the west of the river wharf, around Cameron Hill to Ninth Street, a process which required the demolition of several older industrial buildings along the river. Following the completion of this link, motorists could drive along the river from the Chickamauga Dam to Lookout Mountain along this chain of roadways – Amnicola Highway, Riverside Drive, and Riverfront Parkway. While the highway served to increase the traffic flow and aid industrial access in this area, in recent years thoughts began to turn toward creating a more pedestrian-friendly road here. To that end, in 2001 the roadway was "given" to the city of Chattanooga by the State of Tennessee, opening up the possibility of redeveloping this highway. Current plans include reducing the number of lanes from 4 to 2 in order to create a "Grand Surface Boulevard" aimed at "improving downtown access, matching design to anticipated traffic volume, improving aesthetics and safety and leveraging street design with development opportunities." New intersections are also to be added along the road, at Mabel, Houston, Lindsay, and Lookout Streets, with the long-term goal of creating a park-like atmosphere which will make the road itself an integral part of the Tennessee Riverpark.

Continue along the riverwalk to the **Ross's Landing Park,** ❿ a riverfront park established in 1975 after the area was added to the National Register of Historic Places. Before its designation as a park, this strip of land was long

known as the "City of Chattanooga Wharf," a purpose which it served since the founding of the town by John Ross in 1815. Given the commercial opportunities associated with the waterfront, following the Cherokee Removal a number of individuals leapt to purchase land on or near the landing. In the mid-1840s, much of the landing was purchased by Vernon King Stevenson, the first president of the Nashville & Chattanooga Railroad (and for whom the town of Stevenson, Alabama, is named), who paid $15,000 for 800 feet of riverfront land between Market Street and Pine Street. Richard G. Waterhouse, who came to Ross's Landing from Knoxville, Tennessee, purchased 220 acres on the river (a 220-acre long strip which was only 1-acre wide) from the landing west to Moccasin Bend; he paid 1 penny per acre, or a total of $2.20, for the property. Assigned to collect "wharfage" at the landing was Josiah Jackson Bryan, Jr., an early river trader who later served as a guard at the notorious Andersonville prison in south Georgia during the Civil War, after which he returned to Chattanooga to become mayor in 1872. For a number of years, the wharf continued to operate privately, with wharfage fees charged upon boats docking at the landing.

In 1897, however, diminishing business at the landing led many citizens to call for the creation of a free public wharf to increase business. Although the steep grade was difficult for wagons to negotiate and the wharf would be only 60 feet wide, in 1899 the Tennessee River Navigation Company offered to sell its riverfront property, which was located near Market Street at the current site of the Ross's Landing Park. When the Chattanooga Packet Company consolidated with the Tennessee River Navigation Company in 1906, therefore, the wharf was purchased by the city for $45,000. In 1915, the wharf was paved with the Belgian cobblestones which had previously been used to pave Market Street; a number of these bricks still lie at the boat ramp at the riverfront today. Although Market Street merchants later proposed extending the wharf past Market to Lookout Street, poor access led to this plan being dropped; likewise, a proposal to purchase additional wharfage at the foot of Pine Street in 1915 was not approved. After operating for decades as an industrial landing, in 1972 the City of Chattanooga purchased a 3,100 foot strip of land along the river for creation of the current public park. Presently, a riverfront redevelopment plan contemplates the expansion of the Ross's Landing Park to include additional activities, green spaces, and historic markers tracing the development of Chattanooga from its days as a tiny landing on the banks of the Tennessee River.

The riverfront is also the site of the annual **Riverbend Festival**, a 9-day June festival patterned after the Spoleto festival in Charleston, South Carolina. Inaugurated in 1981 as "Five Nights in Chattanooga" with the "intention of bringing diverse elements of the Chattanooga community together through the common language of music," Riverbend has since been recognized as one of the top 20 festivals in the Southeast. With street performers, several musical stages, a variety of food vendors, a floating stage in the Tennessee River, and a grand fireworks display, Riverbend has become a true Chattanooga "event," drawing 600,000 visitors in 2001.

Several historic plaques are located at the riverfront park, including one dedicated to the **"First Citizens"** of Chattanooga (below). ⓫ By June 1837, 53 heads of households had arrived and settled in the vicinity of Ross's Landing. Including merchants, lawyers, doctors, innkeepers, farmers, and a variety of other occupations.

These "first citizens" were the individuals who ventured into the new community on the heels of the Cherokee Removal (or, in several cases, before it) and created the city of Chattanooga, and many of their descendants remain in the Chattanooga community today.

Near this historic plaque is a large bronze statue which stands gazing out over the Tennessee River as it flows past Ross's Landing. Entitled "Cherokee," this sculpture was created by Bud Hartmann, of Brooklin, Maine, and was installed at this location in 1992. The statue is dedicated to the Lupton family, which has been integrally involved in the development (and redevelopment) of downtown Chattanooga, as well as the memory of the Cherokee people who occupied this area in the years preceding the

arrival of white settlers in the 1830s.

Docked at Ross's Landing (201 Riverfront Parkway, Pier 2) is the **Southern Belle**, ⓬ a 500-passenger riverboat which provides daily cruises along the Tennessee River in Chattanooga. The riverboat offers both sightseeing and dinner cruises throughout the year. For additional information, contact the Southern Belle at 266-4488.

In addition to the boats which tie up at Ross's Landing today, a number of steamers similarly docked at the Chattanooga wharf during the antebellum period, one of which was the steamer *Dunbar*. On September 9, 1863, as the federal army advanced toward Chattanooga, Confederate troops abandoned the town and retreated into North Georgia, where they would eventually meet the federal army at the battle of Chickamauga on September 19-20, 1863. To cover the Confederate retreat, the steamers *Dunbar* and *Paint Rock* were set on fire and scuttled at the landing, and the *Tennessee* and *Holston* were sunk upriver from the town. As you look out across the river, you can imagine the site of the burning ships slowly slipping beneath the surface of the river amid huge clouds of smoke, as the federal army enters the town on the heels of the fleeing rebels. The Union army later raised the *Dunbar* for use as a wharfboat, or floating dock, a purpose which it continued to serve for a number of years following the war.

From this spot, continue west along the riverbank. The second-most severe flood to hit Chattanooga occurred in 1875, when the Tennessee River crested at 53.8 feet, covering downtown Chattanooga with muddy floodwaters. Following the flood, one "Colonel Barlow" suggested that 2 levees be constructed at Chattanooga, one of which would be parallel to the river. Barlow promised that raising Water Street (now Riverfront Parkway) a mere 20 feet would protect against a flood of 60 feet above the low water mark, thereby rendering Chattanooga immune from all but the most catastrophic of floods. Instead, however, the town elected to raise street levels throughout downtown, giving rise to "Underground Chattanooga." This was a significant decision for Chattanooga, if only because a levee would have raised a large obstacles between the river and downtown, changing the face of the riverfront.

Another historic marker located in the Ross's Landing Park ⓭ discusses the **Cherokee**

Removal, in which Indian lands east of the Mississippi River were ceded to the United States in exchange for $5 million and 7 million acres of western lands. Following approval of the December 29, 1835, Treaty of New Echota by only 1 vote in the U.S. Congress, 5 companies of Tennessee volunteers commanded by Colonel Joseph Byrd arrived at Ross's Landing on July 20, 1836. These troops were supplemented by additional soldiers in October 1836. From Ross's Landing, these troops were sent out into the countryside to round up the Indians, who were kept in stockades in various locations nearby. Most Indians did not resist, although on one occasion near Dalton, Georgia, an Indian was observed taking aim at a soldier with a bow and arrow; he was killed, and his body was brought to Ross's Landing. After rounding up the Cherokees, the soldiers prepared to send them west to new reservations in what would later become Oklahoma.

On March 3, 1837, a first group of 466 Indians, mostly volunteers, left on 11 specially-built double-deck flatboats which were towed from Ross's Landing by steamboat. On June 6, 1838, 800 additional Cherokees were loaded into a 100-ton steamboat and 6 flatboats, and on June 13, 1838, 875 Indians were loaded onto boats destined for the west, towed, ironically, by a steamboat named *George Guess*, the English name of the Cherokee Indian Sequoyah, who invented the Cherokee syllabary. Another party of 1,070 Indians left on June 17, 1838, marching overland from Ross's Landing; although General Winfield Scott, who oversaw the removal at Ross's Landing, suspended the remainder of the project until autumn due to heat and low river levels, this group was forced to proceed on, leaving only 2,500 Cherokees in Ross's Landing. The final group began the

famous 800-mile "Trail of Tears" in the fall of 1838. Of the 17,000 Cherokee Indians who embarked on the Trail of Tears, 4,000 died along the way. This path is now commemorated by a 1987 National Historic Trail which extends from Chattanooga to Talequah, Oklahoma, part of which will soon be marked by a large memorial and walking trail which tracks the actual route taken by the Cherokee, crossing the river and proceeding along the

north bank of the Tennessee River from this spot.

Across Riverfront Parkway at this spot are the remains of a significant and long-lived Chattanooga business, the **Loomis & Hart Company**. ⑭ Coming from Nashville in 1865, Union veterans Julius F. Loomis (New York) and

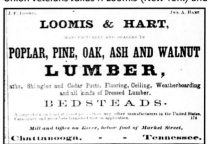

F.J. Bennett (Pennsylvania) purchased a portable sawmill from the federal government and established a business at this location. Originally known as the "Loomis and Bennett Sawmill," the business was "the earliest, the largest, and the most long-lived of the wood processing plants" in Chattanooga. F.J. Bennett left the partnership after the floods of 1867 and 1875 damaged the business, selling his shares to Ohio native and Union veteran John A. Hart, and the business then became known as Loomis & Hart (as seen in the advertisement above and on page 136). By 1876, the plant employed 30 workmen and several wagon teams, and it also began to produce furniture as business grew. In 1882, a new 3-story plant was erected on a 15-acre lot at the river where a number of sawmills had gathered, and by 1884 the plant employed 150 hands and produced $150,000 annually; at that time, it was the fifth largest employer in the city and was one of the 10 largest companies in town. By 1885, the company produced rough and dressed lumber, sashes, doors, and blinds, as well as bedsteads, wardrobes, washstands, and tables. In 1888, moreover, a new 60-by-250 foot brick finishing factory was erected.

Subsequently, the business was acquired by North Carolinian and Civil War veteran Captain Andrew Jackson Gahagan; at his retirement in 1919, the furniture-production business was purchased by Georgia native Gaston Raoul, who previously owned the Keyser Manufacturing Company (which produced the "odorless refrigerator") and the Acme Kitchen Furniture Company. When a fire in 1920 destroyed the former saw and planing mill at this location, they were not rebuilt, as they were no longer necessary.

In 1934, the Tennessee Furniture Company (the name given to the company after its merger with the Loomis & Hart furniture business and the addition of the refrigeration business) received an order from Coca-Cola for an ice chest; by 1948, the business was producing numerous coin-operated refrigerated vending machines, and the name of the company was changed to the Cavalier Corporation (1938). Subsequently, the furniture portion of the business stayed at this location, while the refrigeration plant moved to a new location at Ninth Street and Central Avenue. Due to competition from companies located closer to ready lumber supplies, the company suspended furniture operations in 1961 and closed its 6 buildings on the riverside in order to focus on the cooler business, which continued to expand; by 1979, in fact, the company had produced more than one million soft-drink coolers and dispensers. Two of the old buildings at this site burned in June 1972, and the 1974 completion of Riverside Drive in this area required the city to purchase the remaining structures for $600,000; they were then torn down. The cooler business remained in operation for several years, eventually closing in 2000. Today, parts of the stone foundation of this site are the only existing remnants of this important early Chattanooga business.

Near this site, underneath the Olgiati Bridge, is the spot where **Pine Street** formerly ran to the river. ⓯ This street was eradicated by the West Side development, which altered the natural and urban features of downtown Chattanooga in the 1950s and 1960s. During the Civil War, the Union army constructed a pontoon bridge which crossed the river here. Prior to the construction of the bridges linking Chattanooga to the north side of the river, moreover, a ferry owned by Abe Beason operated here; the ferry was operated by 4 mules and 2 employees, David Hamil and Russel White, who rowed and poled the ferry across the river to several hundred acres owned by Beason on the other side, at the foot of Stringer's Ridge. The ferry has been variously described as the Pine Street or Chestnut Street ferry, and, like other ferries in Chattanooga at the time, it eventually went out of business following the advent of steam-powered ferries in the 1880s. As part of the continued redevelopment of the riverfront in this area, in 2002 it was proposed to connect Pine Street to the river again, this time by way of a boardwalk running to the river from this spot.

Proceed under the Olgiati Bridge to the Ross's Landing boat marina. During the Civil War occu-

pation of Chattanooga, the federal army established a **Shipyard** north of Cameron Hill (pictured above and on page 137), to construct a fleet of steamboats to patrol the river and carry supplies upriver from Bridgeport, Alabama. Several sawmills were erected along the riverbank to supply lumber for the shipyard, which built numerous boats, including the *Chickamauga* (227 tons), *Stone River* (214 tons), *Lookout* (193 tons), *Bridgeport* (184 tons), *Resaca* (182 tons), *Missionary* (115 tons), *Kingston* (93 tons), *Chattanooga* (89 tons), and *Wauhatchie* (89 tons). Most of these boats were sternwheelers, while the last two were sidewheel steamers. Like many of the operations which developed during the federal occupation of Chattanooga, this shipyard helped to create additional river traffic, industrial development, and commercial transportation along the river following the Civil War.

To return to the start of the Ross's Landing tour, walk back through the Ross's Landing Park, crossing Riverfront Parkway at Chestnut Street. At Chestnut and Second Streets, turn left, and proceed to Market Street. The beginning of the tour is on your left.

Broad Street

This tour follows Broad Street from Sixth Street to Second Street. While Market Street was the central thoroughfare within downtown Chattanooga from the beginnings of the community, Broad Street was slow to develop, in part due to a jagged ravine at Third Street which effectively precluded access to the river along that street. In early years, therefore, most of Broad Street was utilized as a railroad spur line for overflow railroad cars, a fact which influenced merchants with stores fronting on Market Street to use Broad Street as a rear loading area for deliveries and merchandise. An open sewer running through the center of the road also hindered the development of Broad Street in early years. As such, even as late as 1883 the city directory listed no businesses along Broad Street between the river and Fourth Street.

Over time, however, the Third Street ravine was filled in, and sewer pipes came to replace the open sewer running along this portion Broad Street. These changes enabled commercial ventures to develop along the street, and several important businesses have since been located along this stretch of Broad Street. With the development of the Tennessee Aquarium in 1992, moreover, Broad Street was redesigned – while the road previously connected to the riverfront, it now dead-ends into the Aquarium tract. The Aquarium project has led to the substantial redevelopment of a number of older buildings along Broad Street, reinvigorating this area and causing a variety of new businesses to open their doors.

8 Broad Street "Gully" during Civil War

to
Railroad Avenue
p. 155

to
Market Street
p. 181

SIXTH STREET

FIFTH STREET

BROAD STREET

2

4

6

1

3

5

chattanooga
ducks
In association with the Chattanooga Audubon Society

Allen Kennedy

4 Chattanooga Ducks

*Chattanooga Coca-Cola
Bottling Plant*

to
**West
Side**
125

7

10

8

THIRD STREET

9

SECOND STREET

to
**Ross's
Landing**
p. 135

10 *Chattanooga Brewery*

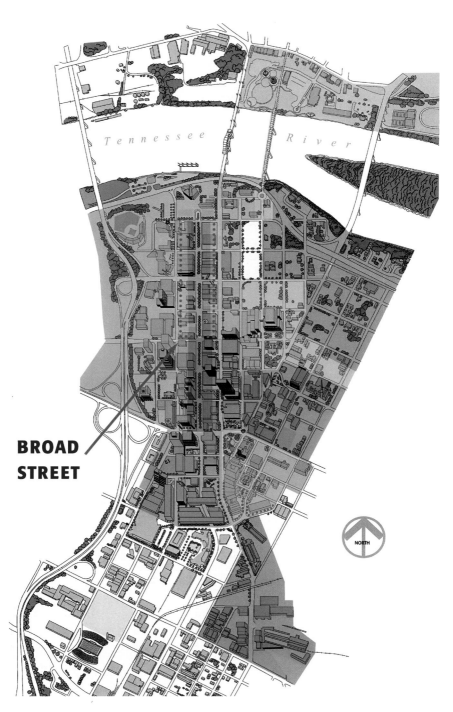

BROAD
STREET

NORTH

The tour of Broad Street begins at the intersection of Broad and Sixth Streets. At the northeast corner of these 2 streets ❶ is the **Market Court** building, which is discussed in greater detail on page 186.

Further down Broad Street, at the southwest corner of Broad and Fifth Streets, ❷ is the **Buffalo Wild Wings** restaurant (511 Broad Street), which is located in a 1-story brick building erected about 1940.

Across Broad Street, at the southeast corner of Broad and Fifth Streets, ❸ is **Sticky Fingers Catering** (500 Broad Street), the catering office for a nearby barbecue restaurant, which is located in a small brick structure erected circa 1910.

From this spot, cross Fifth Street. At the northwest corner of Broad and Fifth Streets ❹ is a 1-story brick building occupied by the **Chattanooga Ducks** (201 West Fifth Street), advertised as "Chattanooga's Most Exciting Ride." At this location, visitors board World War II-era amphibious vehicles, which were used by  the U.S. Army for landing troops on beaches. At Ross's Landing, the vehicles, which float like boats, splash into the Tennessee River, and naturalists from the Audubon Society accompany the vehicle on a tour of nearby MacLellan Island, the Tennessee River, and places of natural and historical interest in the downtown area.

Across Broad Street, at the northeast corner of Broad and Fifth Streets, ❺ is the site of the antebellum **Kennedy House**, an early inn which occupied the current parking lot located between Broad and Market Streets at this spot. Allen Kennedy (right), one of the original settlers in Ross's Landing, initially operated a log inn and tavern near the landing. Following the arrival of the railroad in Chattanooga, Kennedy erected the Kennedy House at this location, near the end of the spur line along Railroad Avenue (Broad Street). This hotel was a large, 2-story frame building with a second-story bal-

cony running the length of the building. After Kennedy died of smallpox, the building was sold, and the name of the hotel was changed to the "Central House." When the Civil War began, the Hamilton Grays, a Confederate unit organized in Chattanooga and known originally as the "Volunteer Company," were presented with their regimental battle flag at the hotel after being mustered into the Tennessee Provisional Army of the Confederate States on April 1, 1861. After the war, the hotel changed hands several times and was known as the Franklin House (advertised as "the next best place to the Crutchfield House"), the Campbell House, and the Planter's House. After the original building was destroyed by fire in 1882, a smaller hotel was constructed on this spot, fronting on Market Street, with a large second-story balcony to the rear of the building. Known initially as the Wisdom House, the hotel contained several rooms on the second floor and a number of first-floor businesses. By the turn of the century, the hotel had been renamed the Thompson House, and it subsequently became known as the American House and the Connor House. By World War II, however, the building ceased to be used as a lodging house. The long-lived structure was torn down in the 1980s, and today the space is utilized as a parking lot.

Immediately to the north of the Kennedy House, approximately where the Buehler's food store parking lot is today, is the former site of the **Waverly Hotel,** a 3-story brick antebellum inn which occupied the narrow spot between Broad and Market Streets at this location. Located opportunistically at the northernmost point of the Western & Atlantic spur line, this short-lived hotel was destroyed by fire during the Civil War. Today, the site of the Waverly Hotel is occupied by Jack's Alley, which is discussed in greater detail on page 187 of the Market Street section.

Further down Broad Street, at the southwest corner of Broad and Fourth Streets, is the **International Towing & Recovery Museum** (404 Broad Street), ❻ located in a brick building erected circa 1910. The museum was opened in 1995 to commemorate the towing industry, which began in Chattanooga when Ernest W. Holmes, Sr., invented the first twin-boom wrecker in 1916. The museum houses a number of historic towing vehicles, including a Bubblenose wrecker, an original Locomobile, and an O'Hare, Chicago, 1929 Chrysler fitted with a Weaver 3-ton crane.

From this spot, cross Fourth Street. On the west (left) side of Broad Street, the block bounded by Broad, Chestnut, Third, and Fourth Streets, which was once occupied by the Forrest Cate Ford Company, is now the site of the $2 million **Haney Building. ❼** This beige brick structure was erected in 1969 by local developer Franklin Haney as part of the Downtown Redevelopment Program to house the TVA Mapping and Survey Branch. Presently, plans are in the works for the TVA to move out, and the building will likely be torn down, ironically, for redevelopment of the property.

Across Broad Street, between Third and Fourth Streets, was an early African-American residential neighborhood which arose in this vicinity following the Civil War. In 1885, the portion of this block on the right (east) was occupied by several small 1-room houses, referred to in an 1885 map of Chattanooga as "Negro Shanties." Conveniently located close to both the river and nearby businesses on Market Street, the lower portion of Broad Street developed quite early as an African-American neighborhood, a trend which continued with the development of the West Side neighborhood in the twentieth century.

From this spot, cross Third Street. As you do, imagine a deep gully running across Broad Street at this location, ❽ preventing rail lines and roads from reaching the river by way of this street. The ditch (pictured below and on page 148), in fact, was so pronounced an obstacle that one visitor from Ohio in 1865 described it as "capable of engulfing Pharoah and his host, with all his horses and chariots." Filled in over time, today no trace of this natural ravine exists

to indicate where it once blocked access to the river along Broad Street.

Running east from this location, Third Street was originally known as Harrison Pike, because the road ran northeast along the river to the former county seat of Harrison, which was completely covered by the Chickamauga Dam erected by the Tennessee Valley Authority in 1940.

To your right, in the block bounded by Broad, Market, Second, and Third Streets, ❾ is a row of brick **Car Barns** erected in 1906 by the Chattanooga Electric Railway Company. Situated within the original Ross's Landing settlement, this block originally housed a small frame store operated by pioneer John P. Long on the west side of Market Street. Though an 1885 Sanborn insurance map of Chattanooga shows the Market Street side of this block as occupied by a number of lunch counters, boarding houses, and the Loomis & Hart furniture warehouse, by 1901 only a few shops and a "negro boarding [house]" were situated in this block, none of which were located on the unpaved Broad Street side of the street. By 1906, however, growth of the city's streetcar system (consolidated in 1891 into the Chattanooga Electric Railway Company), necessitated the creation of additional storage and maintenance buildings near the existing car barns across Third Street. As a result, the current building was erected as repair and maintenance shops for the business, which was subsequently renamed the "Chattanooga Railway and Light Company." The building was divided into 5 fireproof bays with 3 tracks in each bay; also here were shops, work rooms, storage rooms, and maintenance offices, with 1 bay reserved wholly for car washing. In 1926, 2 additional barns were adjoined to these structures for use by the Tennessee Electric Power Company's fleet of 57 city motor buses. The new barns were composed of a steel frame with brick and hollow tile walls, and they included office space as well as bus storage areas.

By 1930, the car barns were joined by a Firestone auto supply store to the north, and a used auto dealership facing onto Second Street was replaced by retail stores. By 1950, the car barns became affiliated with the Southern Coach Lines bus company, and later the property of the municipal CARTA bus company and Seymour Charter Bus Lines. Retail relocation to suburban mall areas eventually led to the closure of the Firestone store by 1990, and this structure, along with the 1926-era bus barns, was demolished after having been acquired by the RiverCity Company for development of the Ross's Landing area. Added to the National Register of Historic Places in 1979, the car barns, which feature 30-foot high ceilings, mahogany beams, and exposed brick walls, reopened in 1993 as the Big River Brewing and Grille Works, a restaurant and microbrewery. This restaurant, which along with the Tennessee

Aquarium functioned as a sort of cornerstone for the development of dining and entertainment facilities near the river, has since been joined by a number of eateries and night spots in the Ross's Landing area.

Near this spot, somewhere close to the southeast corner of Broad and Second Streets (now a parking lot), sat an early pioneer cabin owned by **Billy Gentry**, the ferryman who operated the ferry at Ross's Landing prior to the Cherokee Removal.

Across Broad Street, at the northwest corner of Broad and Third Streets, ❿ is the former site of the **Chattanooga Brewery** (201 Broad Street), established by Conrad Geise and Company in 1888-1889 at an estimated cost of $100,000. This business (pictured below and on page 149) was the first large-scale brewing

company located in Chattanooga and occupied the entire block bounded by Broad, Chestnut, Second, and Third Streets. The brewing house itself was a 6-story brick building, on top of which was placed a mill house. By 1890, the brewery had adopted the logo "Sunny South Brewery," and it produced such beers as "Muenchner," "Liebetchaner," "Family," and "Magnolia," as well as a lager called "Faultless." Chattanoogans at that time were urged to buy the product "not merely because it is a Southern product (which ought to have some weight with you) but because it is beyond question the purest and best in America." The brewery was subsequently purchased by Cincinnati resident Charles Reif in 1890 for $100,000, at which time the name of the company was changed to the Chattanooga Brewing Company. The business continued to expand over the next decade, making $30,000 in improvements to become one of the most modern breweries in the country, and by 1897 over 200 freight cars of brew were produced annually. In 1903, the company commenced

building a 75-by-175 foot storage building south of the main plant at a cost of $200,000, though the undertaking was subsequently scaled down due to new legal developments. When a 1909 state law restricted liquor sales in Tennessee, the brewery chose to focus upon "wet" states as well as drinks with a lower alcohol content, but the brewery faltered after a local plow manufacturer, Newell Sanders, gained a seat in the U.S. Senate and introduced a 1913 bill to prohibit interstate liquor sales. In 1915, moreover, state attorney general Frank M. Thompson filed a nuisance bill against the brewery, alleging that it was violating state laws. Due in no small part to these setbacks, the brewery was closed by the time of Prohibition in 1919.

In 1929, the **Chattanooga Coca-Cola Bottling Company** purchased the site of the old brewing house, the remnants of which were then torn down. During the demolition, members of the Women's Christian Temperance Union held prayers of thanksgiving at the site in observance of the event. A new bottling plant (below) was then designed by architect William Crutchfield and erected at this site. This new facility had the capacity to produce 144,000 bottles of Coca-Cola per day. Through 4 separate expansions, the facility soon came to occupy the entire block. In 1969, the building was sold to the Royal Crown Bottling Company for $450,000, and Coca-Cola moved to a new, larger plant built on Amnicola Highway at a cost of $2 million. Royal Crown then sold the building to the

Hamilton County Board of Education in 1979. Today, the building, which is located in the renewed Ross's Landing riverfront area, has been divided into several restaurant locations. Also located on the former Chattanooga Brewery site is the Bijou Theater, a new downtown theater and parking garage which was erected as part of the redevelopment of the Ross's Landing area.

To return to the beginning of the Broad Street tour, follow Broad Street south to Sixth Street.

Railroad Avenue

Broad Street is one of the main thoroughfares through the downtown Chattanooga area, connecting the riverfront to the growing Southside area. Originally labeled Mulberry Street, during the antebellum period this road was renamed Railroad Avenue in anticipation of a spur railroad line intended to be created along this road. To that end, the Western & Atlantic Railroad obtained a 99-year privilege to maintain a right-of-way down the street, and it was expected that the railroad would connect the railyards to the river landing, where it would also construct a freight-hoisting mechanism. However, partly because of a deep ravine and stream which crossed Railroad Avenue at Third Street, tracks were lain only as far north as Fifth Street, and the road soon became a storage area for rail cars overflowing from the rail yards to the south. As a result, merchants were forced to use their frontage on Market Street for loading and unloading goods, and Railroad Avenue remained underutilized for several years.

Though the rail line along Railroad Avenue was declared a nuisance by the city in 1860, the railroad secured an injunction preventing its removal; a second nuisance order was filed in 1867, though demolition was again stayed. When city officials then attempted to have the rails removed, the railroad had the workers arrested for "maliciously tearing up the rails." By 1875-1876, however, the road was renamed "Broad Street" (it is, in fact, the widest street in downtown Chattanooga), after which the tracks were eventually removed to create a true roadway here. Today, this portion of Broad Street is lined with important historic structures and sites.

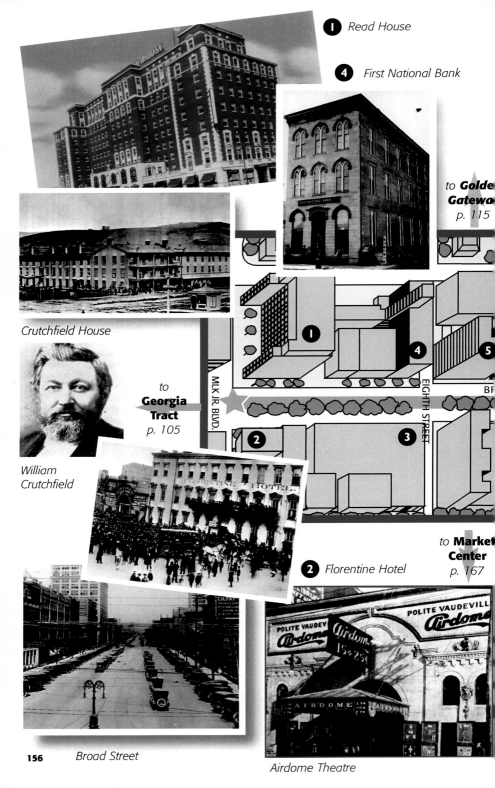

1 Read House

4 First National Bank

to **Golden Gateway** p. 115

Crutchfield House

to **Georgia Tract** p. 105

William Crutchfield

2 Florentine Hotel

to **Market Center** p. 167

156 Broad Street

Airdome Theatre

6 MacLellan Building

9 Hippodrome Roller Skating Rink

to
Broad Street
p. 147

TIVOLI
THEATRE
SOUVENIR PROGRAM

3 P.C. Wilson's Glass House

Charles E. James

157

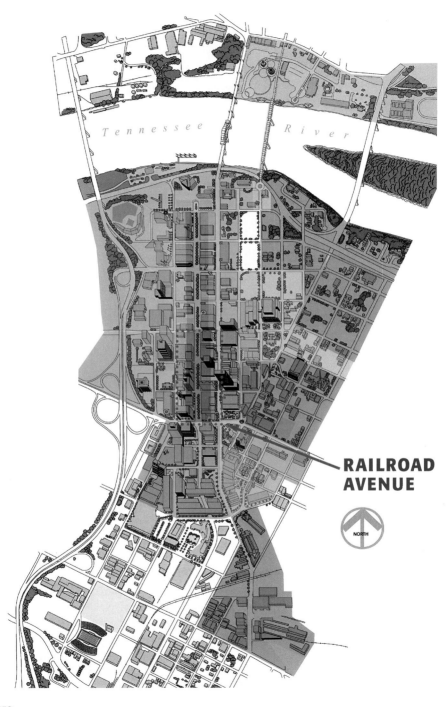

T e n n e s s e e *R i v e r*

RAILROAD
AVENUE

NORTH

The tour of Railroad Avenue begins at the corner of Broad Street and MLK Jr. Blvd., at the **Read House** (827 Broad Street). ❶ This 1926 hotel sits on the site of the Crutchfield House (pictured on page 156), an antebellum hotel erected by Thomas Crutchfield, Sr., the "first professional contractor in the State of Tennessee," who supervised the building of the hotel from a platform placed in a nearby tree. The location of the building was decided upon by an agreement with the Nashville & Chattanooga Railroad, which placed its terminal across Ninth Street (MLK Jr. Blvd.) after learning of Crutchfield's intention to build a hotel at this site. Completed in 1847, the inn was simply referred to as "the hotel" until 1853, when it assumed the name "Crutchfield House."

On the eve of the Civil War, the Crutchfield House was the site of a potentially-significant "near-duel." Visiting the town in 1861, future Confederate President Jefferson Davis gave a speech favoring states' rights from the balcony of the hotel. The crowd then called for a reply from Union supporter William Crutchfield (left),

brother of the hotel's operator; in lieu of debate, Crutchfield simply shouted, "Behold your future military despot!" Although Davis had already departed the room, he returned to overhear further comments made by Crutchfield and replied heatedly, "If there is any person here who will be responsible, I am responsible for what I say." At that point, pistols were drawn, and a duel seemed inevitable. However, cooler heads prevailed, and this near-duel was averted.

During the Civil War, the hotel became the headquarters for Confederate commander Danville Ledbetter, as well as a Union hospital officially labeled the "Ford hospital." The first Union flag raised in the city of Chattanooga during the federal occupation of Chattanooga was from the front balcony of the Crutchfield House. On the heels of the war, another interesting incident took place at the hotel. After mustering out of the Confederate army, Dr. Tomlinson Fort, subsequently a prominent citizen of Chattanooga, stayed at the Crutchfield House for a period of time. With few other clothes in his possession, he was forced to wear his gray uniform much of the time. Wearing a gray confederate jacket to dinner one evening, he found that his normal chair had been removed from

the dining room; when he moved to take another seat, a waiter pulled it away from him, remarking that he would be "damned if he'd wait on rebels." At this, Dr. Fort took up another chair and broke it over the waiter's head, knocking him unconscious. Although the hotel manager berated him and insisted that he leave, Dr. Fort pointed out that he had paid in advance for a week's lodging, and he was allowed to remain at the hotel until the end of the week. (Incidentally, pictured below are original pieces of silverware from the Crutchfiled House, currently on exhibit at the Chattanooga Regional History Museum).

During the great flood of 1867, the river rose at a rate of 1 foot per hour, and railroads discontinued service to Chattanooga by March 9. By the next morning, the town was under 4-to-8 feet of water. As a result, the railroad tracks on Railroad Avenue were lifted by their crossties and carried away; the flood also washed away several bridges which crossed gullies along Railroad Avenue at Fourth, Sixth, and Seventh Streets. Five feet of water rose in the lobby of the Crutchfield

House, and visitors watched a large 100-foot warehouse which had been used by the quartermaster's department during the Civil War float down Railroad Avenue. Small boats were rowed into the lobby of the hotel, taking people to and from the front desk, and the "madam" of the hotel, Mrs. R.A. Bishop, persuaded a milkman who had fashioned a small raft to row her around the first floor of the hotel. When the crowd in the lobby encouraged him to tip the raft, she told him that she would drown him if he did so and, exercising his discretion, the milkman decided to return her safely to the front desk. Manned by Captain Woods Wilson, a small steamboat, the *Cherokee*, attempted to steam up Market Street but, after having been told by the mayor that the waves from the steamer's wake might damage the storefronts in that area, instead ventured up Broad Street to the hotel, where it picked up a group of ladies for an "excursion cruise." By the time the flood receded, it had caused several deaths and a great deal of property damage - although one man made out well when his home was washed away and another, better structure came to rest in its place. Another house which had floated to a new location and was not claimed was sold by the city to benefit flood sufferers. Though the hotel survived the flood, it was not destined to remain long. A prominent Chattanooga landmark in the years surrounding the Civil War, the Crutchfield House burned to the ground in 1867.

One remnant of the Crutchfield House is the persistent rumor that, during the Civil War, a soldier killed a prostitute in Room 311 of the hotel. As a result, it is claimed that Room 311 of the present hotel remains haunted to this day, and several hotel guests have requested a change in rooms after having apparently been visited by the murdered woman's apparition.

On January 1, 1872, the 3-story Read House (below) opened on the former site of the Crutchfield House. Originally, a group of businessmen began construction of a commercial building at the site, but John T. Read, a surgeon in the Mexican and Civil Wars (CSA), purchased the structure prior to completion and converted

it into a hotel. During this period, the Read House came to be considered the "center of all activity in Chattanooga," and in 1880 the hotel, which had been taken over by Sam Read in 1879, was extended along the length of Ninth Street to Chestnut Street; in 1886, a fourth story was also added to the hotel. Impressed by St. Louis' street widening and zoning project, by 1923 Read began to contemplate an addition to the hotel in order to cater to the increasing number of visitors to the city; it was commented at the time that "if building and money conditions are right and if the Nashville railroad consents to widen West Ninth Street thirty feet he will probably start work on this project." Two-thirds of the old building was then torn down and replaced by a new 10-story hotel (as seen in the postcard on page 156) designed in a modernized Georgian style emulating the eighteenth-century manor houses of England.

The base of the structure is granite, with the remainder fashioned of wire-cut variegated red brick with terra cotta trim; the 12 shops on the first floor were fronted with ornamental iron and glass marquises. The vestibule is paneled with American walnut and opens into a 2-story, 45-by-70 foot lobby. In a gesture recognizing the historic lineage of the hotel, the arches in the lobby were keystoned with the Read and Crutchfield family crests. The expanded, 300-room hotel was opened in July 1926, at a total cost of $2 million.

The remainder of the twentieth century witnessed a number of changes to modernize the historic hotel, which has hosted numerous notable guests, including Wendell Wilkie, Winston Churchill, President Miguel Aleman of Mexico, Rutherford B. Hayes, William McKinley, Tom Thumb, Jack Dempsey, Charles Laughton, John Barrymore, Alvin York, Al Jolson, Ginger Rogers, Bob Hope, Bing Crosby, Franklin Delano Roosevelt, Andrew Johnson, Benny Goodman, Dizzy Dean, Al Capone, Andrew Jackson, Liberace, Tallulah Bankhead, Richard Nixon, George Wallace, Dinah Shore, Connie Mack, Bette Davis, and Ronald Reagan.

In 1943, the hotel was sold by the Read estate to the Noe hotel chain, and in 1968 the National Hotel Company began operation of the 520-room hotel after the Provident Life & Accident Insurance Company bought the property. The hotel was then placed on the National Register of Historic Places in 1977. That year, it was purchased by the Chattanooga Choo-Choo Company, which renamed it the "Choo-Choo Read House"; the top 2 floors were renamed "The Towers" and were served with a separate lobby area, and a disco ("Grand Central Station") was temporarily opened in the hotel. In 1981, the creation of a "First Central Business Improvement District" was approved by the city in order to revive the hotel and its surrounding area, and the hotel passed through a number of hands in the 1980s, joining the Radisson chain in the latter half of the decade.

When the name of Ninth Street was changed to Martin Luther King Jr. Blvd. in 1982, the hotel initially altered its address from the Ninth Street side of the building to Broad Street, leading to calls for an NAACP boycott of the hotel. The issue was resolved in 1991, when the address was changed to reflect the hotel's location on MLK Jr. Blvd. The hotel has continued to change hands, having been purchased in 1994 by Tech Motel Ltd., an Atlanta corporation which undertook a $2 million renovation of the hotel to enhance its Civil War theme: as a result, portraits of northern and southern generals hanging in the lobby were supplemented by murals on each floor depicting a specific battle of the war. Today, the hotel continues to serve as an important historic landmark in the downtown Chattanooga area.

One notable building adjacent to the Read House, on the left (west) side of Broad Street, is the brick building located at **819 Broad Street.** This Victorian Commercial structure was erected in 1891. It has housed a variety of commercial offices since its completion, and it continues to serve that purpose today.

From this spot, cross Broad Street. The tree-lined median in the center of this road was added in the 1970s to reduce Broad Street to a "reasonable urban scale." This was not the first time, however, that such a development had taken place on Broad Street. In 1884, in fact, one of the first city park developments in Chattanooga resulted in the creation of a row of

trees along Broad Street, a plan which led to the following criticism: "The movement to lay off Broad Street as a Park was looked upon as a joke until recently when rows of trees were planted in the centre of the street. It is said that this is ornamental. So is a Dude. No one ever said that a Dude was useful, and no one has yet said that this Park business will be useful. Property holders are beginning to look to side streets to build for increasing population, and business is uncertain and yet unsettled in its growth. Can property owners on Broad Street permit their property to be converted from business to park purposes? No city can show four story business houses fronting a park. Broad Street is none too wide for the business that will be done on it in a few years." Subsequently eliminated as automobile traffic increased the demands placed upon downtown streets (above), trees were again planted along the length of Broad Street in the 1970s.

Across Broad Street from the Read House, at the northeast corner of Broad Street and MLK Jr. Blvd., ❷ is the **Market Center** (820 Broad Street), a 4-story, 40,000 square-foot office building erected in 2001, which has been referred to as "the first stand-alone class A office building built downtown in several years." Previously occupying this location in the block bounded by, Broad, Market and Eighth Streets and MLK Jr. Blvd. was the antebellum Grenville flour mill, owned by Augusta, Georgia, native Charles Erskine Grenville. After the Civil War, this corner became the site of the **Florentine Hotel**, a 2-story building erected in 1870 to serve passengers arriving at the nearby Western & Atlantic railroad depot. Initially known as the Carroll House and, later, the Van Horn House, the name of the hotel was changed to the Florentine Hotel after the inn was acquired by A.J. and G.W. Stoops. The Florentine Hotel, which was advertised as "a first class hotel with low rates ($2 per day)," capitalized on its location by offering free luggage transportation between the hotel and the nearby Union Depot. The photograph below shows the hotel as it stood in 1885; in the foreground of this picture, a crowd gathers around the J.H. Lighthall Medicine Show, which arrived in Chattanooga to sell a variety of cure-alls to local residents on September 5, 1885. In 1887, the hotel was purchased by Sarah E. Crow, daughter of Confederate soldier "Wild Bill" Crow, and renamed the Crow House. The building continued to be used as a hotel until 1891, at which time it was sold and leased to the City Bank Block Company for use by the Citizens Bank & Trust Company, in which capacity it continued

to be used until the bank was absorbed by the Hamilton National Bank in the 1910s. Although it was temporarily shut down in the 1930s after having been labeled a "house of assignation," the building was again used as a hotel in later years, the "Kentucky Home Hotel." In 1967, the building (which was in reality 2 separate buildings with a common third story built over both) was sold to anonymous purchasers for $260,000. In 1969, it was demolished to be used as the site for future construction of a new $3 million library; when another nearby site was instead chosen for the new library, the lot was used for parking until the Market Center building was erected in 2001.

Next to the Florentine Hotel (in the picture on page 161) was the **Chattanooga Beer & Ice Company**. Subsequently, Kelly's Barrel House (a wholesale liquor house) acquired this property; after that company was forced out of business by the Volstead Act in 1921, T.O. Duff and Leo Block moved their wholesale business into the spot, which became known as the Duff-Block Building. The original building has since been torn down. Also near this spot, in an open area between 818 and 820 Broad Street, was an alleyway known as "Arcade Alley" which ran from Broad Street through to Market Street. This alley was created after the Kaylor Hall structure at this spot was condemned and torn down in 1886.

Next door to this site is a lot which was at one point occupied by the **Airdome Theater** (below), a "polite vaudeville" theater owned by Fletch M. Catron and Will S. Albert, which

opened in 1909. Advertised as the only theater in Chattanooga built specifically for summer amusements, the theater featured a 12-horsepower cooling plant and a moveable roof. Tickets for shows at the Airdome cost 15 and 25 cents, while matinees were 10 cents. Female patrons received keepsakes at Wednesday evening shows, and during Saturday matinees children were given souvenirs. In 1912, this short-lived theater was merged with the nearby Majestic Theater.

Proceed to the southeast corner of Broad and Eighth Streets. ❸ Boasting that he was the only dealer in the South selling solely glassware, in 1878 P.C. Wilson erected a 4-story

building at this site which, anticipating the twentieth century curtain wall, featured plate glass "from roof to basement" supported by sixteen 1,600 pound iron columns. The building also included a square cupola with "Glass" spelled out on each side, which was topped by an American flag. The sidewalk next to the building was also glass-paneled, allowing light

to enter the basement area. It is said that **P.C. Wilson's Glass House** (left) was destroyed by floating debris during the flood of 1886, after which the business moved to a new location on Tenth Street. In 1892, George Fort Milton, editor of the *Chattanooga News*, erected the present structure in the Richardsonian Romanesque style, which emphasizes the use of heavy masonry. The first floor of the building is of southern Ohio red sandstone, with upper floors of brick. Because the levels of downtown Chattanooga streets were raised in order to address the flooding problem in the town, 12 feet of the building are now underground, in the basement of the structure. In 1976, the building was purchased for $160,000 and renovated; a second renovation was carried out in 1988, at which time the original gabled roof which characterized the building prior to the 1940s was restored. Currently, the "Milton Building" houses a number of private businesses and retail stores.

Across Broad Street, at the northeast corner of Broad and Eighth Streets, is the Chattanooga Bank Building, which is discussed in greater detail on page 175.

From this spot, cross Broad Street to the southwest corner of Broad and Eighth Streets. ❹ **The First National Bank of Chattanooga** was founded in 1865 by a group of Ohio investors, including William P.

Rathburn, Theodore G. Montague, and Union veteran T.R. Stanley, choosing Chattanooga after the Treasury Department refused to grant yet another bank charter for the city of Cincinnati. Due to expanding business, the First National

Bank subsequently erected a 4-story building (below left, on page 162) with an arched stone entrance, designed by R.H. Hunt, at this site. In 1905, the bank merged with the Chattanooga National Bank; it was closed during the Depression and succeeded by the Commercial National Bank, which operated for about 10 years before being taken over by the American National Bank. Temporarily housing the Gottschalk Furniture Company, the original building was torn down when the local Pioneer Bank decided to erect a new building in 1962 at this site. The 6-story building (above) was designed by Mario Bianculli and George Palm, Jr., of Chattanooga; the base is of Minnesota granite, and the upper portion is a "cage" of glass, aluminum, and enameled steel. Currently, the building houses the AmSouth Bank and several private offices.

Cross Eighth Street to the northwest corner of Broad and Eighth Streets, ❺ the site of the **James Building** (735 Broad Street). The Rev. Jesse J. James came to Chattanooga about 1854 and established a farm immediately south of town; initially, "James Place" (now MLK Jr.

Blvd.) marked the southern boundary of Chattanooga. His youngest son, Charles E. James, was an enthusiastic promoter of Chattanooga and is considered the city's "first millionaire." He was involved in the development in 1884 of the "belt line," a rail line which carried freight and passengers throughout outlying areas of the city; this enterprise resulted in significant suburban growth (including the St. Elmo, East Chattanooga, Orchard

Knob, Alton Park, Ridgedale, East Lake, Avondale, and Highland Park neighborhoods) and spurred the real estate boom of 1887-1888. He also became involved in promotion of the City Water Company (1886), a broad gauge railway from St. Elmo to the top of Lookout Mountain (1888), a coal-mining community on Lookout Mountain at Durham, Georgia, and the Hales Bar dam below Chattanooga (1913). He was also instrumental in the development of Signal Mountain, through the creation of the Signal Mountain Inn (1913, now the Alexian Brothers Retirement Home), a 13-mile streetcar line from Chattanooga to the crest of the mountain (1913), and the City of Signal Mountain itself (1919).

One of the most tangible achievements of Charles James, however, was the James Building (below left), Chattanooga's first "sky-scraper" and thus an important milestone for the city. This 12-story, 129,000 square-foot building, which was designed by prominent local architect R.H. Hunt, was completed in 1907. The James Building was constructed in the "Wainwright style," meaning it is a heavy-block "U" shaped building; 1,200 tons of steel and 500,000 bricks went into the completed structure. An additional 48-room annex was completed in 1917. When the TVA entered the Tennessee Valley, the first-floor corner office of the building was occupied by the Electric Home & Farm Authority as a showroom for electric products (1934). The building, which is on the National Register of Historic Places (1980) and has been referred to as the "center of Chattanooga's financial community for many years," underwent restorations in 1982 and 1985, during which the original ornamental entryway, which was sheared off and replaced with "modern" red granite panels in 1960, was replaced. Today, the James Building continues to house numerous offices and retail stores.

Immediately next door to the James Building is the **MacLellan Building** (721 Broad Street). ❻ In reality, this 65,000 square-foot building (right) is actually comprised of 2

separate structures linked by walkways on the first, third, and fourth floors. The original structure, referred to as the James Building Annex, was built in 1913 and later supplemented by the prominent 13-story building constructed in 1924 as the headquarters for the local Provident Life & Accident Insurance Company (1887), founded to provide insurance for "uninsurables," e.g., coal mine, blast furnace, and sawmill workers. The building is named for Thomas MacLellan, who arrived in Chattanooga in 1892 and assumed the directorship of the insurance company. Designed by R.H. Hunt, the building is of Greek Ionic design on the bottom 3 floors and features a sloping green tile mansard roof. In 1951, the 5-story West Building was constructed to the rear of the original building as a needed addition of floor space for the growing company. In 1960, however, Provident relocated its headquarters to new offices near Fountain Square, and in 1981 the building was sold to a limited partnership. In 1993, Provident resumed ownership of the building, which it then sold to a private investor who razed the West Building annex for additional customer parking (1995). Today, the building, which was added to the National Register of Historic Places in 1985, houses a number of private offices and companies.

Next door to the MacLellan Building is the **Tivoli Theater** (709-711 Broad Street). ❼ Once the site of the Truxel & Dunmeyer machine shop, on March 19, 1921, the Tivoli

Theater (named for the Italian Tivoli) opened at this spot with a showing of Cecil B. DeMille's "Forbidden Fruit" and Charlie Chaplin's "The Kid." The theater, designed by C.W. and George L. Rapp of Chicago, cost $750,000 and took 2 years to complete. It was designed as an exact but smaller replica of the Beaux Arts-styled Cincinnati Riveria Theater and featured plaster designs cast in Italy, a domed ceiling, and crystal chandeliers. In 1926, the Tivoli became the first air-conditioned public building in the South when one of the first 5 Carrier air conditioners was installed in the theater. Standing as "Chattanooga's premier movie and variety theater" through the 1940s, the

Tivoli (pictured below left and on page 157) declined in importance following the advent of television in the 1950s, and in 1961 the theater was closed. A local grant enabled it to reopen in 1963, and in 1976 the theater was purchased by the city for $300,000; at that time, the original $30,000 Wurlitzer pipe organ (which had not been played since 1939) was put back into service. Listed on the National Register of Historic Places (1974), the Tivoli again reopened in 1987 after a $7 million renovation to restore it to its original glory. Today, the Tivoli Theater stands as home to the Chattanooga Symphony and Opera Association, the cultural center of the city, and a model for the preservation of historic and cultural properties.

Next door to the Tivoli Theater is the 4-story **Tivoli Center** (above), ❽ also known as the Trigg-Smartt Building (701 Broad Street). The sole structure remaining from the 1887-1888 real estate boom, the 4-story brick and cutstone building was erected by Trigg, Dobbs & Company and the Smartt Brothers & Company shoe store in 1888. In reality, the Victorian Commercial building (which also has strong Richardsonian Romanesque features) was erected as 4 separate units, with a common facade. At the close of World War I, the Sterchi Brothers Furniture Company moved into the building, and in 1939 the Fowler Brothers furniture business took over the location. A subsequent $38,000 renovation of the building was performed by the local architectural firm of Crutchfield & Law, which added pink polished granite, aluminum, and glass to the storefronts of the building, among other exterior and interior alterations. The Fowler's furniture store remained in this location until closing in 1985, and the building was then purchased by the Lyndhurst Foundation, which conducted an extensive restoration of the building. Now know as the Tivoli Center, this building was placed on the National Register of Historic Places in 1986. The building, which was purchased in 2000 by local businessmen for $1.2 million, continues to serve as prime downtown office space at this time.

From this corner, cross Seventh Street. ❾ Referred to as "the largest roller skating rink in the South," the **Hippodrome Roller Skating Rink** (below) was established near the turn of the century by the Stoops brothers at the northwest corner of Broad and Seventh Streets. The

attraction, however, only lasted for 3 years, and today an office building occupied by Blue Cross/Blue Shield of Tennessee sits at this corner.

Across Broad Street, at the northeast corner of Broad and Seventh Streets, ❿ is the former **Miller Brothers Department Store Building,** which is described in greater detail on page 178-179. A remnant of the Underground Chattanooga area created when downtown street levels were raised in the 1870s and 1880s, a tunnel under Broad Street at this point connects this building with the Blue Cross/Blue Shield building at the northwest corner of Broad and Seventh Streets (above).

At the far end of this block, at the northeast corner of Broad and Sixth Streets, ⓫ is the **AmSouth Bank Building**. Following the creation of Miller Park, in 1979 the First Federal Savings & Loan bank was forced to relocate its offices, and the bank thereafter built this 5-story, 55,0000 square-foot marble and glass building, which is today occupied by AmSouth Bank.

If you wish to continue north along Broad Street, turn to page 147. To return to the start of the Railroad Avenue tour, proceed south along Broad Street to MLK Jr. Blvd.

Market Center

Market Center, the historic commercial center of Chattanooga, sits above "Underground Chattanooga," a collection of hidden chambers, basements, and catacombs lying beneath the streets of the downtown area. For decades after the founding of Ross's Landing, the Tennessee River periodically flooded the city, causing significant damage. Although a levee proposed in 1875 was never built, residents raised some street levels, a haphazard arrangement criticized by the *Chattanooga Times* (1886), which reported, "We have hitched up a corner here, a block there and part of a block yonder, each hitch bringing with it a lawsuit for damage...and all this time we have been putting the streets in the most absurd and unattractive shape, confusing builders so they cannot tell what height to put their first floors, and still leaving the grade too low by at least three feet on the average." Following the massive flood of 1886, which crested at 52.18 feet, claimed 2 lives, and destroyed hundreds of homes, the city created a comprehensive plan for raising street levels. By 1890, Market Street was raised by an average of two feet, and in some areas more: it is estimated that the intersection of Market Street and MLK Jr.Blvd. has been raised over 10 feet! Forgotten for decades, in 1978 Underground Chattanooga was "rediscovered" by UTC archaeology professor Jeffrey Brown. Today, the area, which is not accessible to visitors, contains underground passageways between buildings, uneven Civil War-era stone walls, and basements with windows which were the former storefronts of early Market Street businesses.

As part of a 1970s downtown "rejuvenation plan," Market Street between MLK Jr. Blvd. and Sixth Street was redeveloped as the "Market Center." To reduce and slow traffic, Market Street was redesigned as a curving boulevard with large tree planters, information cubes, and sales kiosks. A park-like area in front of the SunTrust Building is part of this design, as is the large fountain near Seventh Street. To introduce visitors to this area, "tall concrete pylons of varying heights" were placed at Sixth Street and MLK Jr. Blvd., to be supplemented with Civil War cannon and night lighting. Though the suburban flight of the 1980s and 1990s left many businesses in the downtown core vacant, today the Market Center is undergoing redevelopment, with a number of historic buildings undergoing renovation for commercial and residential purposes.

New
Orleans
Store

to
**Railroad
Avenue**
p. 155

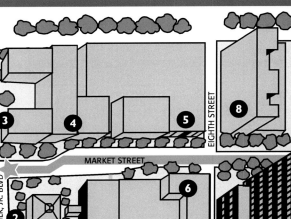

to
Georgia Tract ❶
p. 105

MARKET STREET

MLK, JR. BLVD

EIGHTH STREET

❸ ❹ ❺ ❽ ❷ ❻

❸ Davidson Clothing Store

to
Irish
p. 61

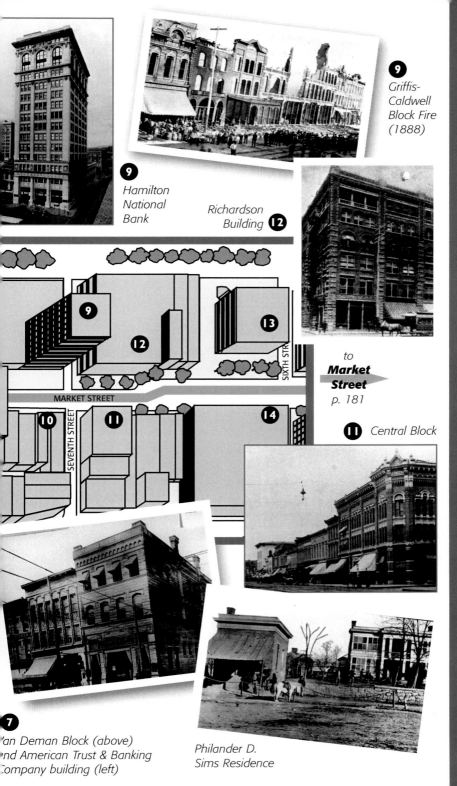

9 Griffis-Caldwell Block Fire (1888)

9 Hamilton National Bank

Richardson Building **12**

SIXTH STREET

13

12

MARKET STREET

SEVENTH STREET

10

11

14

to **Market Street** p. 181

11 Central Block

7 an Deman Block (above) nd American Trust & Banking Company building (left)

Philander D. Sims Residence

MARKET
CENTER

NORTH

Tennessee River

The tour of the Market Center begins at the corner of Market Street and Martin Luther King Jr. Boulevard. ❶ The entrance to the Market Center area is indicated by the concrete columns at the northwest corner of Market Street and MLK Jr. Blvd. These columns are remnants of the urban development plan introduced in the 1970s to create of a "Market

Center" business core for the downtown area, a plan intended to preserve commercial development in downtown Chattanooga at a time when many businesses were fleeing to new suburban areas.

At the northeast corner of Market Street and MLK Jr. Blvd. is **Miller Plaza.** ❷ Originally occupied by a number of buildings known as the "Wisdom Block," this park, which includes a pavilion, stage, and fountains, was created as a $6 million extension of the Miller Park development to the south. Between Memorial Day and Labor Day each summer, the park is the site of the popular Nightfall Concert Series, a free series of shows by a variety of musical artists which draws crowds to this area each Friday evening.

One interesting enterprise which previously occupied the site of Miller Plaza was the **Stag Hotel** (834 Market Street), "for men only," which was established in 1903 by "Colonel" Al W. Stanley and John Bogenshott. This 42-room hotel, which boasted one of the largest pool rooms in the South, cost $30,000 and hosted business travelers arriving at the Chattanooga railyards to the south.

Another important business located near this corner was the **Kress's Department Store** (822-830 Market Street). In 1899, an S.H. Kress store (a branch of the company founded in Memphis in 1896) opened at 808 Market Street, later moving to 706 Market Street (1924). In 1954, however, several buildings in the block bounded by Market, Cherry, Eighth, and Ninth Streets were razed to make way for a new, "modern" Kress's store at this location. This store subsequently became the site of civil rights demonstrations in February 1960, during which several local Howard High School students staged sit-ins at local lunch counters, including this store. These incidents suddenly erupted into violence, and ice cream, potted

plants, sugar bowls, cups, and saucers (as well as fists) were used as weapons until police and firemen with hoses diffused the situation. Thirteen persons, including 12 white and 1 African-American students, were arrested. Similar incidents occurred at other nearby department stores, including Woolworth's (729 Market Street), W.T. Grant Co. (715), and the McLellan Stores (713), and when word spread that additional sit-ins were scheduled to occur after schools let out, stores were temporarily closed at 3:30 p.m. for a time. Although the Kress's store continued in business for several years following this incident, the growth of suburban shopping areas eventually led the business to close, and the building was torn down; today, the site is occupied by Miller Plaza.

From this spot, cross Market Street to the northwest corner of Market Street and MLK Jr. Blvd. ❸ The west side of this block is the site of several interesting buildings with important ties to the history of Chattanooga – though a number of these early structures have since been torn down. For instance, the central amusement hall in early Chattanooga was **Kaylor Hall**, on the west side of Market Street between Eighth and Ninth Streets. This theater, which was managed by Harry Kaylor, was small, with an unimpressive stage which led to an incident in which one performer, actor Edwin Forrest, "cussed out the hall, the stage, the management, his manager, the town, everything and everybody that he could think of to cuss and declared that he wouldn't act in that place." Apparently, a sign reading "Use Eureka Oil" tacked to the drop curtain especially offended the actor. Falling into disuse as other performance halls were built, Kaylor Hall was rented for $100 to the First Methodist Church (1866), and it was used for a time by a volunteer fire company, while the upper floors were used as a meeting hall for ward politicians. Finally, it was condemned and torn down around 1886, leaving an "arcade," or alleyway, between Market and Broad Streets.

The current parking area at the south end of this block was later occupied by the **S&W Cafeteria** (825 Market Street), which opened at this location in 1932 and served as one of the few restaurants in the downtown area for a number of years. This restaurant concocted several intriguing strategies for attracting diners: on Thursday evenings, for instance, the George Rogers orchestra played for patrons, while a movie was shown upstairs for children. In 1952, the restaurant was expanded to Broad Street, and mezzanine seating and a second food line were opened. However, the cafeteria eventually closed in 1981 due to urban flight from the downtown area. Following a remodeling intended to give the building a "Williamsburg look," a Hardee's restaurant opened in the building in 1983; this restaurant also closed in 1987. Subsequently, deterioration (epitomized by bricks which periodically fell from the building onto the sidewalk below) led to its eventual removal, and the site remains a parking area today.

Nearby, the short-lived **Automatic Vaudeville** opened at 835 Market Street in 1907. Capitalizing on the flurry of entertainment devices which were patented at the turn of the century, this $50,000 business featured Mutascopes, Horoscopes, Victor Talking Machines, and an "Automatic Canary Bird." However, the business was soon eclipsed by newer theaters and was closed. The building was then demolished in subsequent years.

Also at the site of this parking lot is the former **Davidson Clothing Store**. Arriving in Chattanooga in 1869 from his native Scotland, Charles Alexander Davidson worked in William Crutchfield's dry goods store and operated the Roane Iron Company store before opening Davidson's Clothing Store in 1881. This business, which advertised itself as a "new cash clothing house" and the local "headquarters for clothing and hats," was the first on Market

Street to feature plate glass windows, "a nine days' wonder which people came from afar and near to see and admire." As the picture to the left indicates, at one point, the business was operated as Davidson & McGrath, offering "dry goods, boots, shoes, and clothing". Following Davidson's death, his sons operated the business until 1946, when it was purchased by Nashville investors. The store went out of business in 1966, and the building was subsequently dismantled.

Next door to this site stood, until recently, the **Patten & Payne** building. Dating to 1865,

Patten & Payne was for many years the oldest store in Chattanooga (a title the business's owners claimed as early as 1925). T.H. Payne was a quartermaster in the Union army who found himself in Chattanooga during the Civil War and stayed at the close of the conflict, opening a book- and news-stand at 523 Market Street. After briefly relocating to the Read House, he moved the business to this location, where he was joined in the business by Z.C. Patten, another former Union soldier who had joined the commissary department after having been injured at the battle of Chickamauga. In 1871, a fire burned most of the buildings on the northern part of this block, after which a new building was completed at this site. A successful business for many years, Patten & Payne opened additional stores in the greater Chattanooga area, including a business machine division located on Amnicola Highway. Ironically, the suburban growth which had allowed the company to expand in the 1960s and 1970s eventually carried business away from the downtown area, and in 1996 the company was sold to U.S. Office Products, which sold the gift shop portion of the business to the local Fischer-Evans company in 1997. After the business was finally forced to close, the building at this site was torn down in 2001.

Next door to the former Patten & Payne site is a recent cause celebre for local preservationists, the stone **Burchay Building** (817 Market Street), ❹ a fine example of Richardsonian Romanesque architecture designed by local architect Samuel McClung Patton in the 1890s. Burchay's Furriers was founded in 1932 by Manchester, England, native Edwin Burke, who had previously served as an apprentice to his father-in-law, Louis Chajage; the name of this new business enterprise was formed by combining the Burke and Chajage names. In 1938, the company moved to this building, which had previously been occupied by the Merchants National Bank, a music teacher, the Cumberland Savings & Loan Association, Joy's flower shop, and, at one time, a saloon. After remaining at this location for 62 years, reduced retail business in the downtown core as well as several consecutive warm winters forced the furrier to close in 2000. Though plans for replacing the building with a parking facility were discussed, developers and preservationists were able to create an innovative plan for the building, removing the rear portion of the building and retaining the elaborate stone tower, which is planned to provide office and residential space in the near future.

Continue north along Market Street. Located at 809 Market Street is the **Hardie & Caudle Building**, erected in 1923. This local clothing shop was founded in 1906 by former restauranteur Charles Hardie and William Caudle, a former salesman for the nearby Davidson Clothing Store. The former business is memorialized by the "Hardie and Caudle" title above the entrance to the building.

Nearby, the 3-story building at the southwest corner of Market and Eighth Streets, ❺ which sits on the portion of this block referred to as the "Poss Block" in old city maps, is the **Fischer-Evans Store** (801 Market Street). This jewelry store was established in 1869 by W.F. Fischer, who came to Chattanooga at age 23 after having worked in the gun shops of the Confederate army in Dalton, Georgia, during the Civil War. "W.F. Fischer & Bro." was initially established in a walled-off corner of a livery stable on this site, with 12-inch interior plank walls papered for "added elegance." With insufficient funds to purchase a safe, the brothers (Will and Lou) reportedly carried home their gems each night in a basket. In 1870, the original building was destroyed by a large fire which engulfed many buildings between Sixth and Ninth Streets, but the business returned to a new, 2-story brick building at this location in 1872; the present building, moreover, was completed in 1925. During the Great Depression, the company was forced to keep no silver in stock, ordering such items only upon special request by a definite buyer. In

1956, the company merged with Evans Jewelers, becoming Fischer-Evans at that time, and it continues to operate at this location currently.

In front of the Fischer-Evans building is the **Fischer-Evans Clock** (pictured to the left and on page 168), a cast-iron timepiece installed at this corner in 1893, which has served as a downtown landmark for more than a century.

Across Market Street, at the southeast corner of Market and Eighth Streets, ❻ is the historic **Loveman's Department Store** (800 Market Street). This corner was originally the site of the Centenary Methodist Church, which was erected circa 1870 at a cost of $2,000 using "machine made bricks." The church, which was set back from the street and reached by way of a board walk over the muddy lot, was a plain structure with a tall spire and a balcony in the rear for African-American worshippers. In 1884, the property was purchased by D.B. Loveman for $35,000. Loveman, owner of the New Orleans Store across Eighth Street (pictured on page 168), then erected a 3-story, 38,000 square-foot brick building to house his new Loveman's department store, which featured

large plate glass windows, high ceilings, and marble drinking fountains throughout the store. The original building was destroyed by fire (1891), after which Loveman built the current 4-story store on the same spot (1892). The first story of the current structure (above) is composed of blue freestone, with upper stories of pressed brick trimmed with stone.

Due to business growth and the need for additional space, in 1904 Loveman purchased an adjacent building, to which he added a fifth story in 1907. In 1932, the store was sold to Thomas & Moore Dry Goods Company, a North Carolina wholesale concern, which continued to operate the store as Loveman's, Inc. In 1940, the first floor was modernized with an exterior of granite and terra cotta, a large 25-by-20 foot vestibule entrance on Market Street, and 3 automatic elevators. The business continued to expand in the 1950s, opening branches in East Ridge, Kingsport, and Oak Ridge, Tennessee, and purchasing adjacent buildings for use as the "budget" section of the store. In 1969, the building was given a "fresh and young personality" through the addition of "ultramodern" insulated aluminum panels as part of a $3 million building project. Branch expansion continued with the installation of mall stores at Northgate (1971), Highland Plaza (1972), Dalton Mall (1979), and Hamilton Place (1987); ironically, this suburban expansion would eventually seal the fate of the downtown store, which closed in 1993. In 1997, the 180,000 square-foot building was purchased with the intention of transforming the structure into retail stores and upscale condominiums; the "modern" aluminum panels have been removed to expose the original brick facade, and at this time the building is undergoing continued renovation.

From this spot, cross Eighth Street to the northeast corner of Market and Eighth Streets, currently the site of the **SunTrust Bank Building** (736 Market Street). ❼ Originally, this entire block was part of the large Thomas McCallie farm which sat on the east side of town. After McCallie sold the property, it passed quickly through a number of hands before being purchased by Alabama resident H.Y. Hall for $2,700.

Subsequently, this corner was the site of the "New Orleans Store," an early department store purchased by David B. Loveman in 1875. The store (pictured below and on page 168) was located in a 3-story brick building with numerous chimneys running along the length of the store, as well as awnings and windows along both street sides to greet and attract shoppers. In 1923, the **American Trust & Banking Company** (1912) acquired a 4-story brownstone building in the Van Deman Block which had replaced the New Orleans Store and was, at that time, occupied by the Hamilton National Bank (see photograph on

page 169). The 60-foot wide structure was constructed of glazed tile and marble, with an interior of east Tennessee gray marble and Circassian walnut. In 1927, however, a destructive fire necessitated the construction of a new building. Planned as the "Taj Mahal of Chattanooga," this elaborate structure, pictured on page 168, was designed by Vitzhum & Burns and built of Georgia marble and Minnesota granite. The structure was intended to display "noble proportions, symmetry of line and perfection of detail," and it featured Corinthian columns, huge cathedral windows, bronze grill work, and a 3-story domed lobby. Around the interior walls of the bank were portraits of Civil War generals, including Forrest, Wilder, Rosecrans, Bragg, Grant, Bate, Johnson, and Lytle. After merging with the Commerce

National Bank in 1941, the bank was renamed the "American National Trust & Banking Company" in 1948.

1957 was a key year for the bank, which added a number of branches, including a new "automatic teller" at Eighth and Lindsay Streets. In recognition of this growth, the decision was made to tear down the building (along with some buildings to the north) and erect a new structure. The building (below) was planned to be 18, then 20, stories (at the time the tallest building in town), with 8 elevators. The concrete-and-steel structure (1968) is covered with granite and precast concrete panels and has anodized bronze window units; the northern wall is of brick and masonry, with a glazed brick logo 18-feet in diameter intended to create "an esthetically satisfying exterior appearance." The original marble American eagle keystone (which is 3-by-4 feet and weighs 3-4 tons), medallions, vaults, and brass designs were salvaged for use in the new building, which boasts an interior of granite, Alabama cream marble, and Italian travertine marble. An 8-foot high sign announcing the name of the bank was also placed on the roof. In the 1970s, Market Street was modified at this spot to create a "park-like" atmosphere, and the current park was developed in front of the building. Today, the building is operated by the SunTrust Bank.

Located next door to this building was the **Gottschalk Building** (732 Market Street), a 3-story building erected by H.Y. Hall. The structure, which was only 25 feet wide but ran from Market to Cherry Street, was later occupied by the Gottschalk & Company furniture store, from which it derived its name. German native and Confederate naval veteran James Gottschalk lived with his wife in an upstairs apartment at this location. In 1915, the American Trust & Banking Company purchased the building for $70,000, announcing that the property, which adjoined the new bank building to be located to the south, would be held for future bank expansion. As expected, the building was later torn down as the bank expanded into the current building located at this spot.

Also in this immediate vicinity (728 Market Street) was a pair of pioneer log cabins built by one of the earliest residents of Ross's Landing, **Isaac Baldwin**. Disabled by a fall prior to coming to Chattanooga, Baldwin died in 1838, and this area soon developed as part of the business center of downtown Chattanooga.

The remainder of the east side of Market Street between Seventh and Eighth Streets, which was listed in old city maps as the **"Sims Block,"** was originally owned by Dr. Philander D. Sims, who erected a home in this vicinity prior to the Civil War. The small brick building in the picture below housed Sims' doctor's office, which sat at

the street in front of the home. Subsequently, this area developed as a commercial area, and today the street contains a number of brick commercial buildings erected in the 1920s (702-712 Market Street) and 1930s (714-724 Market Street). While changing retail patterns and suburban flight led many of the businesses along this stretch of Market Street to close in recent years, the local RiverCity Company, a downtown development enterprise, recently purchased these buildings, announcing plans to renovate the block for use as retail and residential space.

Across Market Street, at the northwest corner of Market and Eighth Streets, is the **Chattanooga Bank Building,** ❽ an 11-story terra cotta building designed by R.H. Hunt and erected in 1927 by the Chattanooga Savings Bank & Trust Company on land leased for 99 years from the Jacob Kunz and William R. Frye estates. At the time the building was dedicated, it was said to be "one of the most beautiful of such structures in the South." With bronze appointments, terrazzo floors, and a lobby of Italian marble, the Chattanooga Bank Building was one of several significant structures built in downtown Chattanooga during the intensive building period of the early twentieth century. In 1958, the building was sold for $1 million to the Fisher-Cooper Company (New York), which reported that its interest in the building was spurred by a recognition that Chattanooga was "a growing

city with an unlimited future." One year later, the building was again sold, this time to a New York syndicate for $1.5 million. Utilized for several years as offices for the Tennessee Valley Authority, in 1987 the building was offered for sale at the asking price of $3 million, and in 1989 it was again sold, after which it underwent a substantial renovation. Placed on the National Register of Historic Places in 1980, today the building continues to house a number of professional offices and retail stores.

One important Chattanoogan who maintained offices in the Chattanooga Bank Building was **Estes Kefauver** (1909-1963), a member of the U.S. House of Representatives (1938-1949) and U.S. Senator (1949-1963). Kefauver's election to the Senate was significant for the state of Tennessee, in that it signaled the end of Memphis mayor "Boss" Edward H. Crump's overwhelming domination of Tennessee politics. During his tenure, Kefauver was heavily involved in the investigation of organized crime, eventually writing a significant book, *Crime in America* (1951), concerning his own findings; he was also an early supporter of civil rights in the South. A popular figure who wore a coonskin cap on the campaign trail, in 1956 Kefauver ran as the Democratic nomination for Vice-President along with Adlai Stevenson, who was defeated by Dwight D. Eisenhower in his bid for the Presidency.

From the corner of Market and Eighth Streets, proceed down Market Street. During the heyday for downtown Chattanooga, this portion of Market Street was considered the busiest commercial district of the city, and a number of businesses maintained space in this area. At 725 Market Street, the present site of the First Volunteer Bank, was located an early drug store opened by **Jo Anderson** (referred to as the "Live Druggist" because of the practical jokes he often played on customers) in 1895. This store, which was originally opened in 1892 in a nearby building, featured a gooseneck soda fountain which had been exhibited at the St. Louis World's Fair in 1904, as well as a drink invented by Anderson called "Pan Pepsin," concocted of panaline, pepsin, and syrup.

Nearby, at 702 Market Street, was the **Theato,** the city's first motion picture theater and the third in the South (after New Orleans and Atlanta). Opened by Howell Graham, who had come from Birmingham, Alabama, with $400 to establish the operation, the theater (left) seated 250 persons in rows of wooden chairs. The

exterior of the theater was very elaborate, with stained-glass windows, large statues, and carved accents covering the entire facade of the building. The theater hosted showings from 10 a.m. to 11 p.m. on a single, one-hand operated projector; a phonograph (a novel invention at the time) was placed in a conspicuous place in the front window to attract a crowd. The first show, a one-reel Edison comedy entitled "The Gay Deceivers," was shown on July 11, 1906, after which a different film was shown each day.

Continue along Market Street to Seventh Street. The intersection of Market and Seventh Streets was for many years considered the commercial heart of downtown Chattanooga, causing one resident to remark that "if he would stand on the corner of Market and Seventh streets long enough he would see everybody in Chattanooga." At the southwest corner of Market and Seventh Street is the **Hamilton National Bank Building** (701 Market Street), ❾ which opened in 1905 with a capitalization of $250,000. Six years later, the bank moved to a 3-story building at this spot which was previously occupied by the Third National Bank (erected 1883), and secured a vault which was "absolutely fire and burglar proof." In 1911, that structure was replaced by the current building, (below) Chattanooga's third "sky-scraper," an R.H. Hunt design which stood 15 stories high and cost $900,000 to complete. In 1920, the bank purchased the stock of the Hamilton Trust & Savings Bank (formerly the South Chattanooga Savings Bank), and in 1929 the two banks merged, forming the largest bank in East Tennessee. In 1940, bank growth demanded that the lobby of the building be extended to Broad Street through a 3-story addition, and in 1950

an additional 2-story expansion occurred, displacing the adjacent Rialto Theater and Federal Bake Shop. A new, 24-foot sign advertising the "Hamilton National Bank" was placed on the roof of the structure in 1960, and in 1965 the building underwent "modernization" as a granite facade was added to the first 2 floors, the upper stories were covered with stainless-steel bronze-colored panels, a sixteenth floor (complete with cafeteria) was added, and the original "L" shape of the building was closed in to make a rectangular structure. Over the years, the Hamilton National Bank seemed to weather every financial crisis which arose, and by 1973 the bank had 24 branch offices, as well as an additional 6-story remodeled building at the northeast corner of Eighth and Chestnut Streets (1973). Nevertheless, the financial downturn of the 1970s took its toll on the bank, which was declared insolvent after heavy real estate loans made by a non-banking subsidiary collapsed along with the real estate market as a whole. The result was the third-largest bank failure in U.S. history. The bank was purchased in 1976 by Memphis-based First Tennessee Bank for $16.25 million. Today, the building functions as office quarters for the First Tennessee Bank, as well as other private companies.

A number of noteworthy individuals occupied office space in this key downtown location over the years. One interesting occupant of the building was found in the 1931 Chattanooga directory, which lists offices 721-723 of the building as occupied by the law offices of **Stephen R. Roddy**. Following the arrest of the Scottsboro Boys in Paint Rock, Alabama, on March 25, 1931, Roddy was hired by the Interdenominational Colored Ministers Alliance of Chattanooga to represent the defendants. Roddy has since been characterized as "unfamiliar with Alabama law and drunk as well" at the trial, and one critic reports that he was "an unpaid and unprepared Chattanooga real estate attorney who, on the first day of trial, was 'so stewed he could hardly walk straight.'" An exchange recorded between the judge and Roddy seems to support part of this conclusion; when asked by the judge whether he was representing the defendants, Roddy replied as follows: "Not exactly. I'm here to join up with any lawyers you name to defend them. Sort of help out." By April 9, 1931, 8 of the 9 defendants were found guilty and sentenced to die; the trial of the ninth defendant, Roy Wright, ended in a mistrial.

Across Market Street, at the southeast corner of

Market and Seventh Streets, ❿ George K. Brown opened **The Palace** drug store in 1907. This interesting building was designed by architects Charles Bearden and Charles Foreman and featured a ceramic tile floor, a special ceiling designed by the Wheeling Corrugating Company, mahogany columns along the walls, and crystal drop lights. The entire 100-foot outer wall was built of solid plate glass. The soda fountain was of Mexican onyx, mahogany, and Italian marble, and it served up such concoctions as a "Tutti Frutti Yum Yum" and the "Palace Special Delight." This intriguing soda shop "was the meeting place and the social pulse of the city until it closed in 1933."

From this point, cross Seventh Street to the northeast corner of Market and Seventh Streets, ⓫ the location of the **Central Block**. Originally occupied by the antebellum home of Dr. Philander D. Sims (pictured on page 169), this lot was purchased by the First Presbyterian Church, which built a large frame building fronted by a tall box-like cupola on the site. The August 1863 shelling of Chattanooga caught General Braxton Bragg and other Confederate officers worshipping at the church; as shells whizzed overhead, the soldiers quickly evacuated the building to prepare for an invasion of the town. In the wake of the Civil War, the church, which was used as a hospital, was left in horrible condition; the seats were all removed, the carpet destroyed, the furnace ruined, and the roof damaged and leaky. As a result, the congregation was reduced from about 150 to 15-20 following the war. Nevertheless, after the federal government eventually paid $4,600 to repair the structure, full services resumed in June 1866. Around 1881, however, the church elected to move to a more serene site, erecting a new church building at the site of the old Daniel Kaylor home in the block bounded by Seventh and Walnut Streets and Georgia Avenue (ironically, next door to a home occupied at the time by Dr. P.D. Sims).

In 1882, an "important sale" took place at this spot, in which two individuals, Prosper Lazard and former Union surgeon Dr. Marx Block, purchased the property for $8,000. Constructed on this site in 1883 was the Block Block (named for Dr. Block), a "magnificent structure" which was labeled "the first pretentious building to go up on Market Street." The brick building (which has since come to be known as the Central Block) has a cut stone foundation and double French plate-glass windows in front. The building (left) is actually shaped like a horseshoe, with an open area on the interior, in which was placed a paved courtyard. Originally, the prime corner storefront of the building was occupied by a storeroom (1885), and after the City Savings Bank occupied this spot for a brief period, the "Live and Let Live Drug Store" then assumed the corner location circa 1892. The third floor of the building was divided into office space, as indicated by a number of fireplaces still located on the upper floor. Occupied for a time by the Liggett's drug store, in 1965 the building was occupied by the Holly Shop florist, and in the 1980s the site became the Hill's Florist shop. "Widely believed to be the oldest commercial structure in the city," in 1987 it was recommended that the Central Block be replaced with a $12 million professional office building (and a $4 million parking garage) to complement the new Justice Building proposed further down the block. As a result, in June 1994 it was planned that the vacant building would be torn down, but in 1995 the structure was "rescued" by the Cornerstones historic preservation group. Placed on the National Register of Historic Places (1995), the Central Block has come to occupy "center stage in [the] city's preservation efforts." In 2000, the building was offered to the United Way of Greater Chattanooga, which currently is renovating the structure for use as office space.

Mute evidence of "Underground Chattanooga" is evident in the Central Block at this corner. Along the Seventh Street side of the building, the edges of former window arches can be seen peeking above the sidewalk. It is believed that the streets in this area were built up after construction of the building, and the original first floor of the Central Block may actually be the current basement of the structure.

Next door to the Central Block, at 9 East Seventh Street, is the 2-story brick **McConnell Block**, constructed by Chancellor T.M. McConnell circa 1885, at a cost of $10,000.

Across the street from this building (14 East Seventh Street) was an early "Ice Cream Factory and Candy Kitchen," though this building was torn down in the 1930s and replaced with the current brick structure, a now-vacant building which last housed Samir's Deli, a local restaurant, before being restored.

Across Market Street, at the northwest corner of Market and Seventh Streets, is the **Griffis-Caldwell Block**. ⑫ In 1887-1888, a temporary real estate "boom" led to feverish land speculation, inflated real estate prices, and the creation

of new subdivisions outside of the Chattanooga city limits. One of the downtown sites which benefited from this event was the Griffis-Caldwell Block, a row of 3- and 4-story brick business buildings erected by Confederate veterans John C. Griffis and James A. Caldwell during the boom period. At 9:45 p.m. on August 9, 1888, a fire broke out at the Bradt Printing Company located on the second floor of one of these buildings and spread quickly. The Lookout fire engine, which was stationed nearby at the corner of Sixth and Market Streets, broke down and was inoperable, and firemen, hindered by a limited amount of firefighting equipment, were unable to halt the spread of the fire. The destructive effect of the fire is evident in the picture above, which shows the damage to the block the following morning. Although the First National Bank building and Joe Simpson clothing business to the north were not damaged, the entire southern end of the block was destroyed by the fire, which killed 2 persons who were trapped inside during the blaze.

Subsequently, Mississippian John P. Richardson, who came to Chattanooga from New Orleans during the 1887-1888 real estate boom, purchased the corner lot and erected the 6-story **Richardson Building** (above right) at this site. The structure, designed by fellow Mississippian

Samuel McClung Patton, was of pressed brick with stone trim. After opening in 1892, the building offered offices for rent at rates of "$5 and up." Also

destroyed by a fire which began in the boiler room and killed 2 individuals, including Patton (1897), the Richardson Building was then replaced by a structure built by Texas natives Gus and Frank Miller, owners of the "New York Racket Store." The Miller Brothers purchased the property and commissioned R.H. Hunt to design a 4-story building (1898) at the site. Offering 110,000 square-feet of space, the store (below), which introduced elevators and air conditioning to Chattanooga, "boasted the greatest display of merchandise that has ever been shown in a Southern store," as well as "the largest stock of mill ends, remnants and 'pound-packages' in the South." The store's owners also referred to it as "the store that made Chattanooga famous."

The remainder of the block, which was thereafter referred to in local maps as the "Phoenix Block," was soon rebuilt, and by 1901 the businesses in this block included grocers, dry goods stores, a hay and feed store, a tin shop, a liquor store, and a number of merchants selling wholesale goods. The Miller Brothers department store, a downtown landmark for decades, stayed in the Miller family until 1973, when it was acquired by the national retail firm of Garfinkel, Brooks Brothers, Miller & Rhoads, Inc., of Washington, D.C. Due to the growth of suburbs and retail malls outside of the downtown area, however, by 1980 most of the small retail stores had left the block, with the larger

department and furniture stores following only a few years later. This store closed in 1986, after closing its annex at Broad and Seventh Streets in 1977. Blue Cross-Blue Shield of Tennessee then purchased both of the buildings (which were joined by an underground corridor, another vestige of Underground Chattanooga) for $1.65 million and renovated the structure, removing the 1967 porcelainized steel covering to reveal the original brick and limestone facade of the building, which was added to the National Register of Historic Places in 1987.

In front of the Miller Brothers building is a historic marker celebrating the achievements of **William "Uncle Bill" Lewis**, who worked as the town blacksmith and wagon maker in a shop located near this corner prior to the Civil War. Born in Winchester, Tennessee, in 1810, Lewis came to Ross's Landing as a slave and reportedly married a Cherokee Indian prior to the Cherokee Removal. He subsequently purchased his freedom from his master, a Colonel Lewis (whose name he took as his own), and then saved up enough money to purchase the freedom of his mother, aunt, 2 brothers, and son; a slave trader also bought his sister for him. He had 8 children, one of whom enlisted in the Union army at the outset of the Civil War. Even as a free man, he continued to face legal challenges in the antebellum South; by law, he could not enter into business in his own name, and he was therefore forced to pay a white man to legalize his business dealings on his behalf. Nevertheless, he became an important part of the antebellum Chattanooga community; referred to as "a rugged man of much intelligence" who "always bore an excellent name for thrift, honesty, and sobriety," by 1860 Lewis was credited with owning real estate valued at $5,000 and personal property worth $2,000. William Lewis stands as an early legacy of the success of African-American residents in the Chattanooga community.

Another business located in this vicinity was Tschopik's Garden, located in the Griffis-Caldwell Block during the 1880s. Russian-born Adolph Tschopik, who emigrated to America in 1857 and arrived in Chattanooga after serving in a German regiment of the Union army, opened a confectionary with a garden in the back which became the "center of society and the trysting ground of the day." Eight wide steps led down from the store to the sunken "**Tschopik's Garden** (right)," which featured graveled walks, goldfish ponds, gardens, and a large fountain; in addition, an open-air stage

hosted amateur shows, charity benefits, soirees, and other events. A center of the local social scene during the 1887-1888 real estate boom, the garden was destroyed in the 1888 fire at the adjoining Griffis-Caldwell Block, after which the site was occupied by the Richardson Building.

Further north, on the left (east) side of this block, are two tall brick buildings (619-621 Market Street), currently vacant, which were erected at the turn of the century and housed a variety of commercial offices and retail stores until changing retail patterns and the growth of suburban shopping areas left many stores in the downtown core empty by the 1980s and 1990s.

Proceed to Sixth Street. **⑬** Surviving the postwar chaos after the Civil War, the **First National Bank** (1866) established a building at the southwest corner of Market and Sixth Streets (601 Market Street), removing the antebellum Chattanooga market house (which had also operated as the public slave market for the town) to make way for the project. After surviving the fire which destroyed the nearby Griffis-Caldwell Block, in 1910 the bank relocated to a new building at Broad and Eighth Streets. Subsequently, this site was occupied by a variety of retail stores, including the "Dixie Shop," a ladies' clothing store. In 1979, the First Federal Savings & Loan bank erected the present structure at this location, which is now occupied by AmSouth Bank.

Across Market Street from this site **⑭** is the **Hamilton County Justice Building** (600 Market Street), which was erected on the site of an early Chattanooga business. Jacob "Pappy" Kunz, a native of Switzerland who came to Chattanooga in 1849, operated a popular grocery store and confectionary at this corner; at the rear of the store was a well which was used by many local citizens, as well as Union and

Confederate soldiers, before the city water-works were created in the wake of the Civil War. In the latter years of the nineteenth century, this spot was occupied by a row of 2- and 3-story brick commercial buildings. In the 1930s, the corner lot came to be occupied by the Effron's clothing store, owned by Lou Effron, who acquired the Southern Salvage Company clothing store and, after expanding the business, moved to this site and changed the name of the business. Effron's eventually went out of business in the mid-1960s, and in the late 1970s the current 100,000-square foot Justice Building, designed by Jack Tyler, was erected at a cost of $9 million to house county courts and offices. This building is constructed of black South African granite and Alabama limestone, with steps of light-gray Georgia marble.

The tour of Market Street between Sixth and Second Streets continues on page 181. To return to the start of the Market Center Tour, proceed south on Market Street to MLK Jr. Blvd.

Market Street

Since the founding of Chattanooga, Market Street has been the main thoroughfare through the downtown area, and from an early date businesses lined themselves along this road. The portion of Market Street between Second and Sixth Streets, however, was close to the riverfront and was primarily occupied by warehouses and wharf-related businesses. Unlike the Market Center to the south, therefore, this area did not develop in tall buildings and business structures.

Following the Civil War, good streets were a rarity. Prior to 1886, the only "paving" on Market Street was the laying of stepping stones across the road. The poor condition of Market Street, in fact, led Alderman James R. Harris to propose changing the name of the street to "Mud Run." After raising money through the issuance of local bonds, however, in 1886-87 Market Street from Ninth to Fourth Street was paved with cobblestones, flagstone crossings were lain at the street corners, and gas lamps were erected along the street and were lit each evening by a man riding on horseback with a blow torch. A $500,000 bond was later instituted, and this portion of Market Street, between Fourth Street and the river, was finally paved in 1891. In 1915, this cobblestone paving was replaced completely by asphalt, to reduce wear and increase the traveling ability of residents; the old Belgian block paving stones were then used in paving the city wharf at the river. By 1920, a local ordinance prohibited the use of horse-drawn vehicles on Market Street, and the automobile then became the predominant means of transportation throughout the entire downtown area.

Several interesting and notable events have taken place along Market Street, including one intriguing contest in 1950. Though it never received the acclaim of the better known "Chattanooga Choo-Choo," that year the song "Chattanooga Shoe Shine Boy," the authorship of which has been claimed by several various individuals, became a national hit. To capitalize on the song, a nationwide "shoe shine contest" was held on Market Street in December 1950, with prizes for "best shoe shiner" and "most versatile shoe shiner"; the winner was sent to Washington, D.C. for an appearance before Congress. A copy of this record is reproduced on page 182.

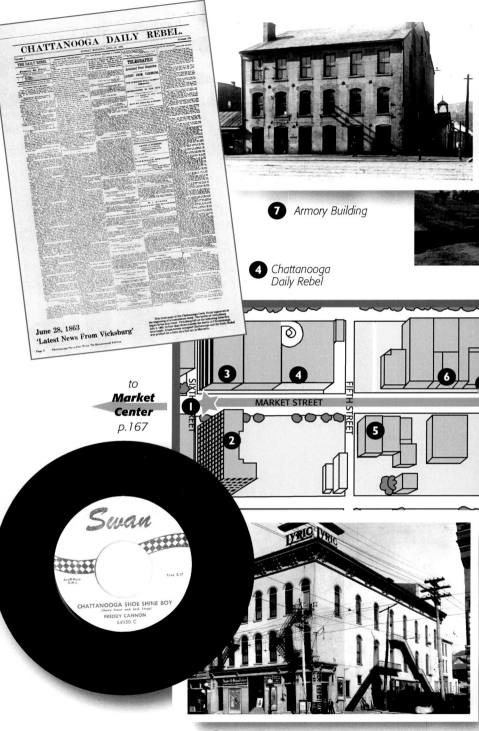

CHATTANOOGA DAILY REBEL.

June 28, 1863
'Latest News From Vicksburg'

7 Armory Building

4 Chattanooga Daily Rebel

to
Market Center
p.167

MARKET STREET

1 **2** **3** **4** **5** **6**

SIXTH STREET

FIFTH STREET

Swan

Time 2:17

Acuff-Rose
B.M.I.

CHATTANOOGA SHOE SHINE BOY
(Harry Stone and Jack Stapp)
FREDDY CANNON
S4050 C

LYRIC LYRIC

2 James Hall/Lyric Theater

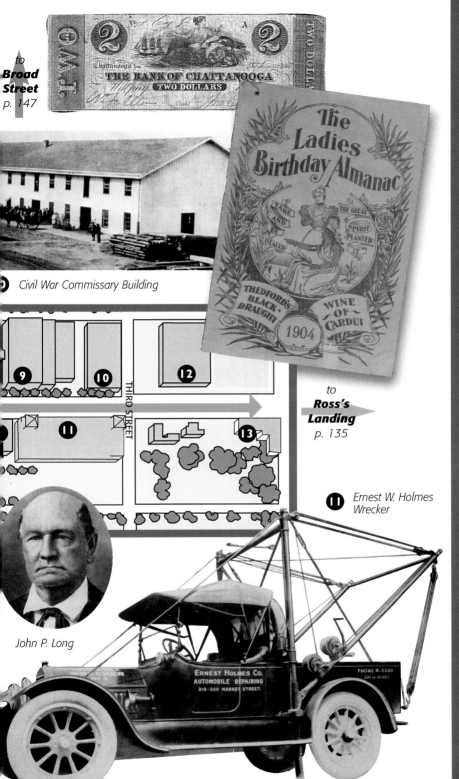

to
Broad Street
p. 147

THE BANK OF CHATTANOOGA
TWO DOLLARS

① Civil War Commissary Building

The Ladies Birthday Almanac

THEDFORD'S BLACK DRAUGHT
WINE OF CARDUI
1904

to
Ross's Landing
p. 135

⑪ Ernest W. Holmes Wrecker

John P. Long

ERNEST HOLMES CO.
AUTOMOBILE REPAIRING
318-320 MARKET STREET.

PHONE M. 6080
DAY or NIGHT

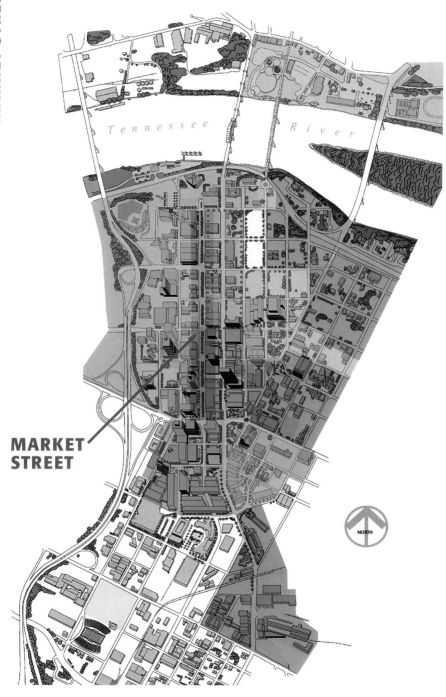

MARKET
STREET

Tennessee River

NORTH

The tour of Market Street begins at the corner of Market and Sixth Streets, ❶ the site of a violent local **Labor Strike** which took place in the early years of the twentieth century. In 1909, the Chattanooga Railway & Light Company was organized to provide trolley service in Chattanooga, utilizing 109 trolley cars along 69 miles of track. After 2 motormen were discharged in 1911 for reckless operation and drunk driving of the trolleys, they contacted the Amalgamated Association of Street & Electric Railways Employees of America; a brief union strike followed, which failed. In 1916, several motormen and conductors again tried to unionize and were discharged. Subsequently, on August 21, 1916, a march accompanied by a brass band proceeded to Market and Sixth Streets, where another strike was scheduled. When one of the trolleys stopped at this intersection, its motorman, W.M. Eaves, announced that he was on strike; the conductor disagreed, and a struggle ensued for control of the car as the streets backed up behind the stalled vehicle. The fire department arrived and hosed down the crowd, and 37 arrests were made. For a number of days, the trolley system operated on a skeleton schedule, and a complete strike soon ensued. After briefly recognizing the union, the company changed course, bringing in strikebreakers to operate the trolleys, and on September 6 the strike resumed. Rioting began the next day: streetcars were abandoned where they sat, company representatives and non-union men were prevented from retrieving the vehicles, trolley poles were pulled down, and rumors spread that the car barns would be burned down. On September 11, 1916, the federal government was called in, and 2 cavalry troops and a machine gun company arrived from nearby Fort Oglethorpe, Georgia, to keep the peace. On September 16, union members pulled strikebreakers from passing trolley cars and beat them; when company guards fired on the crowd, one individual was killed, and 2 others, a boy and a soldier, were wounded. The long strike which began at this corner eventually played itself out, with negative consequences for both sides -- the union gave up and faded away, and in 1919 the company went bankrupt.

The northeast corner of Market and Sixth Streets, ❷ currently occupied by the Electric Power Board building, is the former site of **James Hall** (536 Market Street). After it was determined in 1870 that nearby Kaylor Hall was inadequate for theater facilities, a rough stage was tacked together at this unfinished theater erected by John W. James, and sheets were

used for a curtain as the first performance took place before a capacity crowd. Spectators were forced to funnel through stores and offices to the third-floor stage, which was used at times as a skating rink as well as a theater. After Chattanooga was designated the seat of Hamilton County, the county offices, courthouse, and jail were temporarily housed in this location as well. During the 1887-1888 real estate boom, a number of citizens dissatisfied with the accommodations of the theater (the stage entrance was actually a window with a lowered upper pane) raised $40,000 for renovations, reopening the theater as the New Opera House (it had been called the "Opera House" in the interim period). At that time, the theater seated 1,800 patrons and featured an entrance "enclosed by gates of filigree iron," a grand staircase leading up to the theater (which was moved to the second floor), and a new gallery and balcony for African-American patrons. In 1909, the theater was again remodeled and reopened, this time as the Lyric Theater (pictured above). The building, referred to at one time as "the cultural center of Hamilton County," was also operated as the Grand Theater and as a temporary city auditorium at one time.

Following the organization of the Tennessee Electric Power Company (TEPCO) in 1922, that company purchased this property as the site for its offices. When James Hall was subsequently razed, one reporter wrote that "There is probably no building in all of Chattanooga which is dearer to old residents." TEPCO then built (1923-1924) the 8-story building presently standing at this site. Erected at a cost of $360,000, this structure was designed by Charles E. Bearden to display the different uses of electricity to the best effect, and it was referred to as "the South's finest electrical display room." The first floor of the 60-by-150 foot fireproof building is of trimmed cut stone, the upper floors are of terra cotta, and the lobby floors are of terrazzo. The building was later taken over by the Electric Power Board of Chattanooga (EPB), which in 1939 acquired the city's electricity distribution system for $10,850,000, following the conclusion of a drawn-out legal battle between TEPCO and TVA concerning the provision of electrical services in the Tennessee Valley. Disgruntled by its replacement by a public governmental enterprise, TEPCO issued a newspaper ad upon its demise which stated, "And so private ownership and initiative withdrew in favor of the Government. The Company - pioneer citizen and taxpayer - which for more than half a century served the people of the State of Tennessee, was liquidated. The End." Today, the EPB continues to maintain its offices at this location, although it is currently engaged in the construction of a new office building in the block bounded by Market, Broad, and Tenth Streets and MLK Jr. Blvd; it is anticipated that the building at Market and Sixth Streets will be adapted for residential or commercial purposes in the near future.

Next door to the EPB building is the former site of the **Sterchi Brothers Furniture Company**, a chain furniture store founded by 3 brothers from Knoxville, Tennessee, which opened in Chattanooga in 1910. Following several relocations within the downtown area, the business moved to this spot in 1939, though the building was torn in the 1970s down to create a parking lot for employees of the Electric Power Board.

Across Market Street, at the northwest corner of Market and Sixth Streets, ❸ is the 132,000 square-foot **Market Court** (537 Market Street), a retail and office facility opened in 1989. This lot was originally occupied by an early hotel, the Morgan House, built circa 1871. In 1877 or 1878, Bob and Will Gillespie bought the hotel and changed its name to the Hamilton House Hotel; in 1892, the name again changed, this time to the St. James Hotel, and in 1906 it became the Lighthouse, named for owner Sam T. Light. The 76-room hotel was razed in 1932 in order to create additional space for expansion by the Sears & Roebuck Company, which relocated from Broad Street to this location. In 1948, 2 stories were added to the building, and the basement was extended. In 1971, however, the structure was demolished to make way for a new 4,000 square-foot auto service and retail area, which opened in 1972. In 1981, the 100,000 square-foot building, garage, auto center, and an attached vacant lot were willed to the University of Virginia by attorney Burkett Miller and put up for sale, after which it was

replaced by the current building in 1989.

From this spot, head north along Market Street. On the left, inside the covered parking garage next to the Market Center, is a partly-concealed historic plaque marking the site of the **Chattanooga Daily Rebel**. ❹ Established during the Civil War by editor Franc M. Paul for

circulation among Confederate troops, the 10-cent *Daily Rebel* (pictured above and on page 182) was first produced on August 1, 1862, utilizing the facilities of the defunct *Advertiser* newspaper, including an old-fashioned hand press. Subsequently, the small staff was supplemented by writer Henry Watterson, a volunteer aide to Nathan Bedford Forrest who had previously been a writer in Washington, New York, and Nashville. Other writers were Confederate soldier John W. Faxon and Albert Roberts, a former aide to General John Morgan (CSA). As demand for copies of the paper increased, a power press was secured from Rome, Georgia, and the paper thereafter printed 8,000 copies per day. Entertaining features such as "Mint Julip," "Grapevine Telegraph," and "Bill Arp" were included in the paper. The *Daily Rebel*, however, also included serious pieces, advocating that Chattanooga be made "the great workshop of the Confederate States"; to that end, the paper argued that Chattanooga "was the logical place to locate plants for the manufacture of arms and munitions . . . It was the center of a radiating network of railroads, and in the neighborhood there were 'immense beds of coal and iron.'" Based on these advantages, the newspaper concluded, Chattanooga could become "the Pittsburgh of the South." Some misleading items were also printed in the paper to plant counter-intelligence with the federal army, though the paper did not spare criticism of Confederate General Bragg and other Confederates as well. When Bragg insisted that criticism stop or the *Daily Rebel* would not be allowed to circulate in the army, Watterson resigned rather than take such orders, joining the staff of Gen. Leonidas Polk. During the shelling of Chattanooga in August

1863, local Unionist William Crutchfield pointed out the *Daily Rebel* offices to federal troops, who sent a 12-pound shell crashing into the offices of the newspaper. Sensing that it was time to relocate, Paul secured a railroad car to transport the press south to Atlanta, just missing the advancing federal army. Continuing to stay one step ahead of Union troops, the *Daily Rebel* moved several times, earning the nickname "Rebel-on-Wheels." The paper was finally overtaken by the federal army in Selma, Alabama. Although most of the press was destroyed by a detachment of African-American soldiers, some of the materials were overlooked, and the resilient newspaper continued to circulate until April 11, 1865. The press was then briefly used to print the *Yankee Cavalier*, a federal paper, before meeting its ignominious end: the press was tossed into the Alabama River.

Though much of the remainder of the block between Fifth and Sixth Streets is occupied today by parking facilities, at one time several businesses founded by some of the "First Citizens" of Chattanooga were located in this area. For example, in the late 1840s pioneer M.B. Parham located his dry goods store along Market Street between Fifth and Sixth Streets. Also locating a business in this area were early residents J.B. Nicklin and Dr. Milo Smith, who established a drug business at the corner of Market and Fifth Streets. A Union veteran who later became mayor of Chattanooga in 1887-1888, Nicklin also served as an early president of the Southern Baseball League for a number of years.

From this spot, proceed to Fifth Street. A strange perspective on the growth of Chattanooga may be gained at the corner of Market and Fifth Streets. Despite protests from a number of citizens that this spot was "way out of town," in 1849 the local **Post Office** was temporarily moved to this location. Today, this spot is in the center of the downtown area, and numerous commercial buildings line the street at this point.

On your right ❺ are several 2-story brick buildings erected in the 1920s, which today house businesses and restaurants. One of these buildings (412 Market Street) briefly opened as the Urban Art Institute, a school for aspiring artists in the Chattanooga area.

Across Market Street is the commercial focus of this area: along the west side of the street, an illuminated sign announces **Jack's Alley** ❻ to

passersby. Originally occupied by a series of frame and brick business structures, in 1864-1865 much of this block was demolished by the federal army, which then placed a post corral and prison exercise yard in this area. Over the years, this block developed commercially, becoming the site of numerous small businesses; by 1889, the block was occupied by the Wisdom House hotel, lunch counters, grocery markets, stables, a barbershop, a baking powder factory, a coffee and spice mill, a cobbler, harness shop, and gun shop. By the turn of the century, however, many of these early shops were replaced by the current brick buildings along the west side of Market Street. One popular business along the block was Jack's Army Store, which sat at 425-427 Market Street for a number of years in the mid-twentieth century before going out of business in the 1980s. As plans were formulated to redesign this block, it took on the name "Jack's Alley," after a dilapidated building was demolished to create a walk-through to Broad Street at this spot. Today, this area is a popular destination for local residents and tourists alike, housing a number of restaurants and shops.

One long-time business in the Jack's Alley area is **Buehler's Market** (429 Market Street), a grocery store opened in 1907 by chain meat-market owner Christian Buehler. In Buehler's will, it was specified that profits from his chain of grocery stores would go to support the Christian Buehler Memorial Home for the elderly in Peoria, Illinois. The market moved to its present location circa 1960, after the previous location was torn down to make way for expansion of the Sears & Roebuck store to the south, between Fifth and Sixth Streets.

Also located on Market Street between Fourth and Fifth Streets is the original site of the **Chattanooga Medicine Company** (1879), which was first located in a small building near here. The company began business with two proprietary medicines – "Dr. A.Q. Simmons' Liver Medicine" (1874), which was renamed "Thedford's Black Draught" after a patent suit was filed by a competitor; and "McElree's Wine of Cardui" (1869), which came recommended by McElree's wife's grandmother (or possibly a fellow churchgoer of McElree), who allegedly had received a packet of *Cnicus benedictus* seeds from a Cherokee Indian woman for the purpose of curing female ailments. Of the first shipment of 7,000 units of Wine of Cardui, 6,500 were immediately snapped up by customers. Sales were fueled by advertising booklets such as "The Ladies Birthday Almanac"(1904) reproduced below and on page 183; this booklet, which carried the slogan "Take and be Healed – The Great Spirit Planted It," was in reality little more than an advertisement for the beneficial effects of the company's products. However, such ads did encourage sales, and the company flourished as a result. Around 1889, the company relocated to the St. Elmo neighborhood at the foot of Lookout Mountain, where it continues to operate today with a number of proprietary brands, including Icy Hot, Sun-In, Bull Frog sunblock, and Gold Bond medicated products.

Proceed to the corner of Market and Fourth Streets. In a small building in this vicinity began one of the worst fires to break out in Chattanooga. On June 9, 1887, a fire began at the **Bee Hive Store** in connection with the demonstration of a new gasoline-powered motor, which burst into flames. Although fire crews were successful in controlling the blaze, 2 firemen, Matthew Peak and Henry Iler, were killed when a second blast occurred in the store. Following the fire, a "Fireman's Fountain" near the courthouse lawn was established as a memorial to the 2 men.

The southwest corner of Market and Fourth Streets, ❼ now a parking lot, is the former site of one of the oldest and most historic buildings in downtown Chattanooga. The second brick building built in Chattanooga, the **Armory** (pictured below and on page 182) was built as a storehouse in 1840 by Thomas H. McCallie and R.M. Hooke. It was said by one local newspaper that "At one time this was the most magnificent building in East Tennessee." The building, which was constructed during a period when Chattanooga city streets were 60 feet wide, subsequently sat 15 feet from the curb after streets were narrowed to lower maintenance costs. For a short period, the 2 upper stories were used as a hotel and declared the "home of Chattanooga society."During the Civil War, however, the Confederate army installed bars on the windows and doors to convert the building into a military prison, and the building was used by both armies to house both military and civilian prisoners. Following the war, the building was again used for mercantile purposes until 1870, when it became the temporary Hamilton County courthouse upon the relocation of the county seat from Harrison to Chattanooga. Upon construction of a new courthouse in 1879, the building was converted into the Chattanooga city hall, police headquarters, and "callaboose," or jail; two 1-story jail buildings (one for the not-yet-committed), were placed to the rear, where they were surrounded by a high wooden fence. The building was used for this purpose until 1898, when it was abandoned by the police department. In 1901, the National Guard assumed occupation of the building, at which time it was used as an armory. In 1926, the building was purchased for approximately $100,000 by J.T. Levine, who remodeled the structure for use as an auto sales agency; an auto tire, battery, and radio service store were placed at the rear of the building. The armory was then used temporarily as a basketball sports center, though it was torn down soon thereafter. On this site today is a drive-through banking branch erected in 1981.

The northeast corner of Market and Fourth Streets ❽ is the former site of the **A.J. Fassnacht Wagon Works**, a long-time Chattanooga business. Coming to the United States from Germany in 1855, Andrew J. Fassnacht established a coach and wagon works in Chattanooga after learning the trade in South Bend, Indiana. Located in a 3-story brick building at this spot, Fassnacht built wagons, coaches, and buggies for Chattanoogans for a number of years; although the business was forced to change with the times as automobiles replaced horse travel, A. Fassnacht & Sons thereafter became involved in the manufacturing and distribution of truck equipment, establishing a larger facility for that purpose at Thirteenth Street, and later moved to the suburb of St. Elmo.

Across the street, at 325 Market Street, is the **Chattanooga Lifestyle Center**. ❾ The current building was erected in 1996, using the front facade of the original structure erected here in 1925. That year, the D.S. Etheridge automobile dealership moved from a spot on Broad Street to this location, moving into an eclectic, Italian Renaissance- and Spanish-detailed structure designed by Louis Bull to be set back 35 feet from the street. The *Chattanooga News* described the building as follows: "The design of the building is Italian renaissance, with cut stone base, terra cotta facing, and crowned with green glazed tile canopy. . . The walls are all arched to correspond with the arched display windows on the east and north sides; the base of the walls is mahogany finished paneled wainscoting. Above this wainscoting the arches are finished with Caen stone. The panels within the arches on the blank walls and the ceiling are finished in Italian brocade plaster, colored. The ceiling is heavily beamed with [the] same material as the wainscoting, with consoles at the wall ends of the beams. The floor of the display room is finished with 12x12 black and white rubber tile, laid checker board fashion, with a black cove base at the walls." The building, which was designed as a showroom for the Lincoln automobile line (the "L" placed on the decorative medallions stands for "Lincoln"), also included a tire department, garage, and gas station. Etheridge later sold his Ford business (1941) to the Furlow-Cate Ford Company, and the Newton Chevrolet dealership then took over this site. In 1974, the ornate showroom was taken over by the Chattanooga Cable Television Company after Newton Chevrolet moved to the new Golden Gateway development on the west side of downtown. The building, which was placed on the National Register of Historic Places in 1973, underwent an extensive $10 million renovation in 1996 to create the current "wellness center."

To the left (south) of this structure is a tall, brown building (329 Market Street) which was erected for the Hardwick Buick car dealership, after which it was purchased by D.S. Etheridge to house the Ford portion of his dealership. In the 1960s, the building was converted for use as office space for the Tennessee Valley Authority, after which it was renamed the "John Ross Building."

Proceed to the southwest corner of Market and Third Streets. ❿ During the Union occupation of Chattanooga, the **Quartermaster's Department** erected a number of large storage

warehouses for army goods; the largest (pictured above and on pages 182-83), which served as the principal distribution station for the commissary stores, was at this location. After the departure of the federal army, many of these warehouses were taken over by businessmen who sectioned them off, covered the walls with tent covers pasted over with wallpaper, and opened stores. In 1887, the City Street Railroad Company purchased the property for $15,500 and razed this structure to build a new headquarters at this spot. The current 1-story brick building was built to house the stables, car barns, and offices for the streetcar operation. During its construction, the building was described as "brick with a high stone basement provided with stalls each of which is lighted by a window having in front of it a semicircular brick guard. The brick work will be trimmed with bands of white oolitic limestone, and both the main building and smaller rear extension will be well lighted. The front is simple yet neat and attractive, and as a whole the structure, although massive, will look well and certainly be thoroughly adapted to the use for which it was intended." The building officially opened May 3, 1887, one year before the electric streetcar arrived in Chattanooga. The structure was subsequently taken over by Southern Coach Lines during World War II and utilized as car barns for the city's bus operations, and in the 1970s the site was acquired by the Chattanooga Area Regional Transit Authority (CARTA). In 1978, the building, which is listed on the National Register of Historic Places (1978), was sold to a private group for $375,000, and it now houses the Sports Barn (1979), a fitness center.

Across the street from the Sports Barn is a historic marker commemorating the career of **Ernest W. Holmes, Sr., ⑪** who in 1916 invented the double-boom wrecker, or tow truck (pictured on pages 183 and 189), in a business at this location (318 Market Street) after attaching 3 poles, a pulley, and a chain to a 1913 Cadillac in order to assist a friend. Holmes later became an innovator in military towing vehicles, designing a twin-boom military wrecker which was widely used by the Allied Forces throughout World War II.

Also located at the corner of Market and Third Streets was the first bank to open in town, the **Bank of Chattanooga**, which was established in 1855 near this spot. Following the secession of Tennessee from the Union, the bank began the production of Confederate currency, as seen on page 183; the bills printed by the bank feature a variety of antebellum images, including steamboats, bales of cotton, and other similar scenes. Forced out of business during the Civil War, the bank never reopened.

One notorious destination in the early years of the Ross's Landing settlement was **Taylor's Saloon**, also located in the vicinity of present-day Market and Third Streets. This rough area was frequented by soldiers, rivermen, and other local residents prior to the Cherokee Removal. A brief account of one incident at this tavern serves to illustrate the "frontier" atmosphere which permeated Chattanooga during this period. On one occasion, Sergeant Moses Wells (US) visited the saloon to recover a group of soldiers who had gone to the "joint" and had not returned; receiving no response when knocking upon the door, Wells ordered his provost guard to break down the door. When the door creaked open, an individual referred to only as "a man from Georgia" rushed Wells with a knife, stabbing him in the arm. Following this incident, the assailant then spent 30 days in the military prison, and security was increased at the tavern.

From this spot, cross Third Street. On the left in the block between Second and Third Streets are a series of early **Car Barns** which now house a number of restaurants. **⑫** These buildings are discussed in more detail on pages 152-153.

Across Market Street, at the southeast corner of Market and Second Streets, is a 2-story building erected in 1991-1992. **⑬** This building sits on the site of the **Chattanooga Packing and Milling Company**, a brick corn and flour mill and cooper shop erected here in 1856 by

Charles E. Grenville. Grenville, the grandson of the famous English Lord Grenville, came to Chattanooga from Augusta, Georgia, becoming mayor of Chattanooga on the eve of the Civil War (1860). The mill owned by Grenville became a target for federal batteries during the shelling of the town in 1862 and 1863; the structure was completely destroyed; and Grenville, who lost his fortune, relocated to Charleston after the war. Today, a number of shops and restaurants are located here, including 212 Market, one of the earliest eateries to open in the redeveloped Ross's Landing area.

Located east of these buildings, midway up the hill in the block bounded by Market, Cherry, Second, and Third Streets, is a site where one of the first citizens of Ross's Landing erected his home after arriving by flatboat from Old Washington, Tennessee. Knoxville native **John P. Long** (below) arrived in Ross's Landing on April 18, 1836, where he opened a mercantile store; advertising in the *Tennessee Journal* in Athens, Tennessee, Long's store offered such items as bar iron, "fresh flour," nails, writing paper, "Rio coffee," Tennessee whiskey, champagne, wine, window glass, "Eastern nails," herring and mackerel, saltpeter, tobacco, rope, axes, hoes, and brass kettles, all on "accommodating terms." The store was located nearby, in a frame building on the west side of Market Street between Second and Third Streets, approximately where the car barns are located today. Long, who served in the Second Seminole War and as the Confederate provost marshal in Chattanooga during the Civil War, also operated the town's first post office in the corner of his store. He is buried in the Citizens' Cemetery on the east side of downtown; a photograph of the large monument erected at his grave is reproduced on page 39.

Also at the corner of Market and Second Streets is the former site of the **First Hotel in Chattanooga**, which was established prior to the Cherokee Removal. In August 1833, Daniel Henderson received from Nicholas D. Scales and Pleasant H. Butler "one occupant and possessory right with its appurtanances lying and being in said [Hamilton] County on the south side of the Tennessee River formerly known as Rosses Landing and warehouse now as Scales [etc.]." Along with his wife, Jane, therefore,

Henderson proceeded to Ross's Landing as an appointed U.S. agent to take a census of the Indians in the Cherokee territory. He subsequently left for Virginia with $1,400 to replenish the stock maintained at the landing, but he was robbed and killed by a group of Indians, a fact apparently confirmed by a set of bones subsequently found in a cave on nearby White Oak Mountain. Jane Henderson, however, chose to remain in Ross's Landing, establishing an inn referred to at one time as a "curious little hostelry," composed of several log-hewn buildings with a common porch situated on a 12-acre piece of land near the corner of Market and Second Streets.

To return to the beginning of the Market Street tour, proceed south along Market Street to Sixth Street.

●●‚● ●●‚● ●●‚● ●●‚●

X

Y

Z

PHOTOGRAPHIC CREDITS

Battle of Lookout Mountain (p.12)
reproduction courtesy of National Archives.

Rattlesnake Gorget (p.13) photograph
courtesy of the Museum of the American
Indian.

Cover Art for *Contempt of Court: The
Turn-of-the-Century Lynching That Launched
a Hundred Years of Federalism* (pp.12, 16)
courtesy of Anchor Books.

Newspaper Headlines and photographs
courtesy of *Chattanooga Times-Free Press*:
pp. 18, 76, 81, 92, 182, 186.

Photograph of Bessie Smith Performance
Hall (p.76-77) courtesy of Chattanooga
African-American Museum.

*Colonel and Mrs. James A. Whiteside, Son
Charles and Servants* (p.126) reproduction
courtesy of Hunter Museum of American Art.

Chattanooga Ducks logo (pp.148, 150)
courtesy of Chattanooga Ducks, LLC.